The Economic Thought of Henry Calvert Simons

Drawing on years of research, Gerald Steele delves into the diverse ideas of Henry Simons, a neglected economist whose work in the 1930s on monetary and financial instability is extremely relevant to today's debates about commercial bank credit, the interdependence of fiscal and monetary policy, and financial regulation.

Steele describes the emergence of the first Chicago School of economics and its distinctive difference to the School subsequently associated with the Monetarism of Milton Friedman, and shows how Simons provides the basis for what is now referred to as 'the fiscal theory of the price level' and how this differs from the monetarist attempt to control prices by controlling the supply of broad money.

This book will be of interest to advanced students and researchers of the history of economic thought, economic history, macroeconomics and banking and finance.

G.R. Steele is Reader in Economics at Lancaster University. His research interests include the economics and political philosophy of Friedrich Hayek, and he has pursued a general inquiry into the development of ideas relating to problems of a money economy.

In 2007, he delivered the F.A. Hayek Memorial Lecture, Austrian Scholars Conference, Mises Institute. In 2010, he was Visiting Professor at the University of Economics, Prague, when he delivered the František Čuhel Memorial Lecture, Conference on Political Economy, at the Cevro Institute.

Routledge Studies in the History of Economics

For a full list of titles in this series, please visit www.routledge.com.

196 Economics, Entrepreneurship and Utopia
The Economics of Jeremy Bentham and Robert Owen
Estrella Trincado and Manuel Santos-Redondo

197 War in the History of Economic Thought
Economists and the Question of War
Edited by Yukihiro Ikeda and Annalisa Rosselli

198 Schumpeter's Price Theory
Harry Bloch

199 Economics and Literature
A Comparative and Interdisciplinary Approach
Edited by Çınla Akdere and Christine Baron

200 Economic Analyses in Historical Perspective
Edited by José Luís Cardoso, Heinz D. Kurz, Philippe Steiner

201 Lionel Robbins on the Principles of Economic Analysis
The 1930s Lectures
Authored by Lionel Robbins
Edited by Susan Howson

202 The Foundations of Political Economy and Social Reform
Economy and Society in Eighteenth Century France
Ryuzo Kuroki and Yusuke Ando

203 Asia and the History of the International Economy
Essays in Memory of Peter Mathias
Edited by A.J.H. Latham and Heita Kawakatsu

204 The Economic Thought of Henry Calvert Simons
Crown Prince of the Chicago School
G.R. Steele

The Economic Thought of Henry Calvert Simons

Crown Prince of the Chicago School

G.R. Steele

Routledge
Taylor & Francis Group
LONDON AND NEW YORK

First published 2018
by Routledge
2 Park Square, Milton Park, Abingdon, Oxon OX14 4RN

and by Routledge
52 Vanderbilt Avenue, New York, NY 10017

First issued in paperback 2020

Routledge is an imprint of the Taylor & Francis Group, an informa business

British Library Cataloguing-in-Publication Data
A catalogue record for this book is available from the British Library

Library of Congress Cataloging-in-Publication Data
Names: Steele, G. R., author.
Title: The economic thought of Henry Calvert Simons: crown prince of the Chicago School / G.R. Steele.
Description: Abingdon, Oxon; New York, NY: Routledge, 2018. | Includes bibliographical references and index.
Identifiers: LCCN 2017052867 | Subjects: LCSH: Simons, Henry Calvert, 1899–1946. | Economists—United States—Biography. | Chicago school of economics. | Monetary policy. | Free enterprise.
Classification: LCC HB119.S56 S74 2018 | DDC 330.15/53—dc23
LC record available at https://lccn.loc.gov/2017052867

ISBN 13: 978-0-367-66720-7 (pbk)
ISBN 13: 978-0-8153-6465-8 (hbk)

Typeset in Bembo
by codeMantra

To Catherine and Charlotte

Contents

Preface

If this were a journal article, the abstract would contain the following. Henry Calvert Simons is worthy of interest, for many reasons. He argues that consensus is a necessary preliminary for successful policy initiatives. He held firm to libertarian principles even at the depth of the Great Depression, when others were seeking more radical options. He understands how the application of Keynes's 'solutions' threatens the liberal ethos. He recognises the inescapable interdependence of fiscal and monetary policy. His presentation of fiscal policy is a precursor of the 'fiscal theory of the price level' (aka 'Fiscal Monetarism'). He gave support to the application of monetary rules in preference to discretionary interventions. He argues that the 'near moneys' that are the creation of commercial fractional reserve banking are likely to exacerbate business crises. He backs 100 percent reserve banking (which has affinities with Islamic finance), but anticipates the emergence of new credit extending bodies (aka 'shadow banking'). His influence upon the US tax structure draws from a detailed consideration of a workable basis for income taxation.

To incite further interest in Simons, consider a posthumous collection of his essays and the cogent comments of their editor, Aaron Director: (i) Simons 'had been slowly establishing himself as the head of a "school"'; and (ii) there is a 'failure of professional economists to appreciate his true worth' (Simons, 1948, v). Friedrich Hayek describes that collection of essays as

> one of the most important contributions made in recent times to our problem and as just the kind of work which is required to get discussion started on the fundamental issues. Even those who violently disagree with some of its suggestions should welcome it as a contribution which clearly and courageously raises the central problems of our time.
>
> (Hayek, 1949b, p. 381, fn. 3)

The tenor of that appreciation has endured, as evidenced by the later appraisal of George Stigler: 'Henry Calvert Simons was the Crown Prince of that hypothetical kingdom, the Chicago school of economics' (Stigler, 1974, p. 1). As Stigler later elaborated: it is Simons who provides a 'lucid blueprint of the good society of classical liberalism' (Stigler, 1988, p. 139).

Although better accolades are not readily found, Milton Friedman comes close when he acknowledges Simons as 'a shaper of my ideas' (Friedman, 1967, p. 1). Another former student at Chicago – Friedman's junior by ten years – Don Patinkin writes,

> in my recollections of student days ... it is Simons who stands out sharply as the major source of intellectual stimulation and influence in all that regards monetary and fiscal policy. In the slang of those days, most of us were "Simonised" to some degree or other.
>
> (Patinkin, 1969, p. 52)

Hyman Minsky touches upon a salutary attribute when he describes Simons as a man whose 'prejudices were strong'. He recounts that 'at the beginning of his classes' Simons would read a paper on his philosophical beliefs: 'The point of the exercise was that beliefs and ideology were incisive determinants of policy prescriptions and students had a right to know from where their professor's views were "coming"' (Minsky, 2009, p. 200).

During a period of history when the free world was challenged by the extremes of communism and fascism, and where the liberal-thinking Keynes was finding cause to call upon interventions from the apparatus of the state, Simons held firm to libertarian principles. As one indicator of the relevance of his analysis to modern monetary issues, Simons (by inference) had forecast the demise of the Eurozone project long before its structures had been built:

> Federalism or informal union of states has everything to commend it if the central government confines itself largely to preserving order and free trade among constituent states, and to providing a stable, common currency. But federal governments like our own and the great powers abroad have become a great obstacle to world order. Originating largely as customs unions or agencies for securing free trade within their boundaries ... they have undertaken all kinds of internal policies which must be abandoned if freer world trade is to be achieved.
>
> (Simons, 1944a, p. 3)

When set against the legacy of his published work, the influence of Simons upon those who were fortunate to benefit directly from his ideas is immense. His understanding of the necessity to give careful attention to the institutional structures of money and banking sharply contrasts with that of the current crop of macro-modellers, whose vision is constrained by the mechanistic requirements of dynamic stochastic general equilibrium.

In drawing largely from the publications and online papers of scholars, whose discussions are more tightly focused than the content of the chapters that follow, there has been no burrowing through dusty archives to produce this book. Instead, the significance of Simons's writing to economic concerns of the present day are uppermost. So, readers are urged to remain calm if they feel that the narrative digresses too far from the epoch in which Simons wrote. The objective and the indulgence was to deliver both a broad appreciation of Simons's work and an invitation for others to join the discussion of its relevance.

In October 2015, a conference was arranged at the University of Chicago. Its purpose was: (i) to explore the lasting impact of Frank Knight, Henry Simons and Jacob Viner in giving an initial shape to Chicago economics; and (ii) to show how their influence directed the leading lights of the generation that followed, which includes Aaron Director, Milton Friedman and George Stigler. Salient conference papers and the associated discussions were made available online. As the conference was drawing towards its end and a few questions were taken from their audience, we are told that the panelists 'demonstrated Chicago economics in action: in response to a query about formalism vs. intuitive economics, a hearty argument broke out'.

Work on this book, the beginning of which predates the 2015 conference by two years, was motivated by no thoughtful reflection. As it once first piloted an interest in the work of Friedrich Hayek, this most recent engagement was driven by serendipity. Only by chance was the comment found (which has not gone unchallenged) that Simons 'had committed suicide in despair at the onset of Keynesianism' (Toporowski, 2010, p. 364). No debate: thereafter it was necessary to discover more. In so doing, a remarkable economist was discovered, followed closely by a new research interest aided by a publisher (Emily Kindleysides) who showed patience during the gestation of a book, whose content has benefited enormously from the critical attention provided by my friend and colleague John Whittaker. Of course, he is absolved from any responsibility, as are Mervyn King and David Laidler, who kindly gave their time and attention to questions raised by the author. I acknowledge permission from the Chicago University Press to quote from Henry Simons's *Personal Income Taxation* (Copyright 1938 by the University of Chicago. All rights reserved. Published February 1938. Composed and Printed by the University of Chicago Press, Chicago, Illinois, U.S.A.)

Bibliography

Friedman, M. (1967) 'The Monetary Theory and Policy of Henry Simons', *The Journal of Law and Economics*, vol. X, October, 1–13; reprinted in Friedman, 1969, pp. 81–93.

Friedman, M. (1969) *The Optimum Quantity of Money and Other Essays* (Chicago: Chicago, Aldine Publishing Co.).

Hayek, F. A. (1949) *Individualism and Economic Order* (London and Henley: Routledge)

Minsky, H. P. (2009) 'Beginnings', *BNL Quarterly Review*, vol. 38, no. 154, September, pp. 211–22; cited from https://ssrn.com/abstract=2057575 (accessed 14 June 2013).

Patinkin, D. (1969) 'The Chicago Tradition, The Quantity Theory, and Friedman', *Journal of Money, Credit and Banking*, vol. 1, no. 1, February, 46–70.

Stigler, G. J. (1974) 'Henry Calvert Simons', *Journal of Law and Economics*, vol. 17, no. 1, April, 1–5.

Stigler, G. J. (1988) *Memoirs of an Unregulated Economist* (New York: Basic Books).
Simons, H. C. (1944) 'Some Reflections on Syndicalism', *Journal of Political Economy*, vol. 52, no. 1, March, 1-25, 1-25; reprinted in Simons, 1948, pp. 12–59.
Simons, H. C. (1948) *Economic Policy for a Free Society* (Chicago: University of Chicago Press)
Toporowski, J. (2010) 'Henry Simons and the other Minsky Moment', *Studie Note di Economia*, Anno XV, no. 3, 363–68.

1 Introduction

1.1 Henry Simons

As a junior colleague of Frank Knight at the University of Iowa, Simons had followed his mentor to Chicago in 1927. That a special empathy existed between Knight and Simons might be inferred from the direction of a shared interest. After Knight's attention had shifted in the early 1930s, from cost theory to capital theory, he thereafter published only a handful of 'technical' articles in economics. As is true of Simons, Knight was developing a broader perspective: the application of social science to the defence of a free society. George Stigler describes the situation thus:

> For most present-day economists, the primary purpose is to increase our knowledge of the working of the enterprise and other economic systems. For Knight, the primary role of economic theory is rather different: it is to contribute to the understanding of how by consensus based on rational discussion we can fashion a liberal society in which individual freedom is preserved and a satisfactory economic performance achieved.
>
> (Stigler, 1985, p. 11)

If political freedom is to be protected, the production of resources must be determined by free enterprise and their allocation determined by individual choice, with appropriate legal institutions to promote responsibility in business decisions and to protect markets from restraints and monopoly.

Three criteria set the ethos by which Simons is driven: the highest value is placed upon liberty, 'as both a requisite and a measure of progress'. This is followed next by equality and, finally, by the dynamics of social progress, including progress 'in the criteria themselves' (Simons, 1948, p. 2). Nothing enduring could be achieved without consensus, not least in regard to equality, where Simons voices a strong commitment to progressive income taxation (Chapter 10).

A brief exposition on 'The Tax Exemption Question', published in the *Journal of Business* (March 1923), and a review of *The Economics of Taxation* by H. Gunnison Brown, which appeared in the first published volume of the

Journal of Political Economy (February 1926), indicate the tenor of Simons's early work. That he held that focus throughout his career is evidenced by *Personal Income Taxation* (1938) and the discovery after his death of a manuscript, subsequently published as *Federal Tax Reform* (1951). His reputation in the area of taxation reached its zenith with the *Report of the Royal Commission on Taxation* to the Canadian Parliament (1966), where the recommendations closely follow those outlined by Simons for the US, some twenty years earlier.

On completing his graduate studies at Chicago in 1930, Simons was appointed as an instructor in economics, but he made no immediate impression. It is reported that his progress was slow and that it was only by Knight's support that he withstood strong opposition to the renewal of his appointment.

As the academic discussion of law was increasingly undertaken in the context of contemporary society, arguments became infused with analysis drawn from the social sciences. After the Chicago Law School initiated a broad four-year curriculum for non-graduate entrants, the subject areas of economics, history, political philosophy and other related fields began to be incorporated into the syllabus. Two years after the formal adoption of that programme, Simons accepted a full-time post to teach economics to Chicago law students in 1937, when he was able to show how legal and economic problems are interrelated: problems of bankruptcy, corporate reorganization, antitrust laws, industry regulation and the liability of employers. Shortly before his death in 1946, Simons had been appointed as the first economics professor in the School.

Simons's contributions to economics were made across a period of no more than fifteen years, following which a contemporary assessment is that

> [w]hen he died June 19 in Chicago at the age of forty-six he stood at the height of his intellectual powers but had scarcely come into his own. A twenty-five-line obituary in the *New York Times* was deemed to tell his storey and no doubt accurately reflected his popular fame. New Deal prophets, who had felt the whiplash of his invective, of course knew of and respected him. Businessmen busy about the work of the world were largely too busy to understand his contribution to the system they never tire of eulogizing.
>
> (Davenport, 1946, p. 6)

It is a safe comment, now made more than seventy years after his death, that only a few economists are aware of the writing of Henry Simons. Of those, still fewer have any understanding of his relevance. Indeed, there is little in current career incentives to encourage academic economists to take interest in Simons or, indeed, in the work of those whose arguments have fed the discussion of economics through the twentieth century. Not least, among those whose work in that period *is* widely recognised are Milton Friedman, Friedrich Hayek, John Maynard Keynes and Hyman Minsky. They are here cited, not for the merit of their work *per se*, but for their relevance to any serious narrative relating to Henry Simons.

The author is among those whose ignorance of Simons was little short of total, prior to having chanced upon the following remark: 'Simons, who was prone to melancholy, had committed suicide in despair at the onset of Keynesianism' (Toporowski, 2010, p. 364). Instinctively and instantly, there was motivation to know more about a man who might be so moved. Recent research provides as much information as is likely to be achieved on the event of Simons's death:

> The combination of Simons mentioning suicide, Nef and Samuelson saying he committed suicide, Rose Friedman later claiming that it was "apparently" suicide, and the fact that Simons faced a devastating disappointment less than twenty-four hours before he died, all strongly suggest that Simons committed suicide. Even so, it must be acknowledged that in some ways the archival record is insufficient.
>
> (Van Horn, 2014, p. 532)

Certainly, in the period leading to his death, Simons had been taking medication to alleviate acute depression and insomnia. Irrespective of the fatal overdose being accidental or intentional, it is plausible that the 'melancholy' from which Simons suffered was associated with his fear, not so much that Keynesianism was on the rise, but that the ethos of classic liberalism was being lost. At least, there can be little doubt that Simons connects the two and, in that, he is not alone. Neither Henry Simons nor Friedrich Hayek would have placed any store by the motivation that Keynes provides for having written *The General Theory of Employment Interest and Money* (1936):

> The authoritarian state systems of to-day seem to solve the problem of unemployment at the expense of efficiency and freedom. ... But it may be possible by a right analysis of the problem to cure the disease whilst preserving efficiency and freedom.
>
> (Keynes, 1936, p. 381)

Neither Simons nor Hayek was taken by the idea that government should attempt to engineer 'the economy' in the manner described by Keynes. Instead, and acting more or less independently, they articulated the case for, and sought the means to revitalise, the liberal ethos. In pressing for Aaron Director[1] to return to Chicago to head a 'Free Market Project' (alternatively termed the 'Hayek Project'), Simons had sent a copy of a memorandum to Hayek, in which he had articulated his support. At this same time, Hayek had been contacted by Harold Luhnow of the Volker Fund, where Luhnow was attempting to persuade Hayek to produce a US version of *The Road to Serfdom* (1944).

Simons's proposal for Aaron Director to return to Chicago in 1946 was the more poignant by the fact that Director had been forced to leave in 1935, following acrimonious correspondence between Paul Douglas and Frank

Knight. The issues remain unclear but Simons had been badly affected. As a good friend and a close colleague, he confessed: 'I have been, *qua* economist, alone since Aaron left. Certainly I am worth more to the University with Aaron around than without him' (Simons, letter dated February 20 1939; cited from Van Horn, 2014, p. 529). Simons considered Director to have been unjustly treated. That the pending appointment of Director to Chicago had been lost through a late misunderstanding regarding tenure rendered Simons so distraught that he was unable even to write to inform Director himself. Having shouldered Lloyd Mints with that task, a letter was sent to Director on 18 June 1946, the day preceding Simons's untimely death.

1.2 The Chicago School

That Milton Friedman and Henry Simons are both viewed as 'founders' of the Chicago School (Chapter 3) implies the existence of more than one school. Indeed, that is the case. Friedman was younger than Simons by thirteen years. After a year that lead to a master's degree at Chicago in 1933, Friedman had returned to work as a research assistant for Henry Schultz during the academic year 1934–1935. Thereafter, Friedman held a series of appointments – with the National Resources Committee, the National Bureau of Economic Research, the University of Wisconsin-Madison, the US Department of the Treasury, Columbia University and the University of Minnesota – before accepting a faculty appointment in 1946 to teach economic theory at the University of Chicago, where he remained for the next thirty years.

Not least by the distance which separates the epochs in which the respective reputations of Simons and Friedman were gained, the Chicago School is now widely associated with Milton Friedman, Monetarism and the ethos of laissez-faire. Certainly, a majority of economists would now cite Friedman's interpretation of the quantity theory of money (aka Monetarism) as the epitome of the School (Chapter 8). For a minority, an earlier School of the interwar years defines a group of economists who were reacting in a particular way to the events and issues that were brought to prominence by the Wall Street Crash of 1929. It was then that the institutional structure of commercial banking became a central concern, and there emerged a proposal for 100 percent reserve banking. That proposal quickly became known as the Chicago Plan. The background to the Plan (Chapter 4), pen portraits of the planners (Chapter 5) and the Plan (Chapter 6) are discussed.

The damaging feature of fractional reserve banking is that it 'facilitated and encouraged the use of short-term financing in business generally' (Simons, 1936, p. 10; 1948, p. 168); and it continues to do so across Western economies. Simons opposes the use of short-term debt as the instrument to support both sovereign and corporate activities. With the implementation of the Chicago Plan, short-term lending by commercial banks would be phased out. Although the relevance of Islamic banking to such concerns has no association with the Plan, or more generally with economic events in the 1930s, empirical studies that compare the performance of Western and Islamic banking in the aftermath of the 2008 Credit Crunch raise related issues. The greater resilience to cyclical downturns that is perceived to arise where Islamic precepts govern banking and finance is not so far removed from the motivations of those who endorsed the Plan (Chapter 11).

For the implementation of the Plan, commercial banks would be transformed to become more like investment trusts, holding only two types of assets: long-term bonds and central bank base money (i.e., banknotes and reserves). By implication, lending and investing institutions would then focus upon the provision of 'long-term capital in equity form'. Although the Chicago Plan sits ever upon the 'back burner', from time to time there is recurring interest. Recent examples include a study commissioned by the authorities in Iceland (Sigurjonsson, 2015) and the close examination afforded by a former Governor of the Bank of England (see King, 2016, pp. 261–77). An associated detail relates to open-market operations, where a central bank creates base money in order to purchase interest-bearing sovereign bonds. This activity has conventionally been applied to short-dated bonds, but, as the zero lower bound for short-term interest rates is approached, central banks have seen fit to operate further up the yield curve. The new jargon is 'quantitative easing'. As a central bank creates base money, which it then spends in purchasing long-term bonds, yields fall. Simons argues that this measure is unlikely to counter deflation, and it is here that we find arguments that mark a difference between the principals of the respective Chicago Schools, Simons and Friedman (Chapters 7 and 8). The difference is that, where Simons is implicitly concerned with sovereign indebtedness (i.e., bonds and base money), Friedman's analysis is directed towards broad money aggregates. A citation in Chapter 7 unambiguously shows Simons to have articulated the conceptual basis from which has arisen the fiscal theory of the price level (aka, Fiscal Monetarism).

In the coalescence of the lines of thought that produced the first Chicago School, the roles taken by Hayek and Simons are appraised by Van Horn and Mirowski (2009). Where Hayek is described as 'the prime external contractor', Simons is considered more important as 'the prime architect'. In commenting upon that assessment, Bruce Caldwell explains that it is Simons who transformed an invitation to write 'an American *Road to Serfdom* … into a wholly different vision, the formation of an institute that would establish the University of Chicago as a base for free market ideas' (Caldwell, 2011, pp. 303–305). That same feature is emphasised by David Laidler as the distinctive attribute of Chicago analysis in the 1930s (Chapter 8).

Although Simons has credit as the principal mover in shaping and disseminating details of the Chicago Plan, his intellectual contributions extend beyond that area. A broad appreciation of his relevance must focus as much upon the influence that he brings to the work of others, as upon his direct contributions. The one clear feature of that broader perspective is that it reflects a staunch pragmatic libertarian philosophy (Chapter 2). Yet, it disturbs many that Simons embraces libertarian principles as he argues for progressive taxation to achieve greater income equality. If income inequality is to be mitigated, then Simons insists that taxation is preferable to an array of restraints upon free trade. In an epoch where high unemployment bred support for extremism at both ends of the political spectrum, there is a plausible argument that the edifice of a liberal economic system is more secure in the absence of poverty. Taxation need not place inhibitions upon freedoms. Businessmen may pursue profit, the prosperous may exercise power and market competition may determine prices. Where the focus is upon achieving greater income equality, the primary policy consideration is that of weighing the negative impact of progressive taxation upon work incentives (Chapter 10).

1.3 Fiscal policy

With Simons's persistence in arguing the relevance of fiscal deficit spending (Chapter 7) as the means to counter deflation, many conflate his arguments with the more familiar rationale as propagated by Keynes. With a full-blooded commitment to the insights of his 'Master',[2] Robert Skidelsky suggests that Chicago economists were 'more Keynesian than Keynes' (Skidelsky, 1992, p. 392). Yet, by that assessment, Skidelsky misses the fundamental difference between Keynesian economics and the Chicago ethos. Many economists, having graduated during the twenty-or-so years to 1968, recall Milton Friedman only for textbook entries relating to *A Theory of the Consumption Function* (1957) and the technical relevance of progressive income taxation and state welfare payments as automatic stabilisers. (The gap between tax revenue and rules-based state benefits closes automatically in a recession; the converse occurs in a boom.) Within that narrow context, the nub of Friedman's observations is that 'the multiplier of personal disposable income with respect to autonomous expenditures' (Friedman, 1957, p. 238) is close to unity. At no point did Friedman given his support to fiscal fine-tuning, nor to any attempt to raise the level of government expenditures above 'the community's desire, need, and willingness to pay for public services' (Friedman, 1948, p. 248). It is noteworthy how this citation accords with Simons's view that sovereign debt should have no role in resourcing fiscal expenditure.

Published only two years after Simons's death, Friedman's 'A Monetary and Fiscal Framework for Economic Stability' (1948) carries all the marks of Simons's *credo*: the objectives are 'political freedom, economic efficiency, and substantial equality of economic power', which are best realised by 'a market mechanism within a "competitive order"' (*ibid.*, p. 246). The propositions that Friedman views as 'particularly relevant' are: for the government to provide a monetary framework operating 'under the "rule of law" rather than the discretionary authority of administrators'; and an expressed 'hope that the community would desire to reduce inequality' beyond that determined by competition *per se*. The adoption of 100 percent reserve banking and the elimination of central bank open-market operations would be necessary 'to complete the elimination of the major weapons of discretionary authority' (*ibid.*). Moreover, and contrary to mainstream Keynesian models, Friedman understands the interdependence of fiscal and monetary policy (Chapter 8). It is a matter for regret that, with Friedman's propagation of the relatively narrow perspective of Monetarism, no weight was given to the significance of that interdependence. Furthermore, it allowed Keynesians to give emphasis to Keynes's own speculation that stabilisation policy might be too weak to maintain full employment and that (in disregard of Friedman's insistence upon 'the community's desire, need, and willingness to pay') there might be a requirement for fiscal spending to be permanently raised. With the failure of attempts to fiscally fine-tune economic activity through into the mid-1970s (Chapter 9), attention thereafter became more directly focused upon achieving monetary stability *per se*. Not least was this in association with the single currency project of the European Economic and Monetary Union.

Within the confines of a private conference, a senior Treasury official uttered words that remain with the author after more than forty years: 'No situation is so bad that government intervention cannot make it worse'. Although there are many ways in which that sentiment might be 'unpacked', there is a perversity that arises all too frequently from the need for politicians to be seen to have all the answers. 'Accident and Emergency' hospital units understand well that problems can arise from intervention by invasive surgery, by the side effects of medication and, more generally, by the potential for unintended consequences. For a serious trauma case, the best option may be to allow the patient to experience the natural processes of recuperation.

As a relevant metaphor, this might be the better option than some ill-judged economic policy panacea. Yet, elections are not won by manifestoes that read, 'Leave well alone!' Those with political authority are expected to do something, despite the doubts that must be attached to its likely effectiveness. As an economy slides into recession, or as a speculative housing bubble bursts, or when a key referendum is lost, there may be very little that a finance minister or a central bank governor can do to mitigate adverse consequences. The best on offer may be not to make matters worse. For Chicago economists, that sentiment is consistent with their primary objective of maintaining monetary stability.

Recent innovative directions for monetary policy in the UK have been less than impressive. In the summer of 2013, a newly appointed Governor of the Bank of England gave 'forward guidance': future changes in interest rates would be guided by the state of the labour market. Six months later came the announcement that forward guidance was entering a 'new phase', after which little more was heard of forward guidance. Ever resourceful, the Governor then took it upon himself to signal a cut in the base rate that duly missed its cue. Following that, the impact of an announcement (August 2016) of a new bout of quantitative easing may have been obscured by market reactions to the UK's referendum on membership of the European Union. The argument by which quantitative easing has little relevance as a counter to deflation is a feature of Simons's monetary theory (Chapters 7 and 8).

To underscore the important differences that relate to the relevance of policy options as they were argued in the 1930s, the following benchmarks are provided:

1 position held by Keynes: public works resourced by bond-finance stimulate economic growth
2 position held by Simons and Hawtrey: fiscal deficits counter deflation; public works are mere window dressing
3 position held by Hawtrey: open-market operations stimulate economic activity
4 position held by Simons: open-market operations have little, if any, impact upon economic activity

With the last of these points, open-market operations (quantitative easing) merely displace one type of official debt (bonds issued by the sovereign treasury) with another type of official debt (banknotes and bank reserves issued by the central bank). With that, Simons senses that quantitative easing has little relevance to lifting a recession.

Both Henry Simons and Ralph Hawtrey contemporaneously rejected the argument that fiscal deficits are necessary to create something – equivalent to Egyptian pyramids or to medieval cathedrals (see Keynes, 1936, p. 131) – that would directly raise work opportunities. The relevant force is monetary expansion *per se*, when the better option is for fiscal deficits to lessen tax burdens, thereby to allow the private sector to choose which projects to support. In more recent terminology, the detail laid down by Simons would be termed 'helicopter money', although the parcelling up of banknotes for dispersal from the air (or by post) is an impractical procedure. Tax rebates would do the job equally well at less expense and allowing subsequent decisions on the directions of expenditure to be freely decided. Certainly, new jobs in the domestic economy would not be created if the new money were spent on imported goods or holidays abroad, but the whole point of free trade and competition within a liberal market economy 'is to teach us who will serve us well' (Hayek, 1946, p. 97). The libertarian tenet is that intervention by the state to macro-mange an economy is a road that leads to mediocrity.

1.4 October 1929

The Wall Street Crash of October 1929 had occurred just a few days after Simons had celebrated his thirtieth birthday and a year before his academic appointment to the University of Chicago. As the New York Stock Exchange went into free fall, the ensuing Great Depression would eventually re-reshape the mainstreams of economic thinking. The relevance of the free-market liberal ethos of classical economics and in particular the economics of the

Austrian School (Chapter 9) became heavily discounted. Government spending would play an ever-greater role. One book title catches the point. In *Hayek and the Keynesian Avalanche*, Brian McCormick explains how Keynes's triumph was at the expense of Hayek's poorly presented exposition of business cycle theory and how one final attempt to remedy the deficiency had been 'swept aside by the Keynesian avalanche' (McCormick, 1992, p. xii).

Although neo-Marxist arguments had been developing in the 1930s, new lines of macroeconomic thinking were to become the Siren voices to sway economists away from traditional teaching. Keynes was offering a challenging alternative. In presenting *The General Theory of Employment Interest and Money* (1936), Keynes attempted to show how macroeconomic forces could be managed with minimum damage to the liberal ethos. Bolshevism and Fascism were both to be feared. In the 1920s, the decision to restore sterling to the pre-1914 rate of $4.86 had caused high levels of unemployment throughout the UK and, as that situation was exacerbated by the Great Depression that followed the Wall Street debacle, Keynes looked for immediate and direct action:

> If the Treasury were to fill old bottles with banknotes, bury them at suitable depths in disused coalmines which are then filled up to the surface with town rubbish, and leave it to private enterprise on well-tried principles of laissez-faire to dig the notes up again (the right to do so being obtained, of course, by tendering for leases of the note-bearing territory), there need be no more unemployment and, with the help of the repercussions, the real income of the community, and its capital wealth also, would probably become a good deal greater than it actually is. It would, indeed, be more sensible to build houses and the like; but if there are political and practical difficulties in the way of this, the above would be better than nothing.
>
> (Keynes, 1936, p. 129)

By such interventions, Keynes argued that it would be possible to sustain full employment. With that lead, a new channel was opened that would become the macroeconomics mainstream of 'Keynesianism', which continues to dominate academic and practical discussion of economic policy options. That Simons saw no value in Keynes's panaceas can be inferred from a contemporaneous publication. In delivering 'A Positive Program for Laissez-Faire' (1934), Simons gives shape to the contrasting sentiments that are now recognised as representing the early Chicago School (Chapter 3). Those sentiments are best understood when set against the major tenets of modern economics and the left-right political dichotomy that is readily identified by the analytical bias of economists.

In a clear and widely recognised attempt to counter the influence of Keynes at Cambridge, in 1931 Lionel Robbins had appointed Friedrich Hayek to a chair at the London School of Economics. Through the next fifteen years, both Simons and Hayek worked independently in propagating the philosophy of classical liberalism against the backcloth of an ever-growing conviction among economists of the value of sustained fiscal interventions. The macroeconomic relationships, which Keynes then sketched in the broadest strokes, were eventually to take the form of a deterministic (ISLM) model, in which fiscal and monetary policy are (erroneously and misleadingly) presented as independent options (Chapter 8). For three decades, that presentation drove the discussion and the implementation of economic policy, where the criticisms from a minority attracted little interest. At the zenith of that Keynesian epoch, a persuasive polemic directed to an intelligent lay readership states with little equivocation: 'In *The General Theory* Keynes showed how, by controlling the level of demand, a government could maintain full employment' (Stewart, 1967, p. 206). The only rider that is made by the author is the possibility of incipient inflation and a lower rate of economic growth. The confidence of that Keynesian outlook shows in a contemporaneous comment from a UK Chancellor:

> I sum up the prospects for 1967 in three short sentences. We are back on course. The ship is picking up speed. The economy is moving. Every seaman knows the command at such a moment: 'steady as she goes'.
>
> (James Callaghan, 1967)

In October of that same year, the parlous state of the UK economy brought the devaluation of sterling and the Chancellor tendering his resignation.

1.5 Money matters

As the general stance of post-war budgetary policy in the West caused real currency values to fall and price inflation to rise, the shifting Phillips curve – and the high profile of Friedman's address to the *American Economic Association* (Friedman, 1968) – undermined confidence in Keynes's macroeconomic protestations. When, a decade earlier, Friedman had presented a new transmission mechanism (between money and prices) within the context of the classical quantity theory of money (Friedman, 1956), it had attracted little attention; but as times changed, so did interest in Friedman's interpretation of the quantity theory, not least as it was rebranded as 'Monetarism' (Chapter 8) in 1968.

Even prior to the experience of stagflation in the 1970s, growing doubts over the efficacy of fiscal intervention had centred upon timing. As a prelude to the initiation of policy changes, relevant information has first to be gathered and then assessed. This sets a tendency for measures to be adopted belatedly, often with perverse effects. To address that deficiency, power was acquired to vary UK indirect taxes without the involvement of parliament. There was little success. A further difficulty arises from the democratic process. In the face of recurring parliamentary elections, attempts to fine-tune economic activity gained notoriety in the UK and the description 'stop-go'. As (pre-election) expansionary measures produced trade deficits, (post-election) deflationary measures were necessary to support the international value of sterling.

In a desperate last-ditch 'dash for growth' in 1972, the sterling exchange rate was permitted to float, when a depreciating pound was intended to counter the tendency for fiscal expansion to produce trade deficits. Tax cuts and increased government borrowing were expected to deliver ten percent growth over two years (twice the economy's productive potential). A junior Treasury minister recalls the policy change: 'a diktat came down from No. 10 to the Treasury saying that unemployment should be halved within a year – an absurd and dangerous notion'. He continues,

> it was corporatism gone mad – the belief that intervention could deliver a fair and reasonable basis for proceeding. ... The idea was that you brought about a bargain between the government, the unions and industry – a bargain in which the government said, 'If you, the unions, will moderate your pay claims, and you, industry, will moderate your prices, we, government will give you 5 percent growth.
>
> (Knott, 2002, p. 147–49)

One manifestation of 'corporatism gone mad' was the 'Group of Four' – the Confederation of British Industry, the Trades Union Congress, the National Economic Development Council and the state – which would oversee prices restraint, pay restraint, faster economic growth and lower unemployment. Against mooted doubts within the Treasury, economists at the resolutely Keynesian National Institute for Economic and Social Research were optimistic; they could see 'no reason why the present boom should either go bust or have to be busted' (NIESR, 1973, p. 6). However, the situation proved to be unsustainable. With a policy U-turn in November 1972, incomes policy was imposed to combat rising inflation and (despite the plummeting value of sterling) the escalating trade deficit.

With his counter-revolutionary stand against mainstream Keynesianism, this was the epoch within which Milton Friedman reinvigorated the libertarian principles (Chapter 2) that had been so resolutely defended by Simons. Friedman understood that free markets are the most effective institutional arrangement for coordinating activity. Competitive pricing allocates resources to their most effective uses. Planning and intervention are more likely to aggravate rather than to ameliorate economic difficulties. As markets operate effectively, flexible prices coordinate the rebalancing between consumer demands and entrepreneurial supplies. In that context, the informational damage caused by price distortions and general price inflation is not directly observable and, thereby, too readily missed. In that respect and as the core element of Friedman's Monetarism, a general proposition is endorsed: a requirement for a commitment to effective 'rules' for the implementation of monetary policy (Chapter 7). The primary purpose of rules is twofold: for policy adjustments to be shielded from political opportunism; and for economic agents to have confidence in the rationale and the direction of policy.

With few exceptions, the present chapter is studded with markers to the primary content of the chapters that follow. The pages on taxation (Chapter 10) have proven the least rewarding to their writer, where his direct fears are compounded by the likelihood of that sentiment being shared by his readers. Simons describes *Personal Income Taxation* (1938) as the unlikely combination of two sets of characteristics: those of 'an academic treatise' and those of 'a tract for the times' (Simons, 1938, p. v). With the first, the current writer has no expertise to offer; and, with the second, details are obviously dated. Although 'completeness' is one lame justification for the inclusion of the chapter on taxation, it is one that readers might bear in mind.

Notes

1 Aaron Director's sister, Rose, and Milton Friedman were married in 1938.
2 See *Keynes: the Return of the Master* (Skidelsky, 2009).

Bibliography

Caldwell, B. J. (2011) 'The Chicago School, Hayek, and Neoliberalism', in Van Horn, Mirowski and Stapleford, 2011, pp. 301–34.

Callaghan, J. (1967) 'Budget Speech' cited from BBC News; http://news.bbc.co.uk/1/hi/uk_politics/3288907.stm (accessed 4 November 2016).

Davenport, J. (1946) 'The Testament of Henry Simons', *The University of Chicago Law Review*, vol. 14, no. 1, December, 5–14.

Friedman, M. (1948/1952) 'A Monetary and Fiscal Framework for Economic Stability', *The American Economic Review*, vol. 38, 245–64; cited from Lutz and Mints, 1952, pp. 369–93.

Friedman, M. (1957) *A Theory of the Consumption Function* (Princeton, NJ: Princeton University Press).

Hayek, F. A. (1946) 'The Meaning of Competition', Stafford Little Lecture, Princeton University, May; cited from Hayek, 1949, pp. 92–106.

Hayek, F. A. (1949) *Individualism and Economic Order* (London and Henley: Routledge).

Keynes, J. M. (1936) *The General Theory of Employment Interest and Money* (London: Macmillan).

King, M. A. (2016) *The End of Alchemy: Banking, the Global Economy and the Future of Money* (London: Little, Brown Book Group).

Knott, J. (2002) *Here Today, Gone Tomorrow. Recollections of an Errant Politician* (London: Politico Publishing).

Lutz, F. A. and L. W. Mints (1952) (eds.) *Readings in Monetary Theory* (London: George Allen and Unwin).

McCormick, B. J. (1992) *Hayek and the Keynesian Avalanche* (New York: Harvester Wheatsheaf).

Mirowski, P. and D. Plehwe (2009) (eds.) *The Road from Mont Pèlerin: The Making of the Neoliberal Thought Collective* (Cambridge, Mass.: Harvard University Press).

National Institute of Economic and Social Research (1973) 'Summary and Appraisal', *National Institute Economic Review*, vol. 64, issue 1, May, 1–6.

Sigurjonsson, F. (2015) 'Monetary Reform, A Better Monetary System for Iceland', a report commissioned by Prime Minister Sigmundur David Gunnlaugsson. Reykjavik; www.forsaetisraduneyti.is/media/Skyrslur/monetary-reform.pdf (accessed 28 June 2016).

Simons, H. C. (1936) 'Rules versus Authorities in Monetary Policy', *Journal of Political Economy*, vol. 44, no.1, February, 1–30; reprinted in Simons, 1948, pp. 160–83.

Simons, H. C. (1938) *Personal Income Taxation: The Definition of Income as a Problem of Fiscal Policy* (Chicago, IL: University of Chicago Press).

Simons, H. C. (1948) *Economic Policy for a Free Society* (Chicago, IL: University of Chicago Press).

Skidelsky, R. (1992) *John Maynard Keynes. vol. 2. The Economist as Saviour, 1920–1937* (London: Macmillan).

Skidelsky, R. (2009) *Keynes: the Return of the Master* (London: Allen Lane).

Stewart, M. (1967) *Keynes and After* (Harmondsworth: Penguin Books).

Stigler, G. J. (1985) 'Frank Hyneman Knight', Working Paper 37. Working Papers Chicago, I: Center for the Study of the Economy and the State (Chicago, IL: University of Chicago).

Toporowski, J. (2010) 'Henry Simons and the other Minsky Moment', *Studi e Note di Economia*, Anno XV, no. 3, 363–68.

Van Horn, R. (2014) 'Henry Simons's Death', *History of Political Economy,* vol. 46, no. 3, 525–35.

Van Horn, R., and P. Mirowski (2009) 'The Rise of the Chicago School of Economics and the Birth of Neoliberalism' in Mirowski and Plehwe, 2009, pp. 139–78.

Van Horn, R., P. Mirowski and T. Stapleford (eds.) (2011) *Building Chicago Economics* (Cambridge: Cambridge University Press).

2 Libertarian Philosophy

2.1 Liberalism

It is now possible for the Nobel Laureate Robert Solow to write, with little fear of contradiction, that 'everyone has known for a long time that a complicated industrial economy is either a market economy or a mess' (Solow, 2012). Such comment would have been rare in the depth of the Great Depression, when the attention given to Henry Simons and to others, for their staunch defence of free market economics, was less than fulsome. As politicians then competed on the basis of motley beliefs that it is possible to devise purposeful interventions to raise employment and to alleviate hardships, proponents of minimal government were the few who held the very deepest convictions. It is within that context that Don Patinkin describes Simons's 'A Positive Program for Laissez Faire' (1934) as representing for classical liberalism a combination of 'the same qualities that made Marxism so appealing to so many other people at the time: simplicity together with apparent logical completeness; idealism combined with radicalism' (Patinkin, 1981, p. 4).

Simons describes the ethos that shapes his writing as 'severely libertarian or, in the English-Continental sense, liberal' (Simons, 1948, p. 1). Unless a distinction is explicitly drawn, those adjectives (and that of 'liberalism') are used synonymously. Simons lamented a lack of concern from a 'sophisticated generation', who viewed democracy as 'unfashionable'. His deepest fear was that a 'ruthless dictatorship' might prove the only means to maintain order between uncompetitive organisations, or that a powerful nation would emerge in situations where a populace is 'best disciplined to submission and least contaminated with dangerous notions about the rights of man' (*ibid.*, p. 45).

2.2 Simons and Hayek

Growing fears in relation to the concentration of market and industrial power, the impoverishment of political discourse and the evidence of new totalitarianisms were by no means unique to Henry Simons. Friedrich Hayek was contemporaneously voicing similar concerns. With his editor's introduction to *Collectivist Economic Planning: Critical Studies on the Possibilities of Socialism*

(1935a), Hayek laments that 'there is hardly a political group anywhere in the world that does not want central direction of most human activities in the service of one aim or another' (*ibid*, p. 1).

By the summer of 1940, the remorseless advance of dirigisme had motivated Hayek to embark upon a major endeavour that he called the 'Abuse of Reason Project'.[1] Although the task was never completed, fragments were published separately, including *The Road to Serfdom* (1944), wherein Hayek articulates fears of a widespread threat to civilisation. In then looking back upon the 'mess of things' across the first half of the twentieth century, Hayek expresses a fear that lessons would be lost to a generation yearning for change. *The Road to Serfdom* reached a wide audience after the *Reader's Digest* had published a shortened version, following which a US book club distributed over a million reprints.

Aaron Director was a prominent associate of both Simons and Hayek. He had known Hayek from the late 1930s and significant correspondence between the two had followed in the wake of Director's endeavours to publicise *The Road to Serfdom*. Towards the further promotion of that work, Director had joined with Fritz Machlup (acting editor of *The American Economic Review*) in an attempt to persuade Simons to write a review. The reticence then shown by Simons is as clear as it is puzzling: 'I am reluctant to review Hayek because I like the book so much' (Simons, letter, 17 September 1944; cited from Van Horn, 2013, p. 277); and, in declining a second request some three months later: 'I'm just no good at gilding lilies' (*ibid*.).

As the Second World War was drawing to its end, Simons had become increasingly desperate to establish a secure foundation for libertarian ideals; and he pushed for the formation of an institute of political economy at Chicago, to serve as a hub for both resident and visiting libertarians. Its intended objective would have been to influence professional opinion in the face of a rising tide of collectivist thinking. Retrospectively, it has been described as 'a last-ditch effort to keep alive ideas in danger of being lost' (Coase, 1993, p. 244). To that end, Simons had elicited Hayek's support for Aaron Director to head a new institute.[2]

On a promotional lecture tour of the US in April 1945, Hayek met with Harold Luhnow, President of the William Volker Charities Fund. Although turning down Luhnow's request to work on an American version of *The Road to Serfdom*, Hayek made a counter proposal that became known as the Free Market Project. Hayek wanted that enterprise to be orchestrated by someone who had a greater familiarity than his own with the US economy. It was to be a 'study of a suitable legal and institutional framework of an effective competitive system' (Van Horn, 2013, p. 279), based at the Chicago Law School. The degree to which the Free Market Project was 'at odds' with the prevailing ethos of the early post-war period is evidenced by the lack of any other option: 'Chicago was the only place that was likely to accept such a project, and … the law school was the only part of the University of Chicago that would accept such a project' (Kitch, 1983, p, 181; cited from Van Horn, 2013, p. 279).

The details of the Free Market Project that were approved by Luhnow and Hayek were largely the work of Aaron Director and Henry Simons, with the latter taking responsibility for the original draft and the two memoranda that had followed by June 1945. Director then distributed a research proposal that captured the spirit of *The Road to Serfdom* by setting the general objective: to strengthen understanding of a competitive socio-economic order. Among the policy areas for study that were indicated by Director were antitrust enforcement, tariff policy, corporate policy, labour policy and patent policy.

Although arrangements for Director's appointment to a research/teaching post had been completed soon after Simons's death, the focus that Simons had in mind for a libertarian revival had become diffuse. Or, rather, it was in process of being displaced by movements elsewhere, as Hayek was instrumental in motivating the instigation in 1947 of the Mont Pèlerin Society: an academy of intellectuals whose continuing objective has been 'to reconstruct a liberal philosophy' (Hayek, 1967, p. 149).

Although the ethos of the time was unfavourable, Hayek's influence and advice also led to the foundation in 1955 of the Institute of Economic Affairs (IEA), London. This endeavour originated with Hayek having been asked by Sir Antony Fisher to give advice on measures 'to thwart the ominous growth of socialism'. Hayek had then convinced Fisher of a need for institutions to function as 'second hand dealers of ideas' (Hayek, 1949b, p. 417). Such is the IEA, whose remit is to support 'authoritative studies of the economic theory of markets and its application to practical affairs' (Fisher, 1974, p. 104). Modern counterparts to the IEA include the Institute for Humane Studies at George Mason University (Fairfax, Virginia), the Cato Institute (Washington, D.C.) and the Ludwig von Mises Institute at Auburn University (Alabama).

That Hayek achieved the success that eluded Simons is most plausibly attributed to longevity. Indeed, for a quarter-century or so to the mid-1970s, Hayek was the most significant casualty of that post-war macroeconomic analysis that is structured upon a surfeit of unemployed labour and resources as had been the experience during the Great Depression. As Keynes's new doctrines were then becoming rationalised and popularised as aggregate demand management, *The Road to Serfdom* bore the criticism that it was merely a presentation of a polemic against the new order in which economic advancement would be achieved through fiscal interventions.

One of many affinities between Henry Simons and Friedrich Hayek is the presentation of liberalism as a theory of human progress, with the invisible hand a key element in 'sustaining the vital, creative processes of a free society' (Simons, 1948, p. 3). In like fashion, Hayek identifies in liberalism values that extend beyond the narrowly materialistic: '[p]rogress is movement for movement's sake, for it is in the process of learning, and in the effects of having learned something new, that man enjoys the gift of his intelligence' (Hayek, 1960, p. 41). Further empathy lies with the emphasis placed upon the rule of law, whose purpose is to protect commutative justice,[3] which is the '"natural" basis of co-operation among strangers' (Simons, 1948, p. 5). Hayek

> plan the allocation of resources in order to promote the full utilization of resources.
>
> (Phillips, 1995, p. 34)

This group, which became known as the Brain Trust, was to be influential in shaping the policies of the First New Deal, 1933.

When decisions are no longer driven by profit alone, Keynes argues that corporations are more likely to further the public good, but he is alert and aware that there is no 'unmixed gain' – i.e., that 'a waning of enterprise' might follow. In general, Keynes invokes a sense of optimism as to the net outcome of right-minded managers, but he exhibits a certain *naïveté* in overlooking possibilities for opportunistic behaviour, pressure-group lobbying and the capture of regulatory bodies by vested interests. Other planks of Keynes's broad schema are a need to secure improvements in the coordination of saving and investments for the community as a whole and for greater control over the population, in terms of 'innate quality as well as the mere numbers' (Keynes, 1926, p. 49). The coordination of saving and investments would form the core of Keynes's *The General Theory of Employment Money and Interest*, 1936.

Foremost among perverse state interventions that are identified by Simons is interference with 'the heart of the contract' – i.e., with relative price determination. Whatever the detail of the distortions to market processes that result from the discriminatory imposition of taxation and other levies, Simons identifies a general feature. Regardless of 'economic efficiency or personal justice', governments tend to grab most funds where there is 'least difficulty' (Simons, [1934] 1948, pp. 51–53). Given that the most powerful lobbying is in greatest evidence from business than from consumers, '[a]ll the grosser mistakes in economic policy … arise from focusing upon the interests of people as producers rather than upon their interests as consumers' (Simons, 1944, p. 2). This is evident in the granting of privileges and in the imposition of tariffs and other inhibitions or else when government is simply neglectful in protecting the competitive price mechanism.

An enterprise system requires the state to be active in securing conditions that are conducive to competition. In broad terms, Simons lists these as: a currency that is stable in value; clearly defined property entitlements; and 'many social welfare activities' (Simons, 1948, p. 42). Conversely, in minimising the *necessity* for state interventions, a system of competitive enterprise *allows* the state to be active in pursuing a policy of laissez-faire:

> [t]he representation of laissez faire as a merely do nothing policy is unfortunate and misleading. It is an obvious responsibility of the state under this policy to maintain the kind of legal and institutional framework within which competition can function effectively as an agency of control.
>
> (*ibid.*)

For Simons, 'the decisive argument for laissez faire' rests upon the relative concentrations of power and the inefficiencies that arise with 'government regulation and interference'. That Simons is keenly aware of the necessity to probe the issues that determine the legitimate scope for state intervention is a theme propagated by Hayek. Laissez-faire is not 'the ultimate and only conclusion' (Hayek, 1933, p. 134); and '[p]robably nothing has done so much harm to the liberal cause as the wooden insistence of some liberals on certain rules of thumb, above all the principle of laissez-faire' (Hayek, 1944, p. 13). 'Private property' and 'freedom of contract' do not, in themselves, provide for solutions:

> [o]ur main problems begin when we ask what ought to be the contents of property rights, what contracts should be enforceable, and how contracts should be interpreted or, rather, what standard forms of contract should be read into the informal agreements of everyday transactions.
>
> (Hayek, 1949a, p. 113)

In a free society, those judgements are based upon the defence of liberty for which politics must aspire to identify those rights and duties that promote competitive markets. With the alternative structures of monopoly practices, yields are raised by inhibiting the reallocation of resources from less important uses as judged by market values. With the capacity of monopolistic trade associations to maintain high profits and the capacity of monopolistic trade unions to maintain high wages, the production and allocative inefficiencies that arise in the absence of competition may then leave producers and/or workers with remuneration no higher than would have been achieved under competition, but with consumers in a worse position.

As a first step in the shift of power from particular individuals to the offices of state, the corporate status had been originally granted only to sovereign institutions: 'the state has to be supra-personal, precisely because its task is to defend personal rights' (Van Eeghen, 2005, p. 54, fn. 24). The further extension of the corporate status was initially restricted to private enterprises that were engaged in infrastructure activities of inherent public interest: most obviously the utilities and transportation. With a certain inevitability, the state was lax in preventing extensions beyond those confines but, by the second half of the nineteenth century, most Western states had passed permissive incorporation laws, so allowing the corporation to become the dominate feature of modern capitalism.

The private corporation violates the basic liberal principle of matching personal rights (of ownership) with full responsibility (for failures). By that view, the corporation 'constitutes an illegitimate mixing of the legitimate domains of the private and public sectors' (*ibid.*, p. 56). That the corporation emerges naturally from contractual freedom and efficiency-seeking, and that it is constrained by market forces, is a common liberal defence to which there are a number of counterarguments. Although liberals are generally very content when it ventures from political philosophy into economics. Simons's proposal to nationalise railroads and public utilities,[9] which Coase describes as reminiscent of market socialism, signals 'a strange route to laissez-faire' (Coase, 1993, p. 241). Other proposals that Coase highlights for criticism are: an upper limit to firm size of five percent (of total industrial output) to approximate 'the results of perfect competition'; and the reform of advertising and other promotional activities, because they direct most resources to 'persuading people to buy one thing rather than another' (Simons, 1948, p. 71). Broader indictments are: that Simons provides no supporting evidence for his proposals; shows no appreciation of the information required for their implementation; and makes no investigation of their effects. In categorising Simons as utopian,[10] Coase only tempers this negative appraisal in noting (i) Simons's primary interest to be in monetary theory and policy and (ii) his influence on such high achievers as Aaron Director, Milton Friedman, George Stigler and Gordon Tullock, to which Coase might have added Hyman Minsky[11] and Friedrich Hayek.

Utopian ideals too often take on the tone of a fetish. Where that happens, abuse may be showered upon any sinner who strays from the narrow path. So, for example, Walter Block finds Simons guilty of 'fraud and false advertising' and he suggested that Simons 'would not recognize "economic freedom" if it bit him on the nose' (Block, 2002, p. 28). In setting a backdrop to that abuse, Block describes two categories of libertarians. There is the extreme 'anarcho-capitalist', who accepts no government at all. Then there is the 'minarchist', who admits to a role for government, but in respect only of 'rights to personal safety and to the security of their legitimately held possessions' (*ibid.*, p. 5). It is the minarchist who serves as Block's benchmark in pointing to the waywardness of Simons.

As a preliminary, there are instances where Block allows Simons to pass muster and, in three areas, there is no equivocation. The first is Simons's advocacy of 100 percent reserve banking. With the second, Simons is 'steadfast and eloquent' (*ibid.*, p. 8) in his abhorrence of price controls. In the third, Simons is credited with condemning the anti-market tendencies of Presidents Hoover and Roosevelt. Simons's aspiration for taxation in the low region of ten percent of national income is also applauded.

On free trade, Block argues that Simons is diminished by his willingness to work to that ultimate goal by 'discussion, experiment, and compromise' (Simons, 1948, p. 26). In that gradual approach, the proposition from Simons, that 'legitimate vested interests' might be negotiated away 'over, say, a ten-year period' (*ibid.*, p. 70), is considered no less absurd than '"justified theft," or "proper murder"' (Block, 2002, p. 10). Similarly, the suggestion that property taxes might be retained, when not to do so would confer capital gains upon those already in possession, is likened to allowing neighbourhood crime to continue if its elimination (whereby local property values would rise) would deliver the same outcome. Block cites *caveat emptor* in denying the legitimacy of giving protection to those whose decisions have been taken within an existing regulatory framework. These fine points are moot issues.

It is with taxation that Simons leaves himself open to fierce attack. He minces no words in stating his view: '[t]hat reduction in inequality is per se immensely important' and 'that progressive taxation is … the only effective means to that end' (Simons, 1948, p. 26). That Simons might have a preference for greater equality of income and/or wealth is one thing. That it should be adopted as a political credo is quite another: no 'advocate of free enterprise' could 'elevate this into one of his bedrock principles' (Block, 2002, p. 18). In coming close to conflating bedrock principles with truth, Block misstates the position argued by Simons. Far from a bedrock political principle, this outcome is one that Simons argues must be achieved only by consensus.

The unwavering application of universal principles delivers an unhelpful critique of libertarianism that has little, if any, consequence for policy enacted in the real world. Otto von Bismarck is credited in having observed that 'politics is the art of the possible, the attainable, the art of the next best', where the political context and associated transaction costs lie among a plethora of broad considerations. That unanimity is unlikely to be achieved is a conundrum regularly addressed by libertarians for which reason the law is 'is full of distinctions among kinds of issues that require different kinds of majorities' (Friedman, 1962, p. 24). This explains why libertarians look primarily to markets to lessen the conformity that other systems must build upon; and it is why libertarians are cautious in deciding those areas in which unanimity is an absolute for freedom. For markets to function, the prior presumption is that a framework exists for the maintenance of law, the definition of property rights and the enforcement of contracts. In short, the basic role of libertarianism is

> to provide a means whereby we can modify the rules, to mediate differences among us on the meaning of the rules, and to enforce compliance with the rules on the part of those few who would otherwise not play the game.
>
> (*ibid.*, p. 25)

2.8 Libertarian paternalism

There is no neutral context within which choice can be exercised. In allowing the details of practical situations to intrude, it soon becomes apparent that utopian benchmarks give way to mundane practicalities. That individuals make the best choices for themselves is either tautological or testable, and, when tested, behavioural preferences tend to contradict rational optimisation. In practical situations, the objective of libertarian paternalism is not to coerce anyone into making a decision, but to deter individuals from making inferior choices. In this, a key element is the default option; i.e., if an individual offers no response, the key issue is to decide which option it is best to choose on his/her behalf. For libertarian paternalism, the goal is 'to influence people's choices in directions that will make choosers better off, *as judged by themselves*' (Thaler and Sunstein, 2009, p. 5).

There is a report from a symposium held in 1981 of a number of Simons's former pupils who failed to rise to his defence (De Long, 1990). Harold Demsetz, George Stigler and Milton Freidman are cited as having registered their agreement with Ronald Coase: that Simons's 'interventionism' is a blemish upon the principles of classic liberalism. The report also notes how different those views are to Aaron Director's assessment in the 1947 preface to *Economic Policy for a Free Society*; *viz*. 'Just as Lord Keynes provided a respectable foundation for the adherents of collectivism, so Simons was providing a respectable foundation for the older faith of freedom and equality' (Simons, 1948, p. v).

The difference 'between Chicago then and Chicago today is about what the necessary foundations for a competitive free-market economy are' (De Long, 1991, p. 616). There is no ready prescription by which social order might be achieved. Given the exceptions that blemish the abstraction, Keynes had presented laissez-faire as nothing more than a facile representation in the minds of successful businessmen. Yet, although Keynes was attempting to embellish a richer social philosophy, his understanding of capitalism –

> I think that Capitalism, wisely managed, can probably be made more efficient for attaining economic ends than any alternative system yet in sight, but that in itself it is in many ways extremely objectionable.
>
> (Keynes, 1926, pp. 52–53)

– might be aligned with Winston Churchill's endorsement of democracy: 'Indeed, it has been said that democracy is the worst form of Government except all those other forms that have been tried from time to time' (Churchill, 1947; cited from Hansard, 1947, 207–208).

Notes

1 See 'The Abuse of Reason Project', Chapter 11 in Caldwell (2003).
2 Director had played the key role in securing publication of Hayek's *The Road to Serfdom* (1944).
3 Commutative justice regulates the exercise of rights between individuals and associations, so that exchange is based on equal value.
4 Distributive justice regulates the exercise of rights between a public authority and the individual, in order to achieve an equitable distribution of burdens and privileges.
5 As were many who were moved by the poverty of post-war Vienna, Hayek was inclined towards socialist ideals. Although this was countered under the tutelage of Ludwig von Mises, both Mises and Hayek were alert to wider responsibilities: '[a]nyone with a genuine sense of moral values experiences no hardship in deciding between honour and livelihood' (Mises, 1920, p. 100).
6 Where Adam Smith emphasises gains achieved by the division of labour, so Hayek emphasises gains achieved by the division of knowledge.
7 Keynes catches the sentiment in *The End of Laissez-faire*: '[t]he important thing for government is not to do things which individuals are doing already, and do them a little better or worse; but to do those things which at present are not being done at all' (Keynes, 1926, p. 47). As more recently cited by President Obama,

'I'm a Democrat. But I believe what Republican Abraham Lincoln believed: That Government should do for people only what they cannot do better by themselves, and no more' (Obama, 2012).

8 With the pre-setting of yields that are 'appropriate' to different categories of investment, there are affinities with Islamic finance; see Chapter 11 (the section, 'The social perspective').

9 This proposal relates to fundamental issues relating to the corporate status of business.

10 Simons is far from utopian, for instance with his endorsement of gradualist tariff reforms in giving due regard to 'legitimate vested interests' (Simons, 1948, p. 70).

11 'As a student I was most influenced by Henry C Simons, Oscar Lange, and Josef Schumpeter' (Minsky, 1982, p. 5).

Bibliography

Block, W. (2002) 'Henry Simons Is Not a Supporter of Free Enterprise', *Journal of Libertarian Studies*, vol. 16, no. 4, Fall, 3–36.

Boaz, D. (1997) *Libertarianism: A Primer* (New York: Free Press).

Caldwell, B. J. (2003) *Hayek's Challenge: An Intellectual Biography of F.A. Hayek* (Chicago, IL: Chicago University Press).

Coase, R. H. (1993) 'Law and Economics at Chicago', *The Journal of Law and Economics*, vol. 36, no. 1, April, 239–54.

De Long, J. B. (1990) 'In Defence of Henry Simons' Standing as a Classical Liberal', *Cato Journal*, vol. 9, no. 3, Winter, 601–17.

Friedman, M. (1962) *Capitalism and Freedom* (Chicago, IL: Chicago University Press).

Hansard (1947) vol. 444, HC Deb, 11 November, pp. 203–321; http://hansard.millbanksystems.com/commons/1947/nov/11/parliament-bill (accessed 17 April 2015).

Hayek, F. A. (1933) 'The Trend of Economic Thinking', *Economica*, vol. 13, 127–37.

Hayek, F. A. (1935a) (ed.) *Collectivist Economic Planning. Critical Studies on the Impossibility of Socialism* (London: George Routledge and Sons).

Hayek, F. A. (1935b) 'The Nature of the Problem', in Hayek, 1935a, p. 1.

Hayek, F. A. (1949a) *Individualism and Economic Order* (London and Henley: Routledge).

Hayek, F. A. (1949b) 'The Intellectuals and Socialism', *University of Chicago Law Review*, vol. 16, Spring, 417–33.

Hayek, F. A. (1960) *The Constitution of Liberty* (London and Henley: Routledge and Kegan Paul).

Hayek, F. A. (1967) *Studies in Philosophy, Politics, Economics and the History of Ideas* (London and Henley: Routledge and Kegan Paul).

Hayek, F. A. (1976) *Law, Legislation and Liberty: A New Statement of the Liberal Principles of Justice and Political Economy, vol. 2, The Mirage of Social Justice* (London and Henley: Routledge and Keagan Paul).

Hayek, F. A. (1978) *New Studies in Philosophy, Politics, Economics and the History of Ideas* (London and Henley: Routledge and Keagan Paul).

Hayek, F. A. (1979) *Law, Legislation and Liberty: A New Statement of the Liberal Principles of Justice and Political Economy, vol. 3, The Political Order of a Free People* (London and Henley: Routledge and Kegan Paul).

Keynes, J. M. (1926) *The End of Laissez-Faire* (London: Hogarth Press).

Kitch, E. W. (1983) 'The Fire of Truth: A Remembrance of Law and Economics at Chicago, 1932–1970', *Journal of Law and Economics,* vol. 26, April, 163–233.

Minsky, H. P. (1982) *Can "It" Happen Again? Essays on Instability and Finance* (Armonk NY: Sharpe).

Mises, L. von (1920) 'Die Wirtschaftsrechnung im sozialistischen Gemeinwesen', in *Archiv für Sozialwissenschaften,* vol. 47; cited from 'Economic Calculation in the Socialist Commonwealth', in Hayek, 1935, pp. 87–103.

Obama, B. (2012) State of the Union address, cited from *Denver Business Journal,* 24 January; www.bizjournals.com/denver/news/2012/01/24/text-obamas-state-of-the-union-address.html (accessed 1 November, 2016).

Patinkin, D. (1981) *Essays on and in the Chicago Tradition* (Durham, NC: Duke University Press).

Phillips R. J. (1995) *The Chicago Plan & New Deal Banking Reform* (New York: M E Sharpe Inc.).

Simons, H. C. (1944) 'Some Reflections on Syndicalism', *Journal of Political Economy,* vol. 52, no. 1, March, 1–25; reprinted in Simons, 1948, pp. 121–59.

Simons, H. C. (1948) *Economic Policy for a Free Society* (Chicago, IL: University of Chicago Press).

Solow, R. M. (2012) 'Hayek, Friedman, and the Illusions of Conservative Economics', *New Republic,* November 16; www.newrepublic.com/article/books-and-arts/magazine/110196/hayek-friedman-and-the-illusions-conservative-economics (accessed 11 March 2015).

Thaler, R. H. and C. R. Sunstein (2009) *Nudge: Improving Decisions about Health, Wealth and Happiness,* revised edition (London: Penguin).

Van Eeghen, P. H. (2005) 'The Corporation at Issue, Part I: The Clash of Classical Liberal Values and the Negative Consequences for Capitalist Practices', *The Journal of Libertarian Studies,* vol. 19, no, 3, Summer, 49–70.

Van Horn, R. (2013) 'Hayek's Unacknowledged Disciple: An Exploration of the Political and Intellectual Relationship of F. A. Hayek and Aaron Director (1945–1950)', *Journal of the History of Economic Thought,* vol. 35, no. 3, September, 271–90.

3 Economics and the Chicago School

3.1 Modern economics

Whether detailed by the course set by Henry Simons or that associated with Milton Friedman, the Chicago School sits unambiguously within the classical paradigm. The Chicago School has no empathy with the 'blueprint' that was drawn up and presented by Keynes in *The General Theory*, nor with the many variations upon Keynesian themes that have busied the economics profession ever since.

The general view is that modern economics begins in 1776 with Adam Smith's *An Inquiry into the Nature and Causes of the Wealth of Nations*. The arguments and analysis that followed (from David Ricardo, Thomas Malthus, John Stuart Mill, *inter alia*) are regarded as having set the ethos of classical economics. The core of classical thought is that competitive market forces, which drive the continuous price adjustments of goods, services and factors of production, are the best means to decide the allocation of resources. More formally, the concept of economic efficiency is 'registered' by transient market equilibria that reflect equivalent valuations by marginal sellers and marginal buyers.

Adam Smith's metaphor of the invisible hand is frequently cited, whereby trade is instigated across competitive markets as products are presented for sale that others value. By the mutual gains that market exchanges then achieve, the pursuit of self-interest becomes generally beneficial. Therefore,

> It is not from the benevolence of the butcher, the brewer, or the baker, that we can expect our dinner, but from their regard to their own interest.
>
> (Smith, 1776, book I, chap. 2, para. 2)

> By directing that industry in such a manner as its produce may be of greatest value, he intends only his own gain, and he is in this, as in many other cases, led by an invisible hand to promote an end which was no part of his intention.
>
> (Smith, 1776, book IV, chap. 2, para. 9)

In representing that ethos, socio-economic analysis as generally conducted through to the 1930s 'expressed itself in a distinctive name: it was called the "classic" period of economics'; that is, until

> at a time when the word 'classic' had lost its eulogistic connotation and was beginning to stand for 'obsolete', Lord Keynes used the word in order to denote the teaching of A Marshall and his immediate followers (or simply, pre-Keynesian economics).
>
> (Schumpeter, 1954, pp. 379–80)

Although the original connotation of classical economics was reclaimed, the detail of 'neo-classical economics' was attracting the greater attention. As developed during the last quarter of the nineteenth century, neoclassical economics builds precise mathematical formulations for point-of-time optimisation. A key prerequisite is 'perfect knowledge'. Without that omniscience, there is no information for differential calculus to derive tractable solutions from the mathematical specifications that define the actions of manufacturers and consumers, respectively maximising profits and satisfaction. Within the neoclassical paradigm, competition is redundant because, fully alert to production and consumption possibilities, traders are instantly able to achieve their optimal disbursements.

During that same quarter-century, a second line of development had seen the emergence of the Austrian School. Although the neoclassical thread is evident, the Austrian School does not build from an assumption of perfect knowledge. Instead, it accepts that decision-making is founded upon knowledge that is uncertain, limited and variable across individuals. The Austrian scenario is one in which 'goods are not easily specified … costs were not objectively given … [and] … knowledge is uncentralizable' (Streissler, 1992, pp. 65–66).

The distinctiveness of Austrian analysis is that, by the emphasis that is placed upon competitive entrepreneurial discovery, it is incapable of being summarised by mathematical formulations. Where neoclassical optimisation is achieved by a single point-of-time calculation, the Austrian setting is one in which 'the decisions of many individuals influence one another and necessarily succeed one another in time' (Hayek, 1946, p. 93). Austrian economics is therefore more closely attuned to the older and broader classical context where the term 'political economy' indicates a requirement for robust social institutions. The latter are essential for the presentation of economics as an applied science. Included are a formal legal framework and a moral code wherein implicit obligations and trust determine reciprocal expectations.

3.2 Economics and politics

As classical economics gives emphasis to the interaction between the real economy (i.e., entrepreneurial production and trading) and the facility of money and credit (which improve upon the search costs that are inherent in a barter economy), typical concerns are with monetary institutions and their associated problems: inflation, finance, regulation and civic freedoms.

As developed from ideas elucidated in *The General Theory*, the concern of Keynesian macroeconomics is with boarder features of the nation's economy – national income, full employment, international trade and growth – and the means by which to manage aggregate demand. Having previously censured economists for their long-term view – 'this long run is a misleading guide to current affairs' (Keynes, 1923, p. 80) – Keynes's focus in *The General Theory* is upon the immediate impact of (and the most appropriate response to) falling prices upon real activity.

Monetary deflation, through the 1920s in the UK and across Western economies in the 1930s, had eroded business confidence and caused a retreat into money. This had reduced investment expenditure below the level necessary to sustain full employment, so a recommendation followed for 'a national investment programme directed to an optimal level of domestic development' (Keynes, 1936, p. 349). This would serve as a temporary palliative, but if there were an inherent tendency for the economy to deliver chronic unemployment, then fiscal interventions could redress that outcome.

With that juxtaposition of views, it is possible to categorise two kinds of economists whose respective philosophies are poles apart. Thumbnail sketches now follow. On the political left are those who believe it possible to apply intelligent thought to mould social structures. These are necessary to guide economic interrelationships and, because structures are always capable of being improved, economic systems can benefit from policy initiatives, not only of the kind associated with Keynes's *General Theory*, but also from interventions to regulate money, banking and finance, *etcetera*. This 'constructivist' approach holds that it is feasible for a socio-economic order to be intelligently organised and closely regulated.

On the political right are those economists who believe that the dynamic complexities of modern production and exchange do not support an optimistic view of active policy interventions (including attempts to manage aggregate demand and to forestall bank insolvencies). From that alternative perspective, a cautious evolutionary approach is more likely to give reliable direction:

> If we can agree that the economic problem of society is mainly one of rapid adaptation to changes in the particular circumstances of time and place, it would seem to follow that the ultimate decisions must be left to the people who are familiar with these circumstances, who know directly of the relevant changes and of the resources immediately available to meet them.
>
> (Hayek, 1945; p. 83)

Well-defined legal entitlements to property are essential if the unintended consequences of human action are to enhance rather than to threaten social cohesion. Where livelihoods are reliant upon the interplay of market forces – details of which are beyond any full comprehension or control – it is prudent that individuals should seek to protect gains that they have made. Hence, the requirement for legal protection to claims based upon known rules and procedures that constitute property rights. In effect, all trade consists of an exchange of property rights.

3.3 Credit: saving and bank finance

Few economists would contest the idea that freely-adjusting market prices inform and direct entrepreneurial decision-making. The efficient allocative function of the price mechanism is central to classical economics, where there is no principle to distinguish between inter-spatial prices and inter-temporal prices. Interest rates, which determine the cost of credit arrangements, are inter-temporal prices.[1] It is a typical arrangement for entrepreneurs to require credit to bridge the inter-temporal gap between incurring costs and receiving sales revenue. As with trading generally, the demand for credit (together with its supply) sets a market price.

Entrepreneurs obtain credit that is available from those with the resources (saving) to invest in business ventures. There is no guarantee of success: economic advancement shows primarily as the residual after the *ex post* elimination of entrepreneurial failures.

'Loanable funds' are the *real* resources that are available from savers to finance capital investment projects. In the most rudimentary of a non-money economy, Robinson Crusoe must undertake his own saving. If he wishes to build a raft so that he may catch a greater volume of fish by sailing offshore, he must first create a stockpile of fish caught from his shoreline (i.e., Crusoe must first create a 'wages fund'). After he has salted and saved a sufficient amount of fish, Crusoe may turn his activity to cutting bamboo and vines in order to build his raft. In principle, the same requirement – for real resources (fish) to undertake a real investment (raft) – applies in a sophisticated money economy, where a 'banking' intermediary may be involved. It is easy to see how the necessity for real saving to exist in advance of any undertaking to make real investments may go unnoticed.[2]

If the routine is one in which a bank accepts savers' deposits (say, as gold coins) and is willing to lend that gold to business investors, banking would be a benign activity. Interest rates would find their 'natural' level as competition between savers, bankers and investors achieve that arrangement. In a more 'sophisticated' process, a bank might leverage the volume of its lending upon a relatively small proportion of savers' deposits. This defines a system of fractional reserve banking, where a bank relies upon creating its own liabilities for its clients to use (instead of gold) as the means of exchange. This may be achieved in a number of ways: for example, by a bank printing and distributing its own bespoke banknotes, by the use of cheques or debit cards to transfer balances between bank accounts or by the use of electronic transfer systems. Whatever the means, a bank relies upon depositors accepting a bank's liabilities (rather than gold) as the means of exchange. Of course, savers may demand gold in withdrawing their deposits; and there may be occasions when a bank has insufficient gold to meet those demands. It is upon such occasions that a central bank has relevance.

As a modern substitute for the use of gold, a central bank is a monopolist in the supply of 'base money' (i.e., sovereign banknotes and reserves). If a commercial bank has insufficient reserves to meet the demand from savers for the withdrawal of their deposits, the central bank is in a position to provide the bank with base money. In advancing loans of base money to a bank, the central bank determines the borrowing rate (i.e., the 'market' rate of interest). It is by that decision of the monetary authority (the central bank) that the market rate may diverge from the natural rate. At this point, the empirical is set against the hypothetical. A market rate of interest is observable, but the natural rate is a theoretical concept that would be identified only if it were possible to know when the market for *real* loanable funds is in a state of equilibrium. Indeed, the latter exists when the market rate is equal to the natural rate.

3.4 Keynes's economics (interest rate determination)

For an economy floundering in the depths of a recession, Keynes asserts that 'the concept of a "natural" rate of interest … [had nothing] … very useful or significant to contribute to our analysis'. Rather, its relevance was merely to 'preserve the status quo' (Keynes, 1936, p. 243). In rejecting the relevance of the natural rate as a hypothetical benchmark for the conduct of monetary policy, Keynes presents a novel liquidity preference theory of interest rate determination.

By setting the price at which sovereign bonds are offered for sale to traders across financial markets, Keynes argues that a sovereign central bank could pursue its own 'policy of an autonomous rate of interest, unimpeded by international preoccupations, and of a national investment programme directed to an optimal level of domestic development' (Keynes, 1936, p. 349). In presenting that as a policy option that is open to all, sovereigns generally are in a position to achieve the remarkable result of 'restoring economic health and strength internationally' (*ibid.*).

The necessity for Keynes to create a new theory of interest rate determination arises because the long-standing classical loanable funds theory of interest rate determination is incompatible with a core concept of *The General Theory* – i.e., the income multiplier. If the income multiplier is to be retained, the classical loanable funds theory of interest rate determination must be displaced. Keynes achieves this with his liquidity preference analysis: the interest rate is determined by the choice of assets held within a wealth portfolio.

[1944] 1980, p. 430). That Keynes knew that other options would have to be introduced is indicated by his response, as described by Friedrich Hayek, when he had asked Keynes,

> whether he was not concerned about what some of his disciples were making of his theories. After a not very complementary remark about the persons concerned he preceded to reassure me that he would again quickly swing round public opinion - indicating by a quick movement of his hand how rapidly that would be done. But three months later he was dead.
>
> (Hayek, 1952, p. 348)[3]

In the face of rising inflation coexisting with stagnant economies through into the 1970s, the Keynesian revolution floundered as a counter-revolution was ready to launch. This was associated with Milton Friedman and his insistence that a Chicago oral tradition[4] had remained rooted in classical monetary theory.

3.6 The Chicago tradition

That the credit 'leverage' of commercial banks might drive an economic boom beyond sustainable limits, and that the inevitable retrenchment is likely to be associated with insolvent banks and monetary contraction, gave the motive in the early 1930s for the endorsement of monetary reform by faculty members at Chicago University. The detail of that reform was referred to as the 'Chicago Plan', the wider significance of which is that economists began to link Chicago with a 'school of thought'. Thus, the Chicago School of that period crystallised during the tenure of three economists who were most closely associated with the Chicago Plan (Frank Knight, Jacob Viner and Henry Simons); but, by the 1960s, leadership of the Chicago School had passed to George Stigler and Milton Friedman (see Miller, 1962).

Friedman's growing public persona in the late 1960s and into the 1970s was closely aligned with the angst felt by Keynesian economists over their inability to reconcile the new experience of 'stagflation' with Keynes's assertion of that experience being untenable. Barely a decade earlier, Keynesian economists had been applauding the apparent confirmation of that original assertion, after evidence had been presented in a seminal paper by A.W. Phillips (Phillips, 1958). That publication, which is possibly the most cited paper in the annals of modern economic analysis, defined the Phillips curve: a non-linear inverse association for UK male manual workers, between annual percentage increases in nominal wages and the unemployment rate.

Phillips excited mainstream Keynesians whose research activity was raised, not only to show how different data sets might confirm the 'inflation-unemployment' relationship that is implicit in Keynes's assertion, but also to construct more appealing theoretical explanations for their statistical correlations. That euphoria began to peter out after little more than a decade when, by the demise of the Phillips curve, classical monetary dogma was re-affirmed: money is long-term neutral (i.e., it has no capacity to enhance the long-term performance of a liberal market economy).

Building from his Presidential address to the American Economic Association in 1967, Milton Friedman's new perspectives upon the classical paradigm thereafter received ever-greater prominence. More than a decade after the 'Chicago tradition' first began to be discussed in the context of new presentations of classical monetary theory, the distinctiveness of Friedman's 'The Quantity Theory of Money - A Restatement' (Friedman, 1956) was thereafter described as 'the Monetarist position' (Brunner, 1968, p. 9).

Characteristics that are now most closely associated with that 'Monetarist position' are: (i) that the severity of the Great Depression was a direct consequence of the monetary contraction that followed the Wall Street Crash; (ii) that, by the omission of inflation expectations as a relevant variable, the original Phillips curve was mis-specified; (iii) that the willingness of individuals to 'demand to hold money' is derived from their decisions upon the composition of their asset portfolios; and (iv) that monetary policy should be guided by transparent rules. In short: the broad features of policy recommendations that would comply with the tradition of the Chicago School are monetary discipline, small government and free markets (see Friedman, 1974).

Notes

1 Given that every transaction takes time, all prices are inter-temporal prices. See Chapter 11 (the section, 'Yields: a theoretical perspective').

2 Keynes denies the necessity for real saving in advance of the investment that lifts an economy from recession. Instead, the Keynesian income multiplier shows that the flow of saving, from the income of those newly employed in undertaking investment, exactly equals the flow of investment. The *legerdemain* is that investment (the metaphorical 'cart') comes before saving (the 'horse').

3 There are (at least) two other accounts of that conversation in 1946: (i) 'I had asked him whether he was not getting alarmed about the use to which some of his disciples were putting his theories. His reply was that these theories had been greatly needed in the 1930 but if these theories should ever become harmful, I could be assured that he would quickly bring about a change in public opinion' (Hayek, 1966, p. 103); (ii) 'I asked him whether he wasn't alarmed about what his pupils did with his ideas in a time when inflation was already the main danger. His answer was, "Oh, never mind, my ideas were frightfully important in the Depression of the 1930s, but you can trust me: if they ever become a danger, I'm going to turn public opinion around like this." But six weeks later he was dead and couldn't do it. I am convinced Keynes would have become one of the great fighters against inflation' (Hayek, 1983b, p. 115).

4 The budding of a Chicago oral tradition might be inferred from a four-page review of Lauchlin Currie's *The Supply and Control of Money in the United States*. The reviewer states, 'This book… expounds clearly a set of views which, while firmly established in the 'oral tradition' of some schools are [*sic*] meagrely represented in the accessible literature' (Simons, 1935, p. 555).

Bibliography

Brunner, K. (1968) 'The Role of Money and Monetary Policy', *Federal Reserve of St. Louis Review*, vol. 50, 9–25.

Colonna, M., H. Hagmann and O. Hamouda (1994) (eds.) *Money and Business Cycles, The Economics of F. A. Hayek*, vol. 2 (Aldershot, UK: Edward Elgar).

Friedman, M. (1956) 'The Quantity Theory of Money - A Restatement', in Friedman, *et al.* (eds), 1956, pp. 3–21.

Friedman, M. (1983) 'A Theoretical Framework for Monetary Analysis', in Gordon R. J. (ed.), 1983, pp. 1–62.

Friedman, M., P. Cagan, J. J. Klein, E. M. Lerner and R. T. Selden (1956), *Studies in the Quantity Theory of Money* (Chicago, IL: University of Chicago Press).

Gordon, R. J. (1983) (ed.) *Milton Friedman's Monetary Framework: A Debate with His Critics*, revised edition (Chicago, IL: Chicago University Press).

Hayek, F. A. (1945) 'The Use of Knowledge in Society', *The American Economic Review*, vol. 35, no. 4, 519–30; cited from Hayek, 1949, pp. 77–91.

Hayek, F. A. (1946) 'The Meaning of Competition', Stafford Little Lecture, Princeton University; cited from Hayek, 1949, pp. 92–106.

Hayek, F. A. (1949) *Individualism and Economic Order* (London and Henley, UK: Routledge).

Hayek, F. A. (1952) 'A Review of *The Life of John Maynard Keynes*, by R. F. Harrod', in *The Journal of Modern History*, vol. 24, no. 2; cited from Hayek, 1967, pp. 344–48.

Hayek, F. A. (1966) 'Personal Recollections of Keynes and the Keynesian Revolution', *The Oriental Economist*, vol. 34, no. 663, January, 78–80.

Hayek, F. A. (1983a) 'The Austrian critique', *The Economist*, 11th June, 45–48; reprinted in Hayek, 1995, pp. 247–54.

Hayek, F. A. (1983b) *Friedrich von Hayek*; transcript of interviews completed under the auspices of the Oral History Program, University of California, Los Angeles; www.archive.org/stream/nobelprizewinnin00haye# (accessed 31 October 2010).

Hayek, F. A. (1995) *Contra Keynes and Cambridge: Essays, Correspondence*, vol. 9, edited by B. J. Caldwell (London: Routledge).

Keynes, J. M. (1923) *A Tract on Monetary Reform* (London: Macmillan).

Keynes, J. M. (1936) *The General Theory of Employment Interest and Money* (London: Macmillan).

Keynes, J. M. (1937) 'The General Theory of Employment', *Quarterly Journal of Economics*, vol. 51, no. 2, 209–23.

Keynes, J. M. (1944) 'A Rejoinder to Professor Graham', *Economic Journal*, vol. 54, 429–30; cited from Keynes, 1980, pp. 39–40.

Keynes, J. M. (1980) *Activities, 1941–1946: Shaping the Post-War World: Bretton Woods and Reparations*, vol. XXVI, *The Collected Writings of John Maynard Keynes*, edited by D.E. Moggridge (London: Macmillan).

Miller, H. L. (1962) 'On the 'Chicago School of Economics'', *Journal of Political Economy*, vol. 70, no. 1, 64–69.

Phillips, A. W. (1958) 'The Relationship between Unemployment and the Rate of Change of Money Wages in the United Kingdom 1861–1957', *Economica*, vol. 25, no. 100, 283–99.

Schumpeter, J. A. (1954) *History of Economic Analysis* (Oxford: Oxford University Press).

Simons, H. C. (1935) 'The Supply and Control of Money in the United States by Lauchlin Currie', *Journal of Political Economy*, vol. 43, no. 4, 555–58.

Smith, A (1776) *An Inquiry into the Nature and Causes of the Wealth of Nations*; cited from a compilation by Edwin Cannan, 1904 (Methuen and Co., Ltd); www.econlib.org/cgi-bin/searchbooks.pl?searchtype=BookSearchPara&id=smWN&query=taxation (accessed 7 December 2016).

Streissler, E. W. (1992) 'Hayek on Information and Socialism', *Wirtschafts Politische Blätter*, vol. 39, 258–83, cited from Colonna and Hagmann, 1994, pp. 47–75.

4 The Chicago Plan

The background

4.1 The Federal Reserve

In giving Congress the authority to coin and to regulate the value of money, the US Constitution implicitly requires the sovereign government to underwrite the credit moneys that are issued by commercial banks. With only a fraction of commercial bank deposits backed by base money (banknotes and reserves issued by the sovereign monetary authority – the central bank), bank liquidity is assured only when a central bank provides a 'lender of last resort' facility. With that provision in place, a central bank is committed to provide base money as necessary to meet the withdrawal of deposits from commercial banks. Yet, a central bank has no powers to control an overexpansion of credit moneys that would lead to a shortfall in bank liquidity. *Prime facie*, a central bank has responsibility without power. Whenever they may occur, banking crises show with two characteristics: there is a contraction in the provision of bank credit moneys, and the payments system begins to break down. There was such an event beginning in mid-October 1907.

With the economy already experiencing a downturn, share values on the New York Stock Exchange fell over a three-week period to about one-half of their previous level. The origin of that rapid fall was a rivalry between two copper magnates. By a financial miscalculation involving a ruse that had been intended to facilitate the acquisition of more of its own stock, the share price of the *United Copper Company* collapsed and the company was placed into receivership. Given the banking interests that were associated with *United Copper*, depositors rushed to liquidate their deposits. This led to the collapse of the *Knickerbocker Trust Company* (the third-largest trust in New York City), following which a banking panic spread nationwide.

The response from Congress was to pass the *Aldrich-Vreeland Act* (1908), which established the *National Monetary Commission* (NMC), with a remit 'to inquire into and report to Congress, at the earliest date practicable, what changes are necessary or desirable in the monetary system of the United States or in the laws relating to banking and currency' (NMC, 1912, p. 3). That inquiry was informed by a fact-finding tour of Europe, when the US banking and financial systems were found to be rudimentary by comparison.

Based upon the recommendations that were then forthcoming, the *Federal Reserve Act* was passed in 1913.

The general objective of that *Act* was to establish a national currency and a monetary authority that would bring greater stability to banking and financial systems. Twelve Federal Reserve banks (Boston, New York, Philadelphia, Cleveland, Richmond, St. Louis, Atlanta, Chicago, Minneapolis, Kansas City, Dallas and San Francisco) were each given charge of a district. Seven of their respective heads made up the governing body of the Federal Reserve Board (the 'Fed'), which was empowered to issue banknotes (aka US dollars) and, by implication, given the responsibility to set short-term interest rates. In addition, the Fed was authorised to trade in bonds, notes and bills issued by the US Treasury.

All nationally chartered banks were required to become members of the Federal Reserve System and to purchase specified non-transferable stock in – and to hold non-interest-bearing reserves with – their respective Federal Reserve banks. The Fed would set the required reserve ratio for commercial banks and it would meet their liquidity requirements by rediscounting 'eligible assets' held by the banks. With the authority to hold securities on its own account (where the corresponding yields were to cover the operating costs of the Federal Reserve System), the Fed engaged in portfolio switching – i.e., open-market operations.

4.2 A treasury and a central bank

In reacting to the financial crisis dating from 2008, open-market purchases of sovereign securities and mortgaged assets were at the core of central bank initiatives to counter the deflation that was anticipated. As open-market purchases are made, bond yields fall and commercial bank reserves increase. That a sovereign central bank makes open-market purchases of sovereign (i.e., Treasury) assets establishes a direct link between monetary policy and fiscal policy. The formality of that relationship is signalled by a prescient view that 'the ultimate monetary powers and legislative powers rest with fiscal policy' (Simons 1942, p. 182). The formal *interdependence* of monetary and fiscal interventions is examined in Chapter 8 (the section, 'Broad money and its credit counterparts').

A sovereign power oversees the provision of two categories of debt instruments: those that are highly liquid (banknotes and reserves, which are the liabilities of the central bank); and those that are highly illiquid (undated bonds, which are the liabilities of the Treasury). Despite modern presentations of central bank *independence*, institutional arrangements periodically draw back the curtain. For example, although the US Treasury issued paper currency ('greenbacks') in 1861 to meet Civil War expenses, none has been issued since 1971. In the UK, the *Currency and Bank Notes Act* of 1914 empowered the UK Treasury to issue banknotes to replace gold coins in circulation, and although the intention was to remove those notes from circulation at the end of the

Great War, they were issued until 1928. And for the period since 2009, when the Bank of England has engaged in quantitative easing, HM Government has provided a formal indemnity to cover any losses to the Bank of England from its accumulation of sovereign assets.

4.3 US monetary policy in the 1920s

An eighteenth-century controversy between the Banking School and the Currency School informs alternative perspectives upon the conduct of monetary policy. Relevant issues rest upon the distinction between endogenous (commercial bank) money and exogenous (central bank) money. By the arguments of the Banking School, emphasis is placed upon the 'needs of trade' as the driving force for the endogenous provision of money. From the alternative perspective of the Currency School, the general expectation is that, when exogenous money is increased, prices rather than output tend to rise. In the broadest terms, the 'needs of trade' doctrine explains the passive policy stance adopted by the Fed after its formation in 1913.

The core foundation for the Currency School is the quantity theory of money where, in the early twentieth-century, the influence of Fisher's *The Purchasing Power of Money*, 1911 was seminal, both by its theoretical arguments and by Fisher's persuasiveness in presenting statistical correlations between rising prices and the rising volume of trade. An expansion of exogenous money was observed to *raise* real economic activity. Fisher pointed to an approximate seven months lag between the turning points of rising prices and rising trade. Inspired by his correlations, he conjured a causal connection: that 'a rising price level temporarily stimulates trade and that a falling price level depresses trade' (Fisher, 1925, p. 179). Thereafter, Fisher was vocal in propagating the idea that it would best serve a sound economy if the Fed was were able to deliver price stability. How that might be achieved would remain an enduring theme.

When deflation threatens, monetary expansion is now accepted as an appropriate panacea, but in the 1920s the weight of authority was not aligned with that suggestion. Indeed, during the short-sharp recession of 1920/1921, Herbert Hoover (as Secretary of Commerce) appealed directly to bankers to rein in their credit in the interests of wider social responsibilities. For its part, the Fed 'took particular exception to the suggestion that it could or should require banks to police the ultimate uses to which creditworthy customers put borrowed funds' (Barber, 1985, p. 27).

Herbert Hoover challenged the idea that cyclical downturns were inevitable. During the recession of 1920/1921, he initiated and then organised the President's *Conference on Unemployment*. The general feeling was that, in bringing forward public works programmes, there would be both a direct and an indirect impact upon employment. (In the 1930s and thereafter, Keynes and Keynesians would place great emphasis upon that idea.) With state and local governments responsible for over ninety percent of public sector expenditure, the necessary trigger for an earlier start for public works lay in persuading officials of the net gains from such action. That the proposition failed as a vote-winner was undoubtedly responsible for the reticence of public officials to act: 'much of the foot dragging by politicians stemmed from their reluctance to cede spending powers of government to experts and to formulas' (Barber, 1985, p. 21).

Other practicalities raised further controversies. The authority of the Fed was jealously guarded and there was no enthusiasm for new theoretical structures. From the writing on gold of David Hume (1711–1776), it was deeply embedded within the economic psyche that a trade deficit (surplus) stimulates the specie-flow mechanism, such that a gold outflow (inflow) causes domestic prices to fall (rise), so tending to redress the imbalance of international competitiveness. Yet, the specie-flow mechanism is incompatible with maintaining a constant purchasing power for the domestic money unit, so the operation of the gold standard is at odds with Fisher's recommendation that monetary policy should target price stability. On this and other issues, Hoover was ambivalent: on exchange rate stability under the gold standard; trade protection in defence of stable employment; and caution in the provision of bank credit.

4.4 Complacency

In exercising his responsibilities for commerce over a period of more than seven years from 1920, Hoover had been charged to promote best practice and to eliminate waste. In that regard, free competition sat uneasily with Hoover's predilection that there should be the widest dissemination of information so that commerce might benefit generally. Also dating from 1920, a remit was given to the *National Bureau of Economic Research* (NBER) to produce technical monographs. These would later form the basis for a report in 1929: *Recent Economic Changes in the United States.* Beyond lauding the performance of the economy since the recession of 1920/1921, the report acknowledged that major problems remained. Technological progress and merger activity had raised productivity, but jobs had been lost and market concentration had increased. Government measures (though not financial assistance) had strengthened trade associations in manufacturing, but, under new proposals, farming would receive both encouragement and loan finance. The wishful thinking was that farmer-controlled co-operatives would achieve sufficient marketing efficiencies to enable the co-operatives to become self-supporting bodies. Action in respect of farm import tariffs lacked clarity and was deferred.

Although Hoover remained committed to the principles of free market economics, he was active through the good times and into the early days of the Great Depression in conjuring measures that he thought would best serve the economy. The recovery, that had been the experience from 1922 onwards, was never likely to challenge Hoover's confidence that general economic performance would benefit from improved data and informed exhortations, but those expectations were to be dashed. Even as he was adopted as Presidential Republican nominee in 1928, Hoover had confidently asserted that, 'We in America today are nearer to the final triumph over poverty than ever before in the history of any land'.[1] Not long thereafter and in the wake of the Wall Street Crash, he promised to cut taxes and to expand spending on public works while ensuring that the Federal budget remained balanced.

As Wall Street trading had been pushing stock prices towards a Standard and Poor's peak (29 October 1929), Irving Fisher endorsed a relaxed mood:

> Stock prices have reached what looks like a permanently high plateau. I do not feel there will be soon if ever a 50 or 60 point break from present levels, such as they have predicted. I expect to see the stock market a good deal higher within a few months.
>
> (Fisher, 1929)

Even as stock prices began to fall, Maynard Keynes evinced similar optimism: 'There will be no serious direct consequences in London. We find the look ahead decidedly encouraging' (Keynes, 25 October 1929; cited from Overy, 2010, p. 96). Many others were also disposed to believe they were witnessing the healthy reversal of speculative excesses.

In retrospect, a consensus holds that the monetary policy of the Fed 1929–1933 was perverse. If its primary focus had been upon failing banks and high unemployment, it would have pursued open-market bond purchases and discount rate reductions. Yet, in giving greater attention to the exchange value of 'an ounce of gold for every $20.67 in Federal Reserve notes', the reaction of the Fed when faced by gold outflows 'included raising the discount rate and selling (or at least reducing purchases of) existing bonds' (Fishbank, 2010, p. 387).

From his interest and analysis of business cycles, Wesley Mitchell (as Director of the NBER) had initially regarded the downturn to be in line with historical patterns. With the passing of time, he was more astute in attributing both its depth and its duration to a coincidence of a number of essentially disparate events. As an encompassing assessment, this chimed with the diversity of opinion as expressed by those contributing to the American Economic Association panel (December 1930) on the depressed state of business.

4.5 Unemployment and Keynes

The Chicago Plan and *The General Theory of Employment Money and Interest* (1936) deliver explanations and palliatives for an economy in deep recession. However, where the origin of the Plan clearly lies with events on Wall Street, the origin of *The General Theory* lies with 'parochial' UK policymaking. High UK unemployment throughout the 1920s was a direct result of official policy that was intent upon raising the international value of sterling to the pre-1914 rate of US$4.86. Upon which is based the retrospective conclusion that, '[h]ad the exchange value of the pound been fixed realistically in the 1920s ... there would have been no need for mass unemployment, hence no need for a revolutionary theory to explain it' (Johnson, 1975, p. 110).

With the Bank of England having raised its discount rate from five to six percent in November 1919 and to seven percent in April 1920, swingeing cuts in contemporaneous government spending were such that primary fiscal surpluses were achieved throughout most of the 1920s. Unemployment soared. In a pamphlet published in 1925 (*The Economic Consequences of Mr. Churchill*), Keynes had warned the UK Treasury that its commitment to such a high parity would have deleterious consequences for employment and growth. Having failed to persuade the authorities to set a different course of action, Keynes refocused his attention upon radical initiatives to reduce unemployment.

Although much that Keynes would later formalise in *The General Theory*[2] had been examined in pragmatic terms by 'Americans of Hoover's persuasion in the 1920s', the suggestion that follows – that those individuals 'could rightfully claim that they had anticipated most of Keynes's conclusions' (Barber, 1985, p. 41) – must be disputed. In the US, the broad idea was not, as Keynes would suggest, that a sustained level of fiscal expenditure might be necessary to secure long-term full employment. Rather, the US stance was that the trend of fiscal expenditure should remain unchanged, but that its timing might be better focused to counter cyclical phenomena. To that end, Hoover asked cabinet departments to accelerate spending on projects that had already been authorised. Similar exhortations were made to state governors, municipal authorities and regulated industries. Hoover's general approach had three broad themes: to bring forward fiscal expenditures; to set low interest rates; and to exhort business to maintain wages and prices. However, trade associations overstepped the mark with the backing which they gave to the Swope Plan.

In September 1931, Gerard Swope, then the president of the *General Electric Company*, presented a proposal for recovery whereby the *Federal Trade Commission* would supervise trade associations for each industry. Covering all companies with fifty and more employees, trade associations would regulate output and set prices. Although Hoover had previously given strong support to voluntary trade associations, he castigated the scheme as suggesting 'the creation of a series of complete monopolies over the American people' (Hoover's memorandum of 17 September 1931, cited from Eisner, 2010, p. 293).

With the US economy showing few signs of recovery, the focus began to shift towards banking and finance. Hoover had floated an idea that he felt might arrest rising interest rates and falling equity prices. His suggestion, which fell flat, was that companies might use new bank loans to buy back their own shares. Among other initiatives, a request for greater cooperation between government and bankers led to the creation of the *National Credit Corporation* (NCC) in October 1931. Its broad objective was to enable commercial banks to pool their assets so that small, potentially insolvent banks might borrow against assets that the Fed could not accept as collateral.

Through the decade of the 1920s, enduring fiscal surpluses had substantially reduced the level of sovereign debt, to the extent that subsequent fiscal deficits raised few concerns through to 1931. Although fiscal expenditure was rising sharply, justification could be found in the earlier years of plenty; but that sentiment did not last. With Europe also faltering under the impact of the slump, Hoover proposed setting a one-year moratorium on the repayments of war debt. Against thunderous disapproval from France and others who were averse to any dispensation for German reparations, the moratorium was passed by Congress in December 1931. Congress had also expressed a willingness to mandate the payment of a bonus to war veterans,[3] but the mood changed rapidly as the fiscal budget was being formulated for 1932–1933, when Hoover was motivated to sanction large tax rises and to bring greater austerity to fiscal programmes.

On a more positive note and because the Fed lacked the authority to mandate a number of initiatives, a proposal went to Congress for the *Reconstruction Finance Corporation* (RFC) to be established with a $500 million loan from the US Treasury. By that financial initiative, perceptions were massaged to ease the path of reality: it was assured that 'such outlays should not give rise to red ink in the Treasury's budget accounts' (Barber, 1985, p. 176). In gaining approval early in 1932, the RFC was able to provide loans to smaller banks that were not part of the Federal Reserve System. As with the NCC, the RFC was authorised to make loans against collateral that the Fed would not accept.

Early in February 1932, Hoover failed to achieve any enduring success when he engaged in a general campaign against the hoarding of banknotes, the value of which was estimated to exceed $1.3 billion. His argument was that hoarding had simultaneously paralysed expenditure and depleted bank reserves: for every hoarded dollar, a multiple of bank credit was lost. Given that dishoarding has no direct relevance to the actions of any individual, the proposition proved hard to sell. Through the medium and sponsorship of the *Chicago Daily News*, exhortations by the 'Citizens Reconstruction Organisation' did lead to redeposits of $250 million being made over a ten-week period, but by mid-April, that flow had reversed, leaving the anti-hoarding campaign in failure. Hoover cajoled banks to remain optimistic and to maintain their lending, but demand from credit-worthy borrowers continued to fall and, in the process of rebuilding their cash reserves, banks were switching their loans to fixed-interest government and corporate securities.

With the disappointment of Hoover's monetary measures and exhortations, and as the mood began to favour more direct forms of intervention, the proliferation of advice from various groups of academic economists reached new heights. Among these was a set of recommendations contained in a brief statement (see the Harris *Manifesto* given in the appendix to this chapter) from a collaboration of twenty-four economists, following their participation in a conference held at the University of Chicago in January 1932. The Harris *Manifesto* was the naissance of the Chicago Plan.

4.6 The Norman Wait Harris Foundation Conference

In the immediate aftermath of the Harris Foundation Conference (27–31 January 1932), a *Manifesto* was drawn up to be transmitted to President Hoover. It urged

> that the Federal Reserve be authorized to use government securities as collateral for the note issue, that open market operations be pursued more aggressively, that the Reconstruction Finance Corporation proceed vigorously in aiding the banks, and that the government continue its public works programs.
>
> (Phillips, 1995, p. 29)

The *Manifesto* was signed by twenty-four economists, twelve of whom were affiliated to the University of Chicago and twelve of whom had other affiliations.[4] The economists had identified what they considered to be a key problem: that the cyclical flexibility of credit is accompanied by the cyclical inflexibility of wages and prices. The orthodox neoclassical remedy for unemployment – a reduction in money wages – contradicted the general sentiment that wage levels should be protected. Whatever the merits or otherwise of that neoclassical remedy, it was clear that the moment was not then ripe. Instead, the Harris Foundation economists argued for expansionary fiscal policy. Those measures were not only needed to counter deflation, but they would also be relevant both for the relief of distress and to support projects for public and semi-public improvements. The possibility of a temporary abandonment of gold was not ruled out.

A second statement from the Harris Foundation economists, which quickly followed upon the first, added to that compendium of opinions when it re-emphasised the desirability of loosening credit, greater parsimony within government agencies and increased taxation as the alternative to borrowing. Another lengthy statement from that source in April of the same year was motivated by the perceived need to support prices, which should take 'the form of generous fiscal expenditures financed without resort to taxes'. Other measures within that statement saw benefits in making bonus payments to war veterans and, 'for a time' (*ibid.*) abandoning the gold standard.

The Harris Foundation economists were not alone in supporting policy options of this kind. With an initiative from the newspaper magnate William Randolph Hurst, thirty-one academics put their names to an 'Economists' Plan' that fostered a bill introduced by Senator Robert M. LaFollette. This called for 'an emergency federal bond issue of $5.5 billion' of which $3.75 billion would 'support spending on public works' (Barber, 1985, p. 149). Another group of economists followed Senator Robert F. Wagner with less radical proposals incurring a new bond issue of only $1 billion. With these and a variety of diverse expressions of support and criticism from other sources, the situation is summarised thus:

> three years of depression had dealt a shattering blow to the confidence of the business community and had so shaken the self-confidence of the

> profession's leaders' that, where some continued to support new initiatives, this was 'not because they could offer a persuasive theoretical rationale for them, but from a belief that some action was imperative, even if it meant departing from the rules.
>
> (*ibid.*, p. 155)

Having ceased its open-market purchases in July 1932, the Fed remained largely inactive and many were convinced that the interest of longer-term financial stability required the government to become more closely engaged with the institutional structures of money and credit. Bankers were vehemently criticised, but that political rhetoric was devoid of firm proposals for reform. As the crisis deepened, Hoover increasingly found himself in the role of scapegoat. Although he was moved to breathe life into proposals that he had erstwhile regarded as anathema, during the four months from Franklin D. Roosevelt's election to his inauguration in March 1933, the President-elect opted to stonewall rather than to advance any pre-commitment to policy. In being badly defeated in 1932, 'Herbert Hoover left the White House an embittered man' (*ibid.*, p. 187) and, thereafter, became a strident critic of Roosevelt's New Deal.

4.7 The view from Harvard

In completing his Harvard dissertation on banking theory, Lauchlin Currie had been awarded his PhD in 1931. In January of the following year, he and two Harvard associates (Harry Dexter White and Paul Theodore Ellsworth) issued a *Memorandum* (reprinted in Laidler and Sandilands, 2002b), in which a number of policy recommendations are made for lifting the depression: 'Currie and his associates had concluded that … open market operations alone might not be enough … and argued the necessity of financing budget imbalances with money creation' (Laidler and Sandilands, 2002a, p. 524). Large fiscal deficits coupled with open-market purchases were needed to expand bank reserves. The Harvard *Memorandum* is a document of over 5,000 words, which would compare with the 300 words of the Harris Conference *Manifesto*.

John H. Williams (Currie's PhD supervisor) delivered a paper at the Harris Foundation Conference, held later that same month. That contribution (Williams, 1932) reflects contemporary preoccupations, not least those would subsequently be expressed by Ralph Hawtrey (Hawtrey, 1933) and Friedrich Hayek[5] (Hayek, 1939). Some four years were still to pass before Keynes's would publish his counter to the UK 'Treasury view'. It was Hawtrey who was held responsible for the Treasury View:

> that fiscal policy not financed by money creation would usually be fully crowded out, and that, when deficits were financed by money creation, it was this money creation, and not any direct expenditure associated with fiscal policy that will do the work.[6]
>
> (Laidler and Sandilands, 2002a, p. 524)

The Harvard *Memorandum* is described by Milton Friedman as a 'remarkable and impressive document' that supports the 'position that Chicago had no monopoly on the quantity theory approach to the Great Depression and to measures to recover from it' (letter dated 22 January 2001; cited from Laidler and Sandilands, 2002a, p. 518, fn. 4). Certainly, it can be agreed that, in attempting to reduce their debts by creating fewer deposits, the banking system had exacerbated the fall in money incomes and that, to counter that impact, the reserve banks would need 'to enter upon a vigorous open market purchasing policy' (Laidler and Sandilands, 2002b, p. 536). Given that Friedman had little time for Austrian business cycle theory, it might also be understood how he would applaud the Harvard *Memorandum* for its deprecation of the Hayekian view that 'economic maladjustments' (*ibid.*, p. 534) require those inefficiencies to be purged from the system. Yet, the Harvard *Memorandum* is noteworthy for a number of comments and assertions, which can only be viewed as ultra-Keynesian in their tone:

1 The most salient of these is the implicit acknowledgement of the concept of 'cost-push' inflation[7]: '[i]t is only after much of the present slack in our economic system has been taken up that the danger of inflation becomes real' (*ibid.*, p. 538).
2 Ranking in second place is the income multiplier, where the recommendation could hardly be stronger 'that the Government immediately commerce a program of public construction on a nationwide scale', not least because the 'revival of these industries would involve a secondary increase in employment, which in turn would stimulate recovery in other lines in ever widening circles' (*ibid.*, p. 540).
3 Then, as the *coup-de-grâce:* deficit-finance public works 'does not saddle future generations with a burden… [because]… the capital goods that could be and are not produced deprive the future of the continuous steam of utilities that would have been derived from those capital goods' (*ibid.*, p. 541). *Note bene*: in assuming that those utilities are not traded at full market prices, how are the bond holders to be repaid?

On leaving Harvard in 1934 and with his new status as a naturalised US citizen, Currie joined Jacob Viner's 'Freshman Brain Trust' (a motley group of advisors and strategists to the Roosevelt campaign) at the US Treasury in 1934. Currie became 'a highly visible and leading advocate of expansionary fiscal policy' (*ibid.*, p. 515) as he maintained his focus upon monetary reform by continuing with his work upon the broad principles and administrative details that are relevant to the supply and control of money. With this, Currie's analysis independently delivered the same core tenet as the Chicago Plan: commercial bank sight deposits should be 100 percent backed by reserve assets.

In reviewing Currie's *The Supply and Control of Money in the US* (1934), Simons applauds its 'excellent statistical compilation and analysis'. That observation might reasonably be viewed as gratuitous: any deviations from the results that

Simons might have expected from that investigation would have caused him to cast doubt upon the data, not the theory. Currie's unwillingness to extend the data set beyond the calculation of 'actual circulating media' is criticised by Simons as 'a fallacious simplification of problems'. If the reforms suggested by Currie were implemented, alternative forms of money would appear, just as they had with the emergence 'of checking accounts, after the strict limitation upon note issue'. Above all other considerations, Simons lambasts Currie for resting his policy recommendations upon discretionary powers: '[m]anaged currency without definite, stable, legislative rules is one of the most dangerous forms of "planning"' (Simons, 1935, pp. 557–58). Even so, Simons concludes his review with the comment, 'this book is one of the few economics treatises of recent years which has left the reviewer genuinely grateful and indebted to its author' (Simons, 1935, p. 558).

Working from within Roosevelt's administration through his membership of the Freshman Brain Trust, Currie identified *excess* reserves as a key factor. Given that commercial banks hold excess reserves, a monetary authority might influence the broad money supply (i.e., banknotes in circulation plus commercial bank sight deposits), but only if bank lending were managed to deliver a fixed ratio of reserves. By the impracticality of achieving that outcome, the ratio of *excess* reserves would tend to move inversely to commercial bank lending, with lending rising and falling with the business cycle. The requirement placed upon the Fed, not to vary the ratio of *required* reserves to deposits, together with its authority to discount only real bills, exacerbated the procyclical supply of broad money.

In the process of moving commercial banks to a regime of operating with 100 percent reserves, Currie argued that a gradual adjustment would be served if each bank received a non-interest-bearing note from the Fed, either to be held indefinitely or retired over an extended period. The profitability of commercial banking would be maintained by requiring holders of sight deposits to pay service charges. Federal Reserve notes would replace all existing notes, and the RFC would make secured loans to a lending agency to counter any shortfall in commercial bank lending. Currie again concurred with Chicago: as the preferred alternative to creating a monetary authority independent of the sovereign administration, Congress would define specific monetary policy objectives.

Currie's two associates left Harvard at around the same time, White to the Treasury and Ellsworth into academia, where he would eventually receive retrospective credit for 'the "IS-LM-ization" of Keynesian economics' (Laidler and Sandilands, 2002a, p. 516, fn. 1). Those who remained of the Harvard faculty

> had no positive ideas to offer about the central economic questions of the day [and so] would soon succumb to those who did, namely the young Keynesians led by Alvin Hansen who would quickly come to dominate it after 1936.
>
> (Laidler and Sandilands, 2010, p. 13)

4.8 March 1933: Roosevelt takes office

Throughout his election campaign, Roosevelt championed balanced budgets as he had lambasted Hoover as a deficit spender. Yet, with his legislation for a New Deal, Roosevelt's *National Industrial Recovery Act* (NIRA) authorised a variety of policy initiatives. Greater price stability would provide the *quid pro quo* for cuts to production, where an immunity – given to trade associations against prosecution under antitrust laws – was a ruse to deter price-cutting. In addition, there were codes of fair competition, imposed working standards and rights for labour unions. The NIRA also established a body for administering public works, with funding opportunities for various projects. In general, the NIRA is viewed as having failed, in that it was poorly administered, it promoted monopoly practices and it failed to galvanise business support.

Roosevelt's second major concern was in meeting the argument for general monetary reflation, where Irving Fisher was making waves. With the acknowledged benefit of hindsight, Fisher argued that the US had borrowed too freely in the late 1920s. In order to reduce the real burden of debt and to raise the purchasing power of money, Fisher now gave retrospective support to the open-market purchases that had begun in February 1933. He also recommended that the velocity of money in circulation should be increased by allowing greater flexibility in respect of the required reserve ratio for banking. As a further ruse to dissuade banknote hoarding, he argued for the appendage of a weekly postage stamp to maintain their validation.

In order to stem the withdrawal of bank deposits, a special session of Congress in March 1933 had shut down the banking system as 'a pre-emptive strike … to prevent a further cataclysmic explosion of bank and financial institutional failures' (Phillips, 1995, xi). With his first 'Fireside Chat' on March 12, Roosevelt had sought to persuade his public that the *Emergency Banking Act*, passed three days earlier, would guarantee that 'the banks that reopen will be able to meet every legitimate call' (Roosevelt, 1933).

The President's further promise to cover depositors' losses gave the assurance necessary for the Fed to reopen on March 13 with a mandate 'to issue additional currency on good assets' (*ibid.*). The following day, banks reopened in approximately 250 cities where clearing houses were located; and on March 15, other banks that had been passed fit by examiners also reopened. That same day, trading recommenced, following an extended closure of the New York Stock Exchange. Share prices then soared by a record one-day gain of over fifteen percent. By the end of the month, the public had redeposited two-thirds of $1.78 billion withdrawn from deposits over four weeks ending on March 8.

On 16 March 1933, twelve days after Roosevelt's inauguration as thirty-second President of the US, a six-page academic memorandum was circulated that, in retrospect, is viewed as having launched the Chicago Plan for banking reform.

4.9 Appendix: the *Harris Manifesto*

Recommendations of Twenty-Four Economists

A letter, sent to President Herbert C Hoover on 31 January1931, was signed by Quincy Wright (Chairman) and Donald Slesinger (Secretary) of the Normal Wait Harris Foundation. The letter contained the 'recommendations unanimously adopted by a group of [twenty-four] economists ... following a series of closed discussions on "Gold and Monetary Stabilisation"'. There followed six bullet points listed as follows:

1 We recommend that the Federal Reserve banks give a substantial preference in discount rates to commercial paper eligible as cover for Federal Reserve notes. We recommend further that the Federal Reserve Act be amended to empower the Federal Reserve Board, during the present emergency, to permit, at its discretion, the use of federal government securities on equal terms with commercial paper as cover for Federal Reserve notes.

2 We recommend that the Federal Reserve banks systematically pursue open-market operations with the double aim of facilitating necessary government financing and increasing the liquidity of the banking structure.

3 We urge that the Reconstruction Finance Corporation vigorously and courageously carry out those provisions of the Act which authorise it to give aid to the banks by making loans on assets not eligible for rediscount with the Federal Reserve banks.

4 We recommend that the federal government maintain its program of public works and public services at a level not lower than that of 1930–1931, in order not to counteract the effects of the previous recommendations.

  We believe that some measure of financial co-operation of the federal government with the state and local governments is indispensable to the maintenance of adequate unemployment relief.

5 We strongly recommend the reduction or cancellation of the intergovernmental debts as an essential step toward recovery of world industry and trade, and we regard such a recovery as an important contribution to our own prosperity. We call attention to the fact that the intergovernmental debts, while nominally unchanged since the debt settlements, have increased in real burden as a result of the fall in prices, thus impairing the capacity to pay under normal conditions.

6 We strongly recommend that the government enter into negotiations with other countries, leading toward a reciprocal and substantial lowering of tariffs and other barriers to world trade.

Notes

1 From a speech accepting the Republican Party Presidential nomination, Stanford University (11 August 1928).

2 David Bensusan-Butt – who was tasked to undertake literature searches, references and the index for *The General Theory* (1936) – would later comment that '[a]ny

undergraduate will nowadays write out (what he thinks to be) Keynesian economics in two pages; but Keynes needed 400, wasting no words' (Bensusan-Butt, 1966, p. 32). Henry Simons's 100-line review of *The General Theory* gives a more succinct appraisal of 'the most famous economist of our time', who by popular acceptance is 'one of the authentic geniuses of his generation'. Those courtesies are followed by more pointed remarks: poorly defined terms and unsubstantiated propositions deliver 'a theory of unemployment, interest and money which attains generality by being about nothing at all' (Simons, 1936, p. 91). Simons represents *The General Theory* as a collection of expedients with which wise government must intervene. That deflationary pressures had led to the hoarding of saving is not disputed, but that description is accompanied by no sound 'arrangements for the future'. Although Keynes expresses a preference for a lasting free enterprise economy, he gives not a hint as to how this might be supported by monetary reforms. Instead, he attacks orthodox theory 'with results which will impress only the incompetent' (*ibid*., p. 92). Among the 'sophisticated leg-pulling' of the schemes of 'an army of cranks and heretics', the following are endorsed: 'mercantilism, *autarchie*, social credit, stamped money, fantastic governmental spending, the single tax, underconsumption theories and usury laws' (*ibid*., p. 93).

3 By the *World War Adjusted Compensation Act* (1924), bonuses for war veterans were to be paid in 1945. In 1932, 43,000 individuals marched on Washington, D.C.: 17,000 war veterans, their families and affiliated groups were demanding earlier payment. On July 28, the US Attorney General ordered the removal of veterans from all government property. Shots were fired by the police, leaving two veterans fatally wounded. As marchers and their families were driven out, shelters and belongings were burned.

4 Twelve from Chicago: John H. Cover, Garfield V. Cox, Aaron Director, Harry D. Gideonse, Frank H. Knight, Harry A. Millis, Lloyd W. Mints, Henry Schultz, Henry C. Simons, Jacob Viner, Chester W. Wright and Theodore O. Yntema. Twelve with other affiliations: James W. Angell (Columbia), Irving Fisher (Yale), Max Handman (Michigan), Alvin H. Hansen (Minnesota), Charles O. Hardy (Brookings), Arthur W. Marget (Minnesota), Harold G. Moulton (Brookings), Ernest M. Patterson (Pennsylvania), Chester A. Phillips (Iowa), Charles S. Tippets (Buffalo), John H. Williams (Harvard) and Ivan Wright (Illinois). Those attending but not signing the manifesto: Paul H. Douglas (Chicago), Gottfried von Haberler (Vienna, visiting Harvard) and Henry Parker Willis (Columbia). *Note bene*: four additional names are elsewhere cited (see Barber, 1985, p. 223): Max Handman (Michigan), Frank H. Streightoff (Indiana), Thomas S. Luck (Indian) and Chester A. Phillips (Iowa).

5 This publication gives the content of five lectures delivered by Hayek in 1936, at the Institut Universitaire de Hautes Etudes Internationales, Genève.

6 Laidler and Sandilands comment further on the Hawtrey-Treasury View that, if fiscal expenditure were financed by the issuance of money rather than bonds, sequential rises in public confidence and the velocity of circulation might preclude any crowding out effect of that expenditure.

7 *The General Theory* gives the conditions for cost-push inflation in the following passages:

> It follows that an increase in the quantity of money will have no effect whatever on prices, so long as there is any unemployment, and that employment will increase in exact proportion to any increase in effective demand brought about by the increase in the quantity of money; whilst as soon as full employment is reached, it will thenceforward be the wage-unit and prices which will increase in exact proportion to the increase in effective demand;
>
> (Keynes, 1936, p. 295)

> But, in general, the demand for some services and commodities will reach a level beyond which their supply is, for the time being, perfectly inelastic, whilst in other directions there is still a substantial surplus of resources without employment. Thus as output increases, a series of "bottle-necks" will be successively reached, where the supply of particular commodities ceases to be elastic and their prices have to rise to whatever level is necessary to divert demand into other directions;
>
> (*ibid.*, p. 300)

> When a further increase in the quantity of effective demand produces no further increase in output and entirely spends itself on an increase in the cost-unit fully proportionate to the increase in effective demand, we have reached a condition which might be appropriately designated as one of true inflation.
>
> (*ibid.*, p. 303)

The general accommodation of cost-push inflation within fixed-price Keynesian models sustains a concept that the experience of stagflation and the theory of the expectations-augmented Phillips curve ought to have banished, once and for all:

> I agree with these 'monetarists' in particular … that there is, so far as the economic mechanism is concerned, no such thing as a 'cost-push' inflation-unless one treats as part of the economic causation the political decision to increase the quantity of money in response to a rise of wages which otherwise would cause unemployment.
>
> (Hayek, 2007, p. 79)

Bibliography

Barber, W. J. (1985) *From New Era to New Deal. Herbert Hoover, the Economists and American Economic Policy, 1921–1933* (Cambridge: Cambridge University Press).

Bensusan-Butt, D. M. (1967) (ed.) *On Economic Knowledge. A Sceptical Miscellany* (Canberra; Australian National University Press).

Eisner, M. A. (2000) *From Warfare State to Welfare State: World War I, Compensatory State-Building, and the Limits of the Modern Order* (University Park: Pennsylvania State University Press).

Fishbank, P. (2010) 'US Monetary and Fiscal Policy in the 1930s', *Oxford Review of Economic Policy*, vol. 26, no. 3, 385–413.

Fisher, I. (1925) 'Our Unstable Dollar and the So-Called Business Cycle', *Journal of the American Statistical Association*, vol. 20, no. 150, 179–202.

Fisher, I. (1929) Speech delivered on 17 October, and reported in *New York Times*; cited from Rapp, 2015, p. 52.

Hawtrey, R. G. (1933) *The Gold Standard in Theory and Practice*, 3rd ed. (London: New York & Toronto, ON: Longmans, Green and Co.).

Hayek, F. A. (2007) *Denationalisation of Money*, re-issued edition (London: Institute of Economic Affairs).

Johnson, H. G. (1975) 'Keynes and British Economics', in M. Keynes (ed.), 1975, pp. 108–22.

Keynes, M. (1975) (ed.) *Essays on John Maynard Keynes* (Cambridge: Cambridge University Press).

Laidler, D. and R. Sandilands (2002a) 'An Early Harvard Memorandum on Anti-Depression Policies: An Introductory Note', *History of Political Economy*, vol. 34, no. 3, 515–32.

Laidler, D. and R. Sandilands (2002b) (eds.) 'Memorandum Prepared by L. B. Currie, P. T. Ellsworth, and H. D. White (Cambridge, MA, January 1932)', *History of Political Economy*, vol. 34, no. 3, 533–52.

Laidler, D. and R. Sandilands (2010) 'Harvard, the Chicago Tradition and the Quantity Theory: A Reply to James Ahiakpor', *History of Political Economy*, vol. 42, no. 3, pp. 574–92.

National Monetary Commission (2012) *Letter from Secretary of the National Monetary Commission Transmitting, Pursuant to Law, the Report of the Commission* (Washington. DC: Government Printing Office); www.federalreservehistory.org/Media/Material/Event/60-238 (accessed 20 November, 2015).

Overy, R. (2010) *The Twilight Years: The Paradox of Britain Between the Wars* (London: Penguin Books).

Phillips R. J. (1995) *The Chicago Plan & New Deal Banking Reform* (New York: M E Sharpe Inc.).

Rapp, D. (2015) *Bubbles, Booms and Bust. The Rise and Fall of Financial Assets*, 2nd ed. (New York: Springer).

Roosevelt, F. D. (1933) Fireside Chat 1: On the Banking Crisis (March 12); www.millercenter.org/the-presidency/presidential-speeches/march-12-1933-fireside-chat-1-banking-crisis (accessed 20 November, 2015).

Simons, H. C. (1935) '*The Supply and Control of Money in the United States* by Lauchlin Currie', *Journal of Political Economy*, vol. 43, no. 4, 555–58.

Simons, H. C. (1942) 'Hansen on Fiscal Policy', *Journal of Political Economy*, vol. 50, no. 2, 161–96.

Williams, J. H. (1932) 'Monetary Stability and the Gold Standard', in Q. Wright (ed.), 1932, pp. 3–39.

Wright, Q., (ed.) (1932). *Gold and Monetary Stabilization: Lectures on the Harris Foundation* (Chicago, IL: University of Chicago Press).

5 The Chicago eight, plus four, plus one

The Chicago Plan is associated with eight principal contributors and four minor players. One Nobel Prize-winner in Chemistry also merits inclusion.

5.1 Cox, Garfield (1893–1959)

Born in Fairmount, Indiana, he lived on a small eighteen-acre family farm. He attended Fairmount Academy and Earlham College in Richmond, Indiana, transferring to Beloit College, Beloit, Wisconsin where he graduated in 1917. His teaching career at Wabash College, Crawfordsville, Indiana was broken by service in France with the American Friends Service Committee. In 1920, he joined the faculty of the School of Commerce and Administration at Chicago University. He received his PhD in 1929, for his dissertation on the analysis of business forecast services, which resulted in two publications: *Forecasting Business Conditions* (1927) with Charles O. Hardy and *An Appraisal of American Business Forecasts* (1930). He was named Professor of Finance in 1930. He became acting Dean of the School of Business in 1942 and was formally named Dean in 1945. He resigned that position in 1952 to return to full-time teaching and research. He retired in 1958. In 1935, he was a founder of South East National Bank in the Woodlawn neighborhood of Chicago. He served as Chairman of the Board of the bank from its founding until his retirement in 1959.

5.2 Director, Aaron (1901–2004)

Born in Staryi Chortoryisk, Ukraine, his family emigrated to settle in Portland, Oregon in 1913, where he attended Lincoln High School. In 1924, he graduated from Yale University, returning to Portland in 1926 to teach at the Portland Labor College. In 1927, he left to teach economics at Chicago, Northwestern University and Howard University. His book *The Problem of Unemployment* (1931) was co-authored with Paul Douglas. His sister, Rose, married Milton Friedman in 1938. During World War II, he held positions in the War Department and the Department of Commerce. He was appointed to the faculty of the University of Chicago Law School in 1946. In 1958, he founded the *Journal of Law & Economics*, which he co-edited with Ronald Coase. In 1962, he helped to found the Committee on a Free Society at the University of Chicago, which was established to 'clarify and reinforce the tradition of individual liberty in its economic, political, historical and philosophical dimensions'. He retired in 1965, moving to California, where he accepted a position at Stanford University's Hoover institution. His publications were modest in number, but his contributions to his colleagues' thinking were considerable. George Stigler is cited: 'most of Aaron's articles have been published under the names of his colleagues' (Chicago University News Office, 2004).

5.3 Douglas, Paul Howard (1892–1976)

Born in Salem, Massachusetts and raised in Maine, Douglas graduated in 1913 from Bowdoin College in Brunswick, Maine. After securing a master's degree from Columbia University in 1915, a year of postgraduate work followed at Harvard University after which he gained his PhD at Columbia in 1921. He taught at the University of Illinois, Reed College and the University of Washington before accepting an appointment at the University of Chicago. He was promoted to full professor in 1925. He is best known to economics students as the co-author of the 1928 article with Charles Cobb that first defined the Cobb-Douglas production function (Cobb and Douglas, 1928). In the process of agitating for the enactment of such New Deal legislation as the *Social Security Act*, *Wagner Act* and *Fair Labor Standards Act*, in 1933 he was appointed to a seat on the Consumers' Advisory Board of the short-lived National Recovery Administration. He published *Wages and the Family* (1925), *Real Wages in the United States, 1890–1926* (1930), *Standards of Unemployment Insurance* (1933), *The Theory of Wages* (1934), *Controlling Depressions* (1935) and *Social Security in the United States* (1936). Some of his views on the standards he set for himself and expected of others are contained in his 1951 Godkin Lectures at Harvard, later to be published as *Ethics in Government*. At the age of fifty, he enlisted for the US Marine Corps, rising to the rank of lieutenant colonel. In May 1945, he received a serious arm wound during the battle for Okinawa, the result of which he never regained the use of his left hand. Having resumed his Chicago professorship after the war, in 1947 he was elected president of the American Economic Association. In 1948, he began an eighteen-year Senate career as a member of the Democratic Party. He spoke as forcefully in support of President Truman's Fair Deal containment policy as he had for the New Deal.

5.4 Knight, Frank Hyneman (1885–1972)

Born in McLean County, Illinois, after his early education at the University of Tennessee, he spent most of his academic career at the University of Chicago. He is best known for *Risk Uncertainty and Profit*, which is based on his PhD work at Cornell. With risk, outcomes are determined by probability distributions; with uncertainly, much less is known. Business profits may accrue due to uncertainties, where market perfect competition is empirically irrelevant. Knight made three other important contributions to economics. One is *The Economic Organization,* a set of lecture notes originally published in 1933. Here, he laid out the circular flow model of the economy and emphasised that investments will be made until the returns to investments in each use are equal at the margin. Those details are to be found in today's textbooks. In a well-cited article 'Some Fallacies in the Interpretation of Social Cost', Knight's political disposition might be inferred from his rejection of the notion that road congestion invites government intervention. Knight favoured privately owned roads and tolls to reduce congestion. Knight was a critic of Austrian capital theory, not least for the concept of an average period of production. As a firm believer in freedom and as a strong critic of social engineering, Knight saw threats to liberty from increases in monopoly power and income inequality. Milton Friedman, George Stigler and James M. Buchanan were students of Knight at Chicago.

5.5 Mints, Lloyd Winn (1888–1989)

Born near Bushnell, South Dakota, his family moved to Bolder Colorado, where he obtained his bachelor's (1914) and master's (1915) degrees. After teaching in high school for two years, he left for Washington to work as an analyst in a federal office. In 1919, he entered a graduate programme at the University of Chicago, where he found that he had been assigned to teach even though he had not been interviewed for the post. From the mid-1920s, he participated in regular informal discussions held at Frank Knight's home, often over or after Sunday lunch, when Garfield Cox and Aaron Director were regular contributors. With his memorandum on 'Banking and Currency Reform', Mints gives special credit to Henry Simons (for policy ideas) and to Frank Knight (for philosophical inspiration). Mints remained at Chicago until his retirement in 1953.

5.6 Schultz, Henry (1893–1938)

Born in Szarkowszczyzna (now part of Belarus) to a Polish family, after his family moved to the US, Schultz completed his primary education and undergraduate studies at the College of the City of New York. Although he received a BA in 1916, his graduate work at Columbia University was interrupted by World War I. In 1919, he received a scholarship, by which he was able to spend time at the London School of Economics and University College London. In 1920, he returned to the US, where he resumed doctoral studies at Columbia, while simultaneously conducting statistical work for the War Trade Board, the US Census Bureau and the US Department of Labor. He received a PhD (*The Statistical Law of Demand as Illustrated by the Demand for Sugar*) from Columbia in 1925. In 1926, Schultz went to the

University of Chicago, where he was to spend the remainder of his career. He was one of few economists of the time who was able to combine a rigorous theoretical understanding of neoclassical general equilibrium with the ever-widening application of statistical methods. His former student Milton Friedman worked as his research assistant for a year in 1935. In 1938, Henry Schultz died in a car accident, in which his wife and two daughters also perished.

5.7 Simons, Henry Calvert (1899–1946)

'Lector si monumentum requiris circumspice.'[1]

5.8 Viner, Jacob (1892–1970)

Born in Montreal, Quebec to parents of Romanian descent, Viner obtained his undergraduate degree from McGill University in 1914. He enrolled for graduate studies at Harvard University, earning his MA in 1915. After serving as an instructor at the University of Chicago, he became an assistant professor in 1919. He was promoted to associate professor in 1923 and to full professor in 1925. He obtained his PhD from Harvard University in 1922. Written under the supervision of Frank Taussig, his dissertation – *Canada's Balance of International Indebtedness* – set the style for a series of studies on the working of international financial mechanisms. At various times, he taught at Stanford (1937), Yale (1942–1943), the University of California (1945), the Institut Universitaire de Hautes Etudes Internationales in Geneva (1930–1931 and 1933–1934) and the National University of Brazil (1950). Between 1934 and 1942, he periodically served as special assistant to the US Secretary of the Treasury, Henry Morgenthau, Jr. During World War II, he served with Alvin Hansen as co-rapporteur to the Council on Foreign Relations of the 'War and Peace Studies' project of the economic and financial group. In 1946, he left for Princeton University. Although retiring in 1960, he spent a year at Harvard University (1961–1962) as the Taussig Research Professor. In 1965, he was elected a distinguished fellow of the American Economic Association. A noted opponent of Keynes, Viner considered his analysis to be flawed. Perhaps his most influential articles are reprinted in *The Long View and the Short* (1958): 'No matter how refined and how elaborate the analysis, if it rests solely on the short view it will still be… a structure built on shifting sands'[2] (Viner, 1958, pp. 112–13). Mark Blaug describes Viner as 'the greatest historian of economic thought that ever lived' (Blaug, 1985, p. 256).

… plus four minor players

5.9 Gideonse, Harry D. (1901–1985)

Born in Rotterdam, Netherlands, his parents brought him to the US in 1904. He received his bachelor's (1923) and master's degrees (1924) from Columbia

University and a Diplome des Hautes Etudes Internationales from the University of Geneva (1928). He filled posts as assistant professor of economics at Rutgers University and associate professor of economics at the University of Chicago. In 1939, he was appointed President of Brooklyn College, a post he served for nearly thirty years. In 1966, he became Chancellor of the New School for Social Research, a position he held until retirement in 1975.

5.10 Millis, Harry Alvin (1873–1948)

Born in Paoli, Indiana, he received his BA in 1895 and his MA in finance in 1896 from Indiana University. After joining the sociology programme at the University of Chicago in 1896, he switched to economics in 1898, receiving his PhD the following year. After a three-year period as reference librarian, he was appointed assistant professor of economics at Stanford University in 1904. He left Stanford in 1911 to join the economics department at the University of Kansas. In 1916, he became assistant professor of economics at the University of Chicago. Appointed chair of the department in 1928, he became professor emeritus in 1938.

5.11 Wright, Chester Whitney (1879–1966)

He studied at Harvard University, where he obtained his AB in 1901, his AM in 1902 and his PhD in 1906. After graduation in 1906, Wright began his academic career at Cornell University. In 1907, he moved to the University of Chicago as assistant professor of political economy, rising eventually to full professor. He retired in 1944.

5.12 Yntema, Theodore Otte (1900–1985)

He obtained an AB degree from Hope College in 1921, an MS in chemistry from the University of Illinois in 1922, an AM in business in 1924 and a PhD in economics from the University of Chicago in 1929. He was professor of statistics in the School of Business, from 1930 to 1944, and professor of business and economic policy, from 1944 to 1949. He then joined the finance department of the Ford Motor Credit Company, eventually becoming chairman of the board.

… plus one 'outlier'

5.13 Soddy, Frederick (1877–1956)

Born in Eastbourne England, he studied in Aberystwyth at the University College of Wales and at Merton College, Oxford, where he graduated in 1898 with first class honors in chemistry. A Nobel Prize was awarded to Soddy in 1921: 'for his contributions to our knowledge of the chemistry of radioactive substances, and his investigations into the origin and nature of isotopes'.

In fearing the destructive potential of atomic energy, Soddy gave deep thought to economic forces and to the institutions that might safeguard humankind. However, he drew no insights from established economic analysis, where he criticised the like treatment of wealth and debt. In Soddy's presentations, value has a physical dimension. As a tangible asset, a pig is a pig; but where there is a liability – i.e., to be owed a pig – there is no physical dimension. An asset is a tangible item; a debt is an imaginary item. Wealth is governed by the laws of thermodynamics and the natural decay of physical structures (entropy). Debt is a mathematical concept, with no physical dimension. By the natural physical degradation of an asset, its limiting value is zero; but when compound interest is applied to debt, it grows at an exponential rate, with a limiting value of infinity. As science advances, increasing reliance is placed upon past accumulations from energy sources; but the extent to which current flows can be stored is limited. The socio-economic practice of converting wealth into debt in order to derive income in the future carries inherent risk; i.e., Soddy presumes that the growth of income will not match the rate at which debt accumulates. That being so, the repudiation/cancellation of debt becomes inevitable.

By the presumption that wealth cannot grow as fast as debt, interest needs to be curtailed. Given the impossibility for everyone to live on debt interest, no one should be permitted to do so. Unsurprisingly, therefore, Soddy is critical of commercial banking practice that is inherently structured upon extending credit at interest. Fractional reserve banking is malevolent.

On the basis of his socio-economic perspective, Soddy is regarded as a crank. A notable exception to those holding that view is Frank Knight. Without Knight's review of Soddy's *Wealth, Virtual Wealth and Debt* (1926), it must be doubted that any relevance to the Chicago Plan would have been noted. Although Soddy's arguments are not without coherence, he probably overplayed his hand in attributing 'war and all other evils to fractional reserve banking' (Daly, 1980, p. 470). Even so, his understanding of key banking issues was sound, as his reviewer acknowledges:

> The practical thesis of the book is distinctly unorthodox, but is in our opinion highly significant and theoretically correct. In the abstract, it is absurd and monstrous for society to pay the commercial banking system "interest" for multiplying several fold the quantity of medium of exchange when (a) a public agency could do it at negligible cost, (b) there is no sense in having it done at all, since the effect is to raise the price level, and (c) important evils result, notably the frightful instability of the whole economic system and its periodical collapse in crisis, which are in large measure bound up with the uncertainty of the credit structure if not directly the effect of it.
>
> (Knight, 1927, p. 732)

The impact of variations in the supply of bank credit money is to thwart official attempts to stabilise prices. In a period of rising business activity, 'impecunious borrowers' acquire wealth that is expropriated from the community as a whole, when the purchasing power of money is caused to fall. Once 100 percent reserve banking is introduced, it would be for the state to adjust the provision of base money to stabilise an official price index: 'Soddy makes an analogy between the price index and the governor on a steam engine. Both provide a mechanism of stabilizing feedback' (Daly, 1980, p. 481).

Soddy's recommendations closely match those emanating from Irving Fisher. Yet, apart from Knight's review, there is no acknowledgment of Soddy's prescience of the Chicagoan precepts for monetary stability: for 100 percent reserve banking and the application of monetary policy targeted upon a constant price index and flexible exchange rates. Soddy's comment in 1943 on 'the near identity of [Fisher's] plans as an interesting and encouraging coincidence … in no way suggests that Fisher had copied or even been influenced by him' (Daly, 1980, p. 484).

Notes

1 This Latin phrase describes a person's legacy. Its general meaning is that what we leave behind best represents our life. Carved on a slab of black marble, it covers a tomb in St Paul's Cathedral, in which lies the body of the architect: Sir Christopher Wren (1632–1723).

2 The fundamental core of Viner's position might be embellished as the antithesis of Keynes's approach: '[a]re we not told that "since in the long run we are all dead", policy should be guided entirely by short-run considerations? I fear that these believers in the principle of après nous le déluge may get what they have bargained for sooner than they wish' (Hayek, 1941, p. 410).

Bibliography

Blaug, M. (1985) *Great Economists since Keynes* (Aldershot, UK: Edward Elgar).

Chicago University News Office (2004) 'Aaron Director, Founder of the field of Law and Economics', 13 September; www-news.uchicago.edu/releases/04/040913.director.shtml (accessed 30 March 2017).

Cobb, C. W. and P. H. Douglas (1928) 'A Theory of Production', *The American Economic Review*, vol. 18, no. 1, Papers and Proceedings of the Fortieth Annual Meeting of the American Economic Association, March, 139–65.

Daly, H. E. (1980) 'The Economic Thought of Frederick Soddy', *History of Political Economy*, vol. 12, no. 4, 469–87.

Hayek, F. A. (1941) *The Pure Theory of Capital* (London and Henley, UK: Routledge and Kegan Paul).

Knight, F. H. (1927), 'Review of Frederick Soddy's *Wealth, Virtual Wealth, and Debt*', *The Saturday Review of Literature*, vol. 3, no. 38, April 16, 732; www.unz.org/Pub/SaturdayRev-1927apr16-00732?View=PDF (accessed 11 September 2015).

Viner, J. (1958) *The Long View and the Short* (Glencoe, IL: Free Press).

6 The Chicago Plan

6.1 US money and banking

In a money economy, core liquid assets are the banknotes/reserves that are the monopoly product of the central bank. When a commercial bank's liabilities are backed by anything less than 100 percent reserves, their viability is guaranteed only if the central bank is willing to lend to the bank against its assets. For libertarians, there is an obvious problem with an arrangement in which a monopoly provides the lubricant for commercial activity. A second concern is that of moral hazard. When a commercial bank facing a liquidity crisis can expect to be 'bailed out' by the central bank, the likelihood increases that such a bank will have need of support.

In the early days of banking, the asset considered most eligible for rediscounting was identified by the real bills doctrine. That doctrine is supported by erroneous beliefs: that short-term, self-liquidating commercial loans provide adequate security; that lending against sound commercial paper ensures an equi-proportional variation in real output and bank money; and, by that latter relationship, price inflation is impossible. The error lies in ignoring the two-way interaction between money and prices. As monetary expansion tends to raise prices, rising prices tend to generate further requirements for bank loans to finance trade. From that perspective, the implication of the real bills doctrine is that money and prices are free to chase each other in an upward spiral.

The desire to provide a secure 'anchor' for the value of money attracted Simons towards a solution that would emulate the practice of early goldsmith bankers, whose deposits had been backed by 100 percent reserves. Except for one important detail, this might have been achieved in the UK by the *Bank Charter Act* of 1844. In adopting David Ricardo's 'Plan for the Establishment of a National Bank' (1824), the *Act* split the Bank of England into a money-issuing department and a banking department that would advance loans.

Although the Bank of England had been founded in 1694, it was only by the *Bank Charter Act* that it acquired the monopoly of sovereign banknotes and reserves. As the issue department traded in gold at a fixed price (issuing and retiring banknotes accordingly), the banking department undertook the commercial activity of taking deposits and making loans. Initially, the issue department was restricted to a note issue to the limit of the amount of the value of its vault gold plus a 'fiduciary issue' of £14 million. The latter value was determined by the level of current loans to the UK government.

By the other details of the *Act*, no new commercial bank was permitted to issue banknotes and the current circulation of country banknotes was limited to their existing levels. However, demand deposits were exempt from the 100 percent reserve requirement. With that final exemption, the *Act* did not end fractional reserve banking, but merely changed its focus from banknotes to demand deposits. By that omission, bank credit-led booms and their consequential busts remained as likely events. In drawing upon that lesson, Simons viewed the 100 percent 'scheme' as a 'first step toward reconstruction of our whole financial organisation' because, as an isolated measure, it would deliver only a 'crank scheme' that would be undermined by evasion (see Simons, 1936, p. 19, fn 17; 1948, p. 173, fn 17).

Although the *Act* constrained the degree to which the Bank of England could finance government activity, the rules were loosened whenever it was opportune to do so. Thus, the *Act* was suspended during the panics of 1847 and 1857, when the Bank was permitted to exceed the limits of the fiduciary issue.

6.2 Fractional reserve banking

A description of bank credit creation is a general feature of economics textbooks. Within an effective bank clearing system, base money remains in the collective possession of commercial banks, held either as banknotes (till money) or as 'bank reserves' held at the central bank in the accounts of the commercial banks. With everyday transactions, a bank's clients make withdrawals from their accounts in order to make payments into accounts held by other individuals. Net balances between the respective banks are periodically cleared, and it is only when clients demand to withdraw banknotes from their accounts that the total reserves (of base money) held by commercial banks fall.

Given the unlikely event of requests for bank deposits to be withdrawn in their totality, a commercial bank may be confident that, in holding less than 100 percent of its assets as base money, its ability to meet withdrawals on demand is unlikely to be threatened. This allows a bank to put the bulk of its assets to profitable use, such that base money is 'leveraged' to extend loans to a much greater value. As those in receipt of bank credit increase their spending, a higher volume of 'broad' money circulates, with an ever larger volume finding its way into others' bank accounts. This is the process of bank credit creation that is made possible by fractional reserve banking – i.e., by the 'leverage' that is applied to reserve assets.

In practice, the textbook details do not apply; i.e., the notion of a trusted high-street branch manager waiting patiently for deposits to accrue to the bank, before permitting loans to be extended within the constraint of fractional reserve requirements, is a myth. If a bank wishes to make a loan, it typically credits a business account with a deposit (the bank's liability) as it simultaneously records the loan as an asset held by the bank. By that bookkeeping process, the ratio of deposits to reserve assets then falls. If a bank considers it commercially sound to expand this activity, it can bid for short-term wholesale deposits (of liquid assets) to extend the process of bank credit creation. The bank implicitly relies upon wholesale deposits being 'rolled over' into a further term, if it wishes to sustain the level of its banking activity. If a bank finds that its reserves are falling below a 'safe' level, it can obtain liquidity from the central bank by refinancing. By the 'lender of last resort' facility that was established in the UK during the nineteenth century, the central bank is willing to rediscount 'good' collateral; i.e., a commercial bank is able to obtain the liquidity it requires, but it then expects to pay a borrowing rate that is higher than the rate paid on wholesale deposits.

If refinancing is not available, a bank may be forced to 'liquidate' such assets as it currently holds. If there is significant competition between banks to liquidate funds, loans may become heavily discounted (as in a 'fire sale') and depositors may begin to doubt the capacity of banks generally to repay deposits, so inducing depositors to withdraw rather more banknotes than otherwise. To be absolutely confident of meeting demands for deposit withdrawals, banks would need to hold reserves equal in value to their liabilities – i.e., 100 percent reserve banking. By such an arrangement – which is the essence of the Chicago Plan – banks would no longer be free to create bank credit money.

When there is a requirement to hold 100 percent reserves, banks are obliged to revert to their earlier function – i.e., to provide safe-care of their clients' deposits (warehousing) with fees charged for that and other services. Banks would then operate as true intermediaries – i.e., as investment trusts providing loans that are financed by savers' deposits, with loan instruments taking the form of either debt obligations or equity investments. Although lending would remain a banking function, a commercial bank would be unable simultaneously to enter a new debit and new credit onto its balance sheet. Instead, bank loans would require a transfer of existing banknotes (or bank reserves) from a bank's vault (or central bank account) to borrowers. By the elimination of bank credit, the circulation of money would then vary primarily by the amount of base money that is supplied by the central bank. With the removal of the leverage by which bank credit is created, the only remaining points of slippage in a monetary authority's overall control are in respect of variations in the velocity of circulation of base money and payments effected by transfers of private third-party debt. The latter are the chink in the armour of effective central bank control over the monetary system.[1]

6.3 The Plan

With the unprecedented level of bank failures that followed in the wake of the Wall Street Crash of 1929, proposals for 'emergency relief' and 'permanent banking reform' were discussed widely and at length. One set of reforms, in which interest was particularly strong, became known as the Chicago Plan. Simons was in the vanguard, but he and three other individuals who were most closely associated in propagating the Plan (Frank Knight, Jacob Viner and Lloyd Mints) were as firm in their commitment to competition within markets as they were to monopoly in the provision of money. With the addition of Garfield Cox, Paul Douglas, Aaron Director, A. G. Hart and Henry Schultz, there were eight signatories to a six-page memorandum that was distributed on 16 March 1933. The accompanying letter contained the following:

> The program defined in the statement is one which we believe to be sound, even ideal, in principle. What its merits may be, in the light of political consideration, we frankly do not know. We are sensible, moreover, of an obligation not to broadcast publicly any statement which might undermine confidence in Administration measures, or impair their chances of successful operation. On the other hand, we feel, that the statement may merit deliberate consideration, among people of interests like our own; also, that it may suggest measures which might usefully be incorporated in other, and perhaps less impractical, schemes.
>
> (Cited from Allen, 1993, p. 705, fn. 9)

With an initial circulation limited to some forty individuals, the memorandum brought a total of 320 responses from 157 universities. Over seventy percent of those responding gave general agreement to the proposals with fewer than fifteen percent registering disapproval (see Zarlenga, 2005). Prominent supporters included Maurice Allais, Irving Fisher, Milton Friedman and Frank Graham. The proposals itemised three key features:

1 a Federal guarantee of bank deposits to halt the fall in 'circulating media'.
2 a programme of banking reforms to prevent a recurrence of banking crises.
3 a policy to induce a rise in wholesale deposits, as a prelude to 'some explicit criteria for long-run currency-management' (Phillips, 1995, p. 192).

The memorandum made five general recommendations towards achieving those goals:

1 Federal government to take ownership and management of the Federal Reserve banks.
2 Federal Reserve banks to supervise and guarantee deposits with member banks.
3 Federal Reserve notes to be issued to meet depositors' withdrawal demands.
4 Federal Reserve notes to be legal tender for all debts.
5 Non-member institutions to be provided with generous support.

The 'major problem' that remained to be addressed was long-term currency management, but the expedient of short-term 'price-stabilization' had general support among the eight signatories. Thereafter, there was a requirement for policy to be directed towards reflation at a rate appropriate to setting the economy on the path to 'normality'. Contrasting views on the appropriate magnitude for reflation emanated alternatively from the authors of the Plan (who wished to raise the general level of prices) and from Fisher (whose primary concern was to restore the debtor/creditor relationship). Where Simons viewed the impact upon employment as the decisive concern, Fisher was convinced that major booms and slumps were systematically associated with over-indebtedness and deflation.[2] While there was no dispute that measures were needed to lift the general level of prices, there was no consensus even on a 'ballpark' magnitude. By Irving Fisher's calculation, a general price index had fallen from 100 in 1926 to 56 in 1933. So, where the Plan eventually settled upon the recommendation of a fifteen percent rise, Fisher had wanted a sixty percent rise. Setting that difference to one side, once normality was achieved, the 'Planner's' desire for no further inflation was in line with Fisher's wish to keep a retail price index within narrow limits. In responding to the circulation of the Plan, Fisher had given support to the introduction of a deposit guarantee scheme, but only as a temporary expedient pending permanent reform. While he was not immediately attracted by the core element of 100 percent reserve banking, he evinced some flexibility. Fisher's involvement is discussed further as follows.

Within a matter of days, Secretary of Agriculture Henry Wallace had alerted Roosevelt to the existence of the Plan. That there is no record of his reaction causes no surprise given the caution of a President who had only recently assumed office. At his first press conference four days after his inauguration, Roosevelt announced that: 'questions in writing' would not be taken; 'direct quotations' would not be used; background information would 'not be attributed to the White House'; and information given 'off the record and confidential' should not be repeated to those who were not present to hear it (see American Presidency Project, Press Conference, 8th March 1933).

Two innovations were incorporated into the *Banking Act* of June 1933. The first was Federal insurance, by which the government guaranteed a proportion of each bank deposit, where the motive was to restore confidence and so to dissuade hoarding. The second was a separation of commercial banking from investment banking. Retail deposits were no longer to be used by bankers to finance speculative investments. In removing that option, little attention was given to alternatives for underwriting investment. That the *Banking Act* was no more than a staging post is clear. In October, Roosevelt announced that his primary policy objective was to restore the general level of prices and thereafter to defend the purchasing power of the dollar. As the means to those ends, the initiation of a gold purchase programme stirred controversy within the financial community, but that outcome was to be achieved by another *Banking Act* in 1935.

Written by Simons, but representing proposals and conversations among members of the group, a Chicago memorandum was circulated in November 1933. The original eight all signed the seven-page document, 'Long-term Objectives of Monetary Management', with its six-page appendix, 'Banking and Business Cycles'. Their arguments opened with an accusation and a complaint: that 'government has, in a significant sense, allowed the commercial banks to usurp its primary function of controlling the currency'; and that fractional reserve banking allows money to be 'created when it should be destroyed, and destroyed when it should be created' (Allen, 1993, p. 707).

The key focus of the initiative was upon the means to tighten the Fed's monetary control, which is undermined when commercial banks are permitted to create deposits by a bookkeeping transaction whereby (as described before) a bank loan is made to a customer (a debit) as the bank writes the same value against the customer's account (a credit). In describing this outcome as fostering 'an unreliable and unhomogeneous medium' to serve as money, Simons states his preferred alternative (to the 'outright socialization' of banking) as the 'outright abolition of deposit banking on the fractional reserve principle' (Simons, 1933; cited from Phillips, 1995, p. 64).

The instability that results from fractional reserve banking invites both simple and complex explanations. In the early 1930s, the complex possibilities that were in the early stages of further elucidation as 'Austrian business cycle theory'[3] were never likely to attract the attention of practical bankers or, indeed, many economists. In the Chicago November memorandum, Simons posits an alternative simple narrative: rising business profits in a cyclical upswing encourage bankers to meet a rising demand for business loans, which, by their association with even higher profits, encourage further lending. With the implicit premise that this process must eventually end, a crisis is then to be expected as banks find it necessary to curtail their lending. A downward spiral of monetary contraction, falling prices and falling incomes then ensues. In 1933, real income was some thirty percent below its previous peak.

The practical options that would be open after the elimination of bank credit creation needed careful consideration. Existing banks would face the choice of operating either as deposit banks or as investment banks. Thereafter, any shortage in the volume of money transfers that needed accommodating might be met by extending the government's postal savings system. Options by which monetary expansion (and control) might operate include: (i) the conversion of interest-bearing federal debt to non-interest-bearing debt; (ii) open-market operations by Reserve Banks; and (iii) increases in federal expenditure and/or cuts in taxation. A further suggestion was that any commitment to a permanent monetary policy rule might be deferred to allow full examination of the issues. In the interim, the Plan would set a temporary monetary policy rule that would follow a precise price-level objective.

A significant response to the November memorandum came from Fritz Machlup, who had arrived from Vienna on a Rockefeller scholarship at the beginning of 1933. Machlup had previously studied economics under both von Mises (who had guided his dissertation on the gold-exchange standard) and Hayek at the University of Vienna. In agreeing generally with the Chicago proposals for banking reform and in noting that the business cycles appendix was a close match to his own published work,[4] Machlup emphasised exchange rate stabilisation over price stability. His classic liberal credentials also told against holding any expectation of sound monetary management if the ultimate policy control was under the aegis of the state.[5]

In December 1933, Robert Hutchins (as President of Chicago University) sent a copy of the November proposals to Senator Bronson Cutting. Although Cutting was viewed as influential among those senators who were likely to force progress towards 100 percent reserve banking, his relevance was to be terminated by a fatal airliner crash in May 1935. In response to Hutchins, Cutting had signalled his general agreement and had suggested a draft bill. When, in the following January, Roosevelt asked Congress to give thought to the detail of legislation to deal with current 'monetary matters', the Chicago group put themselves to the task.

6.4 A federal monetary authority

Although the innovation of deposit insurance settled the fears of bank depositors, lending remained in the doldrums. More generally, rising burdens of debt led to Congressional calls for some alleviation by monetary inflation. In acceding to Roosevelt's request, Congress passed the *Gold Reserve Act* in January 1934, whereby titles to gold and gold certificates were vested with the state. The very next day, the Treasury duly expropriated wealth from erstwhile holders of gold by announcing a 7.5 percent currency devaluation. The combination of new regulatory constraints on banking with a reluctance of banks to extend credit to business bought ambitious demands for loans to be forthcoming from the RFC. A more modest proposal from Senator Glass saw loans totalling $580 million from the RFC and the Fed.

With Senator Cutting pressing Hutchins for a status report on the draft proposals from Chicago, Simons was sent to meet him in Washington in March 1934. Shortly following that meeting, Cutting organised a final draft of a bill that was presented to Congress in June. Among its details were: the segregation of demand deposits and savings deposits (where the respective reserve ratios were 5 percent and 100 percent); and a Federal Monetary Authority (FMA) with full control over (i) the note issue, (ii) trading in government debt and (iii) the dollar gold price. Commercial banks would raise the necessary reserves by swapping their debt with that of the FMA.

In order to first raise and then to hold the general level of prices at the level of 1926, the FMA would purchase sovereign bonds. Following a key Chicago principle, the expansion of base money would be at a fixed annual rate. The objective would be to take base money to a level where the mean holding of commercial bank deposits was $250 per head of population. Owing to the rancour (a legacy of divergent opinions on veterans' pensions) that existed between Cutting and Roosevelt, it was anticipated that support from the President would be lukewarm. For that reason, Cutting regarded these proposals as 'tentative', serving primarily as a catalyst for 'criticisms and suggestions'.

Research undertaken by the Treasury thorough the second half of 1934 provided the basis for the *Banking Act* of 1935, which addressed broad issues relating to money and credit. The lack of bank credit to business raised two policy options: to restructure the Federal Reserve System or to expand the role of the RFC. In believing that economic revival was being stifled by the reluctance of banks to lend, Roosevelt's disposition was aligned with Hoover's earlier motivation, which had brought the inauguration of the RFC in January 1932. A more general argument related to the relative weight that might be attached to the unwillingness of banks to lend and the reluctance of business to borrow. Given the opposition that existed to a long-term role for the RFC, Roosevelt followed the advice of his principal 'Brain Trust' advisor, Adolf Berle, whose recommendation was for the countrywide credit banks to increase their provision of finance to small business.

6.5 The Plan: Lauchlin Currie

Jacob Viner was acting as special assistant to Henry Morgenthau, then newly appointed in 1934 as Secretary of the Treasury, when Morgenthau asked him to convene a research group (the 'Freshman Trust') whose task would be to focus on general matters relating to money, banking and public finance. Among the studies then undertaken was one by Lauchlin Currie. With a paper on 'Monetary Control in the United States', Currie argued that it was only by an accident of history that the supply of money had become associated with the act of lending money. Currie further argued that a dispersed system of government agencies might purchase/sell sovereign debt instruments as and when it was considered appropriate to expand/contract money deposits. Although money should be controlled by government, Currie was adamant that political considerations should have no bearing upon monetary policy. Not least in achieving that end, legislation would be necessary to define the objectives and the means of monetary control.

Currie regarded the separation of money and credit to be the core reform. He therefore proposed a stepwise development towards a position where inter-bank deposits and cheque deposits would be backed by 100 percent reserves and non-cheque deposits by zero reserves. Service charges would be paid by those holding 100 percent reserve-backed deposits. Federal Reserve banknotes would replace all other banknotes and the RFC would be authorised to address any liquidity shortages that were the consequence of implementing the 100 percent reserve requirement. The FMA would control the money supply by conducting open-market operations. Reserve banks would issue non-interest-bearing notes so that commercial banks could meet the 100 reserve requirement without loss of profit. That debt as newly provided by commercial banks would be retired over an extended period. On balance, Currie argued against the FMA having the status of an autonomous body, believing that democracy would best serve the general interest.

As Morgenthau had received Currie's report on 100 percent banking in September 1934, Roosevelt had passed Fisher's memorandum to him on the same subject (see Phillips, 1995, p. 101). Thereafter, Currie became engaged with the Treasury in working on the *Banking Act* of 1935, which was the beginning of his association with Marriner Eccles. Morgenthau had recommended Eccles to Roosevelt to head a reconstructed Federal Reserve system. In responding to a request from the President, Eccles and Currie submitted a memorandum in November: 'Desirable Changes in the Administration of the Federal Reserve System'. In working from the current clearing house system towards the creation of a central bank, Currie gave full backing to 100 percent reserve banking. Among others of his recommendations was that the Federal Reserve Board should be responsible for monetary policy, including the conduct of open-market operations and short-term emergency funding.

6.6 The Plan: Irving Fisher

Irving Fisher's acclaim as 'the leading economist of his generation' was matched by the financial acumen that had allowed him to accumulate 'a fortune of millions' – that is, until 'the fateful autumn of 1929' (Allen, 1993, p. 703). Devastating personal financial losses then no doubt inspired the 'almost frenetic effort' by which Fisher sought explanations, devised measures, addressed public meetings, wrote academic manuscripts and drafted legislative proposals, through to his death in 1947.

Fisher was slow to acknowledge the relevance of 100 percent reserve banking. As a part move in the direction of bringing greater security to bank deposits, he did give backing to the separation of retail banking from investment banking. In welcoming Fisher's 'sympathetic comments' on the March Memorandum, Simons gave further elucidation to the detail of the Plan in terms of twin objectives: (i) the elimination of private credit within the exchange system; and (ii) to achieve greater 'homogeneity' within the exchange system (see Simons to Fisher, March 24 1933, in Simons Papers, as cited by Phillips, 1995, p. 50). Beyond those points, however, Simons experienced great difficulty in explaining to Fisher that the problems associated with commercial banking 'might easily reappear in other forms of financial arrangements' (Allen, 1993, p. 708).

On reflection, Simons rued the omission from the Chicago Plan of any worries that the evolution of deposit banking 'might render our drastic reform quite empty, nominal, and unsubstantial' (Simons to Fisher, 9th January 1934, Simons Papers cited from Phillips, 1995, p. 89). On this, there was support from Hayek, who argued that it is not possible 'to regulate the quantity of all media of exchange' nor 'any arbitrarily selected part' (Hayek, letter to Simons dated 1st December 1934, Simons Papers cited from Phillips, 1995, p. 91).

Simons agreed and his response was emphatic: 'I have completely repudiated the position taken in the Addendum to the mimeographed memorandum … as to the merits of fixing the supply of *circulating media*' (Simons, letter to Hayek dated 18th December 1934, Simons Papers cited from Phillips, 1995, p. 91).

Simons was exasperated by Fisher's inability to see that the ease with which demand deposits currently served as a ready substitute for base money would be matched by the ease with which 'savings-deposits, treasury certificates, and commercial paper' could do likewise. Fisher remained unmoved and insistent: to consider interest-bearing savings deposits on the same basis as sight deposits was 'quite preposterous' (Fisher, letter to Simons dated 14th December 1934, Simons Papers cited from Phillips, 1995, p. 92).

By his propensity to court self-publicity, Fisher did not enamour himself to those who were in the vanguard in promoting 100 percent reserve banking. When eventually Fisher began to show the zeal of the newly converted, Simons attempted to dampen his enthusiasm, advising him by letter (29 March 1934) to give more attention to 'special students' and less to 'popularization'. In summary, it is argued that

> [w]hereas the Chicago economists had provided a theoretical rational and Currie had given a proposal for policy implementation, Irving Fisher picked up the cause of banking reform and actively sought to promote legislation and educate the public.
>
> (Phillips, 1995, p, 107)

Certainly, as ever-widening discussion saw support increasing for the 100 percent reserve proposal, caution and scepticism were meliorated. Simons acknowledged that legislative bills submitted to Congress were 'much less bad than I had expected them to be – and not ill-suited to their immediate purpose of initiating discussion' (Simons, letter to Paul Douglas dated 2nd October 1934, cited from Allen, 1993, p. 710). Fisher also felt that Congress had fallen for the idea, and he repeatedly urged Roosevelt to discuss the issues with him; but, in the end, Fisher formed the view that 'the President is afraid of the bankers' (Fisher, letter to his family, dated 24th February 1935, cited from Allen, 1993, p. 710).

Fisher's eventual backing for the Chicago Plan was primarily for its likely effectiveness in preventing debt deflation.[6] More particularly, his efforts towards refining explanations of the trade cycle and in devising policies for recovery and stabilisation became enduring commitments. Fisher's distinctiveness from the Chicago economists is marked by the higher level of reflation that he considered to be necessary to secure recovery.

6.7 The Plan: Maynard Keynes

Given the rising profile of Keynes, whose explicit reformulation of monetary theory and novel ideas for aggregate demand management were increasingly taking attention, Fisher had cause to express concern that 'younger economists' were being 'swept along in the movement toward managed economy'; and he countered with the argument that most of the ills, which those budding Keynesians feared, would be 'prevented by managed *currency*' (Fisher, letter to Richard A Lester, dated 24th February 1936, cited from Allen, 1993, p. 713, fn. 38).

On the last day of 1933, the *New York Times* had published an open letter from Keynes to Roosevelt. Polite and often deferential, Keynes nevertheless admonished Roosevelt for 'a wrong choice in the order of urgencies', and he accused Roosevelt of having given too much attention to reform and insufficient to recovery. Keynes's preferred option was 'to increase the national output and put more men to work', to which end it was imperative for individuals to 'be induced to spend more of their existing incomes'. Given that this was unlikely to occur on a sufficient scale and that business was unlikely to invest sufficiently, the 'public authority must be called in aid to create additional current incomes through the expenditure of borrowed or printed money'. Rising prices were to be encouraged, but only those 'which are the natural result of an increase in the nation's purchasing power'.[7] In short, '[t]he stimulation of output by increasing aggregate purchasing power is the right way to get prices up; and not the other way round' (Keynes, 1933, pp. 4–6). Nothing would be gained simply by increasing the quantity of money that Keynes describes as 'like trying to get fat by buying a larger belt' (Keynes, 1933, p. 11).

Keynes's tight focus upon the need for the government to spend more is clear from his correspondence with Roosevelt; and there no evidence that he gave any serious attention to the Plan, either in 1933 or a decade later when Fisher approached Keynes in July 1944, at the time of the Bretton Woods negotiations. Fisher had then suggested that the adoption of 100 percent reserve banking would be a natural counterpart to the international arrangements then being discussed. In his reply, Keynes voiced 'some considerable reservations':

> In my judgement deflation is in the near future a much more dangerous risk than inflation. I am afraid of your formula because I think it would certainly, in England, have a highly deflationary suggestion to a great many people.
>
> (Keynes, letter to Fisher, dated 7th July 1944, cited from Allen, 1993, p. 715, fn. 49)

Not least by the fact that both Fisher and Keynes were dead before another three years had passed, their relevance to further developments to the Plan was minimal. Although the structure of Keynesian economics was thereafter for others to determine, Keynes had left warnings that much remained to be resolved:

> This that I offer is… a theory of why output and employment are so liable to fluctuation. It does not offer a ready-made remedy as to how to avoid these fluctuations and to maintain output at a steady optimum level. …

> Naturally I am interested not only in the diagnosis, but also in the cure; and many pages of my book are devoted to the latter. But I consider that my suggestions for a cure... are on a different plane from the diagnosis. They are not meant to be definitive; they are subject to all sorts of conditions of the time.
>
> (Keynes, 1937, p. 39)

6.8 The Plan: Jacob Viner

In a brief appraisal of the banking legislation that culminated in the *Banking Act* of 1935, Jacob Viner argues that credit contraction in the US had been considerably more severe that elsewhere, which he attributes to 'parish-pump banking'. Interstate branch banking had continued to be thwarted by a variety of pettifogging jealousies: from small bankers, agrarians, state officials and small-town people. However, their removal would have required political battles of a kind that the Administration had 'no eagerness to wage' (Viner, 1936, p. 107).

The severity of credit deflation post-1929 had been driven by the panic withdrawal of deposits. Thereafter, the innovation of a (maximum $5,000) deposit guarantee had provided a safeguard. The *Banking Act* of 1933 had established the Federal Deposit Insurance Corporation (FDIC), but this was entirely at the initiative of Congress and against opposition from Roosevelt, who saw dangers in the government becoming 'liable for the mistakes and errors of individual banks' (Public Papers, 1937; cited from Phillips, 1995, p. 38). Chicago economists gave their support pending more radical reform.[8] One obvious concern was that the insurance premium paid by banks was a mere one-twelfth of one percent of their total deposits, which was 'certain to prove insufficient … even in the absence of recurrence of major depressions' (Viner, 1936, p. 111).

With the exception of restrictions upon private currency, commercial banks in the UK were constrained only by the generality of commercial law. By contrast, four overlapping federal authorities and forty-eight state authorities supervised and regulated US banking. More generally, the value of such control has to be questioned when risk assessment is based upon 'favourable conditions of the moment' (Viner, 1936, p. 109). In failing to place 'any new mandate upon any authority' and in not changing the 'objectives to be pursued', the *Banking Act* of 1935 fell short of providing 'one central agency' to strengthen and extend 'credit control power' (Viner, 1936, p. 113).

Perhaps the greatest controversy relates to the central control of credit. Although academic economists were seeking 'a major reconstruction of the banking system, and adoption of some simple statutory rule of credit control', Viner felt that the *Act* went

> as far as it is wise to go in the present state of public opinion, of our monetary standard interregnum, and of imperfect knowledge and experience as to the most expedient objectives and methods of credit control.
>
> (Viner, 1936, pp. 112–13)

Not least by the Treasury's facility to engage in 'operations equivalent to the open market operations of the Federal Reserve system', it would have been premature to have invited the Fed to administer a 'definite mandate' relating to the procedures and objectives of credit control. Complex and uncertain practicalities were an impediment to having 'procedures proscribed in detail in the law' (Viner, 1936, p. 117). However, it is clear that a monetary system is undermined if banks are forced to liquidate assets in a depression. To remain solvent, a bank requires the assurance of a central bank that is willing to lend against the bank's assets; but the underlying proviso is that 'liquidation or expansion of the system as a whole should be controlled by the central bank and not by the wishes or exigencies of the individual banks' (Viner, 1936, p. 118).

6.9 The Plan: Milton Friedman

The potential for Milton Friedman's Monetarist counter-revolution (Friedman, 1956) was stirred by the widespread experience of stagflation in the 1970s, when it became clear that a singular assertion demanded re-examination – i.e., Keynes's insistence that 'an increase in the quantity of money will have no effect whatever on prices, so long as there is any unemployment' (Keynes, 1936, p. 295). In gaining impetus from Friedman's 1967 Presidential address to the American Economic Association (Friedman, 1968), the Monetarist counter-revolution showed how the original statement of the Phillips curve relationship was deceptively simplistic.

For the quarter-century during which Keynesian dominance went generally unchallenged, Friedman's early reputation had been built upon his seminal paper on stabilisation policy. In this, he presented a set of theoretical arguments for a monetary and fiscal framework that, while compatible with efficient resource allocation and economic growth, had the objective of minimising cyclical variations in the levels of employment and output. In this paper, Friedman's references to 'aggregate demand', 'effective demand', 'national money income' and the 'average propensity to consume' must not be allowed to mislead. That Friedman's exposition draws deeply from the writing of Simons is indicated by the itemisation of primary goals: political freedom, economic efficiency and a 'substantial equality of economic power'. Furthermore, the onus would not rely upon the discretionary authority of administrators to provide 'a monetary framework for a competitive order' (Friedman, 1948, p. 246), but upon a government structure operating 'under the "rule of law"'. That Friedman's paper is pointedly antipathetic to Keynesian economics is signalled by the fact that no credence is assigned to 'the doctrine of stagnation or economic maturity that is now widely held' (*ibid.*, p. 262). That point is re-enforced by the argument that, given significant lags – between prognosis, identification of measures, legislation and action – discretionary interventions by the authorities were likely to be destabilising (*ibid.*, p. 255).

With a design that would allow automatic fiscal adjustments (and changes to the money supply) to offset other variations in aggregate demand, Friedman's framework again reflects Simons's writing when it stipulates:

1 no discretionary action by the central monetary authority (e.g., the elimination of changes to reserve requirements, rediscounting, open-market operations and credit controls).
2 government expenditure to be set 'entirely on the basis of the community's desire, need, and willingness to pay for public services' (*ibid.*, p. 248).
3 fixed welfare transfer entitlements, so that absolute outlays 'vary automatically over the cycle' (*ibid.*).
4 taxation predominantly from progressive personal income tax, so that (with welfare transfers) automatic countercyclical variations deliver a balanced budget at a hypothetical full-employment level of income.
5 government expenditure to be financed only by raising taxes and issuing money.
6 if the highest taxation levels are not feasible (as in wartime), interest-bearing sovereign debt might be justified 'to offset the inflationary pressure of abnormally high government expenditure' (*ibid.*, p. 250).

With this framework in place, a fiscal surplus in the boom phase of a peacetime cycle (higher tax receipts and lower welfare payments) would be matched by a fall in the money supply. Conversely, in a cyclical downturn, by increasing the 'real value of the community's stock of assets' (*ibid.*, p. 260), a rise in the money supply would be expected to stimulate consumption expenditure. In this fashion, variations in the money supply would be 'automatically determined by the requirements for domestic stability' (*ibid.*, p. 252). In a recession (and conversely in a cyclical upturn), the cumulative effect of money-financed fiscal deficits would be to offset falling prices. Since falling prices raise both the real value of government expenditure and the real value of assets, the incentive to save also falls: this is the 'Pigou Effect' (see Pigou, 1943). Thus, by changing the real value of money assets and the proportion of income consumed, rising/falling prices produce additional countercyclical features. While no claim is made to address the impediments to full-employment that are caused primarily by inflexible prices, Friedman's framework would nevertheless eliminate 'the uncertainty and undesirable political implications of discretionary action by governmental authorities' (Friedman, 1948, p. 263).

In keeping with the core element of the Plan, Friedman accepts that an ideal world would have '100% reserve requirements, abolition of discount lending, a constant money growth rule, and market determined short-term interest rates' (Nelson, 2013, p. 64). However, given the inevitable operational constraints that apply in practice, theory must defer. In that context, 'Friedman frequently presented his constant money growth rule without including 100% reserve banking as part of the package' (*ibid.*, p. 65). The stark explanation is that Friedman sets aside the core feature of 100 percent reserve banking to focus upon reforms that he believed were more likely to be achieved.

Perceived differences between the respective positions articulated by Henry Simons and Milton Friedman are largely, if not entirely, explained by Friedman's pragmatism. As Friedman's elaborations became ever more obviously targeted upon the practicalities of implementation, his policy objective of a growth target for base money segued into a focus upon board money. Moreover, although Friedman came to accept that the conventional operations of a central bank are in short-term debt, he stresses the importance for aggregate spending of 'portfolio effects on long-term bond yields' (Nelson, 2013, p. 67). It is here that Friedman's practical considerations differ radically in their empirical detail from any presentation given by Simons.

With Simons's endorsement of the Plan, the status of money is not shared with that of credit. In further detail, the relevant interest rates that are associated respectively with the provision of money and the provision of credit are then obviously different. For example, whether in the form of business investments, domestic investments or the purchase of consumer durables generally, the acquisition of tangible property is relevant to the demand for credit. The price of the latter is unlikely to be determined in the market for sovereign bonds, where the decisions of a fiscal authority and the central bank are paramount. Therefore, with the adoption of the Plan, the decisions of policymakers are at some distance from any implications that they might have for the demand for credit.

Where money/bonds are traded in open-market operations that are conducted by, or on behalf of, a central bank, the average time-to-maturity of sovereign debt is altered. Yet, that process of changing the relative proportions of bonds (issued by a sovereign treasury) and money (created by a central bank) leaves the magnitude of aggregate sovereign debt unchanged. The terminology relating to this operation has hardened in recent years. Following the financial crisis that broke in 2008, quantitative easing was effected by the creation of base money by the central bank to be used to purchase sovereign bonds. The idea is for this to be undertaken in sufficient volume that yields on long-term bonds are significantly reduced in a situation where short-term borrowing rates have already been taken to their zero lower bound.

By Simons's judgement, such action constitutes the 'feeble, inadequate, and anomalous implementation of monetary policy' (Simons, 1942, p. 167). The more effective option is for fiscal deficits to be directly oriented towards increasing the circulation of base money, so that the latter rises *pro rata* the rise in sovereign debt. It is by this route that Simons argues that the '[u]ltimate control over the value of money lies in fiscal practices' (Simons, 1936, p. 22; 1948, p. 175).[9]

Bondholders are obviously alert to the potential for the capital loss that can arise with any need to liquidate long-term bonds. As a safeguard, they might choose to hold cash and short-term assets jointly as 'reserves' alongside their holding of long-term bonds. By implication, 'imperfect asset substitution' becomes a feature of financial portfolio adjustments with the further implication that, *for any given level of the short-term rate*, a central bank has scope to affect long-term rates. Friedman therefore suggests that the 'portfolio balance channel' is relevant to delivering a stimulus to aggregate spending: '[d]irect central bank purchases of longer-term securities … offer themselves as an operation that can both raise the money stock and make longer-term interest rates lower *in relation to the expected path of short-term rates*' (Nelson, 2013, p. 67; italics added). By that reduction in longer-term rates, business expansion might then be facilitated by lower yields on corporate bonds.

It is the combination of agents (such as pension fund managers) whose positions are 'hold-to-maturity', with others (including commercial bankers) who are reluctant to hold long-term assets without augmenting their holdings of liquid reserves, that fuels Friedman's argument that the long-term interest rate is determined by 'imperfect asset substitution'. By alternative descriptions, this situation has been described as 'preferred habitat' or 'market segmentation' (Nelson, 2013, p. 68).

This is the context in which Friedman sees two dimensions to the potential instability of a bank credit system: (i) unstable demand parameters; and (ii) over-leveraged creditors. If the banking system were sound, conventional open-market operations at the short end would give the authorities the option of leaning into any monetary wind; and when a banking crisis threatens, the potential of a destabilising flight into liquidity would be neutralised in the presence of deposit insurance. The one impediment that would then remain – the consideration that banks and others give to their reserves-to-deposits ratio – might be countered, either by central bank refinancing against lower-grade collateral or by quantitative easing. By either means, a central bank would be able to maintain its money-market goals in the face of a potential for credit-market instability.

Friedman's close attention to the empirical practicalities of investors' portfolio choices are rooted in the theoretical core of the Plan and is motivated by the potential instabilities that arise from the provision of credit, not money:

> Let me clear up my position on one-hundred reserves and zero reserves. … In my opinion, either extreme is acceptable. I have not given up advocacy of one-hundred percent reserves. I would prefer one-hundred percent reserves to the alternative I set forth. However, I believe that getting the government out of the business altogether or zero percent reserves also makes sense. The virtue of either one is that it eliminates government meddling in the lending and investing activities of the financial markets. When I wrote in 1948, we were already halfway toward one-hundred percent reserves because so large a fraction of assets of the banks consisted of either government bonds or high-powered money. One-hundred percent reserves at that time did not look impossible of achievement. We

> have moved so far since then that I am very sceptical indeed that there is any political possibility of achieving one-hundred percent reserves. That does not mean that it is not desirable.
>
> (Friedman, 1985; cited[10] from Phillips, 1995, p. 174)

In establishing 100 percent reserve banking, the need to create additional base money sufficient to fully cover banks' liabilities would reduce the total of sovereign bonds in matching proportion. This detail can be represented as the transference of seigniorage from the banking system to the state, and this is likely to increase the cost of banking services. The explanation is that, where a fractional reserve banking system functions within a competitive market, only normal profits are earned. All manner of bank fees are competed away, as inter-bank rivalry erodes the monopoly profit of seigniorage. The argument that consumers of bank services and users of bank payments systems should bear the full market price of those facilities sits comfortably within the ethos of the Chicago School.

6.10 Summary thoughts

Entrepreneurial activity implies the extensive instrumentation of money and finance. Money presents competing options: a sovereign currency (base money) or bank credit money or (*pace* Hayek) private currencies. For sovereigns, there is an open temptation to profligacy in suppling base money to avoid raising taxation or paying interest – and, more recently, in attempting to meet macroeconomic goals. Bankers, who extend credit on the basis of fractional reserve holdings, may find that their enterprise is threatened by defaults on their loans or by large withdrawals by their depositors. Finance is essential in order to fuel the imagination of entrepreneurs. Across the multiple structures of banking and finance, recurring successes and failures motivate insurance, counter-strategies, regulation, gaming and moral hazard. That general interplay of economic activity in the face of fundamental uncertainties motivates a recurring interest in the Chicago Plan, of which more follows in the next chapter.

Notes

1 See Chapter 9 (the section, 'Shadow banking').
2 Fisher first stated his debt-deflation theory in *Booms and Depression* (1932).
3 Elements of Austrian business cycle theory are covered in Chapter 9.
4 When Machlup was asked if Hayek's analysis of the onset of the Great Depression was correct, his reply was emphatic: 'Yes, I do, absolutely. I have always accepted it. The stable price level during the early twenties was the beginning of our downfall; this was a period of particularly fast growth of total output and, to keep price levels from falling, one had to create a good deal of money which was all fed into investment and this high rate of investment turned out to be unsustainable in the long run' (Machlup, et al., 1980). Hayek's case is that easy money

in the period 1927–1929 had prolonged an unsustainable boom. Idle plant and machinery in the 1930s was the consequence.

5 That view is also aligned with that of Machlup's erstwhile tutor: '[a]ll history contradicts the belief that governments have given us a safer money than we would have had without their claiming an exclusive right to issue it' (Hayek, 1978, p. 224).

6 By Fisher's broad calculations, liquidations in the period 1929–1933 had reduced indebtedness by twenty percent, but the dollar had appreciated by seventy-five percent, so causing real debt to rise by forty percent. Fisher ventured the tentative opinion that 'in the great booms and depressions', when set against '*over-indebtedness* to start with and *deflation* following soon after', there were only subordinate roles for the more usual suspects: 'over-production, under-consumption, over-capacity, price-dislocation, maladjustment between agricultural and industrial prices, over confidence, over-investment, over-saving, over-spending, and the discrepancy between saving and investment' (Fisher, 1933, pp. 340–41).

7 The relevance of that condition lies with the necessity for labour to be 'involuntarily unemployed'. It is regrettable that modern Keynesians gloss over the context in which Keynes set the rationale for 'demand side' action. See Chapter 7 (the section, 'Involuntary unemployment and make-work schemes'). It is necessary for real wages to fall in order to price labour back into work, but not by cutting money wages. The alternative action, of raising aggregate demand, induces a rise in unit costs as production bottlenecks begin to have effect and so lead to a modest rise in retail prices ('the price of wage-goods'). If money wages remain constant, real wages fall.

8 A Federal guarantee of bank deposits was the first of three general recommendations in the memorandum of 16 March 1933, with the second item delivering the proviso 'only as part of a drastic program of banking reform' (Phillips, 1995, p. 192).

9 See Chapter 6.

10 Cited only as 'an article published in Challenge in 1985'.

Bibliography

Allen, W. R. (1993) 'Irving Fisher and the 100 Percent Reserve Proposal', *Journal of Law and Economics*, vol. 36, no. 2, October, 703–17.

American Presidency Project (1933) Presidential News Conferences, Franklin D. Roosevelt, March 8; http://www.presidency.ucsb.edu/ws/index.php?pid=14672 (accessed 19 June 2015).

Fisher, I. (1933) 'The Debt-Deflation Theory of Great Depressions', *Econometrica*, vol. 1, no. 3, 337–57.

Friedman, M. (1948) 'A Monetary and Fiscal Framework for Economic Stability', *The American Economic Review*, vol. 38, 245–64; cited from Lutz and Mints, 1952, pp. 369–93.

Friedman, M. (1956) 'The Quantity Theory of Money – A Restatement', in Friedman, *et al.* (eds), 1956, pp. 3–21.

Friedman, M. (1968) 'The Role of Monetary Policy', *The American Economic Review*, vol. LVII, no. 1, March, 1–17.

Friedman, M., P. Cagan, J. J. Klein, E. M. Lerner and R. T. Selden (1956), *Studies in the Quantity Theory of Money* (Chicago: University of Chicago Press).

Hayek, F. A. (1978) *New Studies in Philosophy, Politics, Economics and the History of Ideas* (London and Henley: Routledge and Keagan Paul).

Keynes, J. M. (1933) 'An Open Letter to President Roosevelt', *New York Times*, December; http://newdeal.feri.org/misc/keynes2.htm (accessed 9 April 2015).

Keynes, J. M. (1936) *The General Theory of Employment Interest and Money* (London: Macmillan).

Keynes, J. M. (1937) 'The General Theory of Employment', *Quarterly Journal of Economics*, vol. 51, no. 2, 209–23.

Lutz, F. A. and L. W. Mints (1952) (eds.) *Readings in Monetary Theory* (London: George Allen and Unwin).

Machlup, F., J. T. Salerno and R. M. Ebeling (1980) 'An Interview with Fritz Machlup', *Austrian Economics Newsletter*, vol. 3, no. 1, Summer; https://mises.org/library/interview-fritz-machlup (accessed 29 April 2016).

Nelson, E. (2013) 'Friedman's Monetary Economics', *Journal of International Money and Finance*, vol. 38, 59–83.

Phillips R. J. (1995) *The Chicago Plan & New Deal Banking Reform* (New York: M E Sharpe Inc.).

Pigou, A. C (1943) 'The Classical Stationary State', *Economic Journal*, vol. 53, no. 212, December, 343–51.

Samuels, W. (1933) (ed) *Research in the History of Economic Thought and Methodology*, Archival Supplement, vol. 4. (Greenwich, CT, USA: JAI Press).

Simons, H. C. et al. (1933) 'Banking and Currency Reform' *ms.* edited by C. J. Whalen, in Samuels, 1933, pp. 21–49.

Simons, H. C. (1936) 'Rules versus Authorities in Monetary Policy', *Journal of Political Economy*, vol. 44, no.1, February, 1–30; reprinted in Simons, 1948, pp. 160–83.

Simons, H. C. (1938) *Personal Income Taxation: The Definition of Income as a Problem of Fiscal Policy* (Chicago: University of Chicago Press).

Simons, H. C. (1942) 'Review of Alvin H. Hansen, *Fiscal Policy and Business Cycles*', *Journal of Political Economy*, vol. 50, no. 2, April, 161–96.

Simons, H. C. (1948) *Economic Policy for a Free Society* (Chicago: University of Chicago Press).

Viner, J. (1936) 'Recent Legislation and the Banking Situation', *The American Economic Review*, vol. 26, no. 1, Supplement, Papers and Proceedings of the Forty-eighth Annual Meeting of the American Economic Association, March, 106–19.

Zarlenga, S. (2005), 'The 1930s Chicago Plan and the 2005 American Monetary Act'; www.monetary.org/wp-content/uploads/2014/04/Chicago-Plan-and-American-Monetary-Act.pdf (accessed 20 May 2015).

7 Monetary rules

In modern debates on inflation targets, nominal GNP targeting, variants of the Taylor Rule and the relevance of forward guidance, Simons produced the seminal paper on a broad theme: that monetary policy should be determined by rules rather than through the exercise of discretion.[1] Yet, beyond an occasional deferential reference to Henry Simons (from ageing members of the economics profession) details of his contributions are generally neglected. That is a pity. His presentation is rich and 'modern' in a number of disparate aspects.

The gestation of 'Rules versus Authorities' (Simons, 1936/1948) is contemporaneous with Keynes's *General Theory* and Hayek's development of Austrian business cycle theory.[2] Although Simons cites the work of neither of these two great rivals,[3] his antipathy to Maynard Keynes and his empathy with Friedrich Hayek can be inferred from the tenor of various comments. In respect of Keynes and his associates, disparaging remarks relate to 'the stupid schemes of plausible reformers'; and, in respect of a concept later to be utilised by Hayek, Simons refers to neutral money[4] as 'the most stimulating contribution to recent discussion' (Simons, 1936, p. 4; 1948, p. 163). With regard to the 'plausible reformers', Simons is contemptuous of their 'almost diabolical ingenuity' in conceiving a world system in which nations with 'similar credit pyramids (and narrowly nationalistic commercial policies) adopt the same commodity as the monetary standard' (*ibid*., p. 11; p. 168). The essence of that objection (see Hayek, 1939) is as follows.

When a proportional reserve banking system operates under the gold standard (or any other fixed exchange rate system), a general shortfall of reserve assets can be made good only as commercial banks compel their creditors to repay loans. Unless an imbalance in international currency flows quickly corrects itself, the reserve position of a central bank may become endangered. To counter that threat, a central bank may raise domestic interest rates, so bringing added pressure (generally and indiscriminately) upon outstanding loans. In responding to higher domestic rates, international capital flows would also adjust, so strengthening the reserve position of the central bank.

Secondary reactions then involve those to whom banks would have lent and those who would have benefited from expenditure facilitated by that bank lending. Even leaving aside the impact of higher interest rates upon international capital flows, domestic deflation simultaneously reduces payments abroad and (by lowering the price of domestically produced goods) diverts expenditure from foreign products. In this fashion, discretionary credit contraction shortens the period of adjustment. However, the broad conclusion is that 'it is the necessity of "protecting" international reserves rather than letting them go (i.e., using the conversion into gold as the proper method of reducing the internal circulation) not the methods by which it has to be done, which is evil' (Hayek, 1939, p. 33). In short, under the gold standard, monetary instability arises because a central bank must provide reserves whenever they are needed to meet a withdrawal of commercial bank deposits. Otherwise, the payments system fails. Yet, until that need arises, a central bank has little control over the expansion of bank credit money.

The previous commentary (drawn from Hayek, 1939) is in full alignment with the contemporaneous writing of Simons, who further condemns the 'reformers' for their 'irresponsible proposals for indefinite inflation, based on the notion that our ills are traceable to deficiency of consumer-purchasing-power' (Simons, 1936, p. 12; 1948, p. 169). Against the option of bond-financed public works as championed in Keynes's *General Theory*, the mainstream classical response (as caught by David Ricardo's perception of the equivalence between sovereign borrowing and taxation) is that, when resources are taken for public works, this diminishes the 'resources of the investment market for other purposes' (Hawtrey, 1925, p. 45). This would enter the lexicon of economics as either the 'Treasury view'[5] or 'crowding out'. Although, by issuing paper currency, a nation might 'escape an intensification of unemployment by letting its exchange rate depreciate', this builds no reputation for financial stability: in 'a gold using world, countries with paper currencies do not count for much in the investment market' (*ibid.*, p. 47). Yet, this *is* the essential feature of Keynes's remedy for chronic unemployment – i.e., a 'policy of an autonomous rate of interest, unimpeded by international preoccupations, and of a national investment programme directed to an optimal level of domestic development' (Keynes, 1936, p. 349). With that solution arguably open to all, Keynes paints an implausible scenario of 'restoring economic health and strength internationally' (*ibid.*).

In regard to the theoretical concept of neutral money (i.e., that which is commensurate with monetary equilibrium), Simons notes that any translation to a workable proposal is unlikely to prove easy.[6] Yet, he laments the little progress that had been made in identifying 'what kind of money rules might be adopted to make capitalism a more workable system' (Simons, 1936, p. 4; 1948, p. 163) and the absence of specific proposals for 'an adequate monetary system based on simple rules' (*ibid.*, p. 12; p. 169).

7.1 Monetary reform (1936)

In following the classic liberal tradition, the objective for Simons is that monetary policy should be benign (*vide*, neutral money) where the sole pragmatic requirement is to counter general price rigidities:

> [w]ith adequate price flexibility, we could get along under almost any financial system; with extreme rigidities (reflecting widespread partial monopoly), the most drastic monetary and financial reform … could not protect us from serious disturbances of production and employment.
>
> (*ibid*., p. 14; p. 170)

In arguing that money is a prime driver 'of extreme industrial fluctuations' (*ibid*., p. 163) and by his desire for capitalism to become a more workable system, Simons proposes three reforms to dampen economy-wide fluctuations in output and employment: (i) a flexible price structure; (ii) a fixed quantity of 'circulating media'; and (iii) strictly limited short-term financing. The motivation for the first and second proposals is that, in the face of variations in both the quantity and the velocity of money in circulation, wage and price rigidities inhibit necessary adjustments to real economic activity.

As a stopgap measure and in recognising a requirement to accommodate changes in the velocity of money in circulation, Simons favours targeting prices (the 'price-index rule'), which he recognises as 'the more expedient solution unless and until a highly competitive economy is realized and the structure of private money contracts drastically modified' (*ibid*., p. 18, fn. 16; p. 172, fn. 16).[7] One-half century later, the Medium Term Financial Strategy (1979–85) for UK monetary policy would illustrate how the strategy of targeting a money aggregate that is inclusive of endogenous bank money can be undermined by new banking technologies, regulatory changes and variations in inter-bank competition for market share.[8]

In regard to the third proposal – for strictly limited short-term financing – Simons envisages a financial structure where 'the volume of short-term borrowing would be minimised' and where only the government would effect changes in the volume of 'effective circulating media'. Among measures reviewed by Simons is that of fixing the aggregate of currency (aka 'base money') plus demand deposits; but a weakness lies in the availability of 'abundant money substitutes during booms' (*ibid*., p. 9; p. 166) and for sharp changes on the velocity side. The nub is that, when bank liabilities have become established as a means of payment, 'the banking system acquires in effect the prerogative of currency issue and places the government under the practical necessity of giving the private obligations virtually the status of public debts' (*ibid*.). Here, Simons touches on the source (as indicated before) of monetary instability: in order to protect the payments system, a central bank must provide reserves as necessary to meet withdrawals of commercial bank deposits.

It is the use of endogenous money in business financing that exacerbates cyclical instability. During a cyclical downturn, the potential for insolvency is precipitated as banks attempt to keep ahead of preferential creditors. By the liquidation of loans that were extended during a cyclical upturn, banks themselves become exposed to insolvency. Hence, a core requirement is to address the financial structure as a 'source of aggravation in booms and depression' (*ibid.*, p. 7, fn. 6; p. 165, fn. 6).

Ideally, this would be achieved by the abolition of short-term borrowing. Yet, it is the next-best option of 100 percent reserve banking that gained status as the 'signature' Simons proposal – i.e., for banks to be limited to holding and transferring base money, with limits placed upon endogenous money. In addition, measures would be required to prevent other institutions taking on that prerogative when it is denied to banks, as illustrated by the recent rapid growth of shadow banking.[9] In drawing a comparison with the regulation of monopolies, Simons is fully alert to 'the reappearance of prohibited practices in new and unprohibited forms' (*ibid.*, p. 17; p. 172). This is a ubiquitous feature: patching over regulatory loopholes is a Sisyphean exercise.[10]

An additional characteristic, by which the banking problem can be exacerbated, is the low ratio of owner equity to the volume of unsecured lending. To ameliorate that source of instability, Simons's recommendation is for all the capital of a bank to be 'held in a residual-equity or common stock form', so that 'no one would be in a position either to create effective money-substitutes … or to force enterprises into wholesale efforts at liquidation' (*ibid.*, p. 6; p. 165). Closely aligned to that ideal is the proposal for borrowing to take the form of 'contracts in perpetuity' (i.e., consols), which, by their widely varying prices, would have little appeal as money substitutes.[11]

7.2 The Great Depression

By the evidence that he draws from the Great Depression, Milton Friedman gives little weight to the impact of endogenous money. In Friedman's view, events immediately prior and subsequent to October 1929 were driven not by the liquidation of commercial bank loans but by policy decisions of the Federal Reserve. Friedman argues that, from mid-1928, monetary constraint was 'not restrictive enough to halt the bull market yet too restrictive to foster vigorous business expansion' (Friedman and Schwartz, 1963, p. 298; cited from Friedman, 1967, p. 9). Only subsequently, as stock prices were plummeting, was monetary contraction brought about 'entirely by a decline in Federal Reserve credit outstanding. No part whatever was played by weakness in the banking structure, attempted liquidation of loans by banks, or an attempt to convert deposits to currency' (*ibid.*, p. 10).

Beginning with a series of bank failures in December 1930, Friedman notes that, although a run on banks did lead to the liquidation of assets, it was only when the Federal Reserve's role of lender of last resort gave way to deliberate deflation that a second banking crisis (beginning in March 1931) was turned into a catastrophe.[12] It is Friedman's contention that, in not knowing 'the facts as we now know them' (*ibid.*, p. 12), Simons's thoughts followed a path similar to those of Keynes, by the emphasis that he placed upon the need for fiscal intervention. (On this, more is written in the next chapter.)

From the perspective of Austrian business cycle theory, Hayek contests Friedman's assessment when he argues that

> the common element in the doctrines of Simons and Keynes was the influence of the Great Depression..... [Rather] all the elements of the theories that were applied to the Great Depression had been developed during that great enthusiasm for "business cycle theory" which preceded it.
>
> (Hayek, personal letter; cited from Friedman, 1967, p. 8, fn. 7)

Hayek argues that economic growth to 1927 gave no reason to expect other than a mild recession to follow. That this did not happen, he attributes to the deliberate action of the authorities who

> succeeded, by means of an easy-money policy, inaugurated as soon as the symptoms of an impending reaction were noticed, in prolonging the boom for two years beyond what would otherwise have been its natural end. And when the crisis finally occurred, for almost two more years, deliberate attempts were made to prevent, by all conceivable means, the normal process of liquidation.
>
> (Hayek, 1935, p. 162)

Friedman disputes both Hayek's appraisal of the events of the late 1920s and, more generally, the value in Austrian business cycle theory (on the latter, see Garrison 1996). Friedman also suggests a 'difference in temperament' between Keynes and Simons: that when the financial structure was viewed as a threat to stability, Keynes looked to the immediate solution of replacing 'where necessary private investment by government spending'. By contrast, Simons 'regarded a large measure of laissez-faire as an essential requisite for the preservation of political liberty'; and, for that reason, he was inclined to go to the root of the problem 'by reforming drastically the financial structure' (*ibid.*, p. 9). In mapping the detail of that reform, Simons has much to say about fiscal policy; but the relevance of fiscal policy to Simons could not be more different to the position taken by Keynes in *The General Theory.*

7.3 Sovereign expenditure

For Keynes, the priority is to use deficit-financed state investment to counter the effects of (i) high liquidity preference and (ii) low business confidence. Respectively, those predispositions emasculate (i) attempts by a central bank to reduce long-term rates and (ii) the impact of low interest rates in stimulating business investment. The counterargument (the 'Treasury view', or 'crowding out') is that state expenditure 'financed by genuine loan subscriptions (aka "real saving") cannot do any good'. Rather, it 'can only stimulate activity in some localities at the expense of others' (Hawtrey, 1932, p. 446). By the Treasury view, the remedy lies with expenditures that are financed by newly provided commercial bank credit. As the economic guru of the UK Treasury, Ralph Hawtrey argued that this can be achieved by open-market asset purchases:

> When the Bank of England buys securities, the total of bankers' deposits [aka 'reserves'] is increased. The joint-stock banks, holding more cash [aka 'base money'], become ready to increase their advances and discounts. Thus when the stimulus of cheap money offered to the *borrower* is insufficient, the stimulus of redundant cash reserves can be applied to the *lender.*
>
> (*ibid.*)

As bondholders are enticed to sell sovereign bonds to the central bank, commercial bank holdings of base money (reserves) must increase to the same degree. It is implicit in the above that Hawtrey expressly assumes that commercial banks 'become ready to increase their advances and discounts'; but that is an empirical question.

It is uncontroversial that, by the sale/purchase of sovereign bonds, a monetary authority has direct influence over interest rates when it engages in open-market operations. Yields fall/rise as bond prices rise/fall. Whether applied at the short-end of the market, or with longer-dated securities, those operations have become the primary (even sole) instrument of macroeconomic stabilisation. With the onset in 2008 of the Great Recession, asset purchase programmes (quantitative easing) by central banks were initiated (in the US, the European Union, Japan, the UK, Switzerland and Sweden), with a consequential expansion of reserves held by commercial banks. A stimulus to business activity was anticipated: (i) that commercial banks would be motivated to increase advances and discounts; and (ii) in consequence of a general competitive reduction in corporate borrowing rates. However, if banks are subsequently intent upon rebuilding their balance sheets and/or are wary of the inadvertent acquisition of 'toxic' assets, they may show themselves as reticent lenders. The anticipation was that the fall in corporate borrowing rates would have the greater effect.

The general assessment from Simons is that open-market operations are unlikely to lift an economy from a deflationary process. At one level, he merely notes the expedient of 'such injections of fiscal stimulants as may be necessary to prevent recurrence of wholesale liquidation' (Simons, 1936, p. 19; 1948, p. 173); but in a more significant and forceful passage, he states:

> Ultimate control over the value of money lies in fiscal practices - in the spending, taxing, and borrowing operations of the central government. Thus, in an adequate scheme for price-level stabilization, the Treasury would be the primary administrative agency; .... The powers of

> the government to inject purchasing power through expenditure and to withdraw it through taxation - i.e., the powers of expanding and contracting issues of actual currency [aka 'base money'] and other obligations more or less serviceable as money - are surely adequate to price-level control.
>
> (*ibid.*, p. 22; p. 175)

For Simons, central bank open-market operations, which merely alter the ownership and the term-structure of sovereign debt (substituting base money for interest-bearing debt), are unlikely to prove adequate as the means to counter deflation. It is this argument that marks the divide between Simons and Friedman; and the difference relates to the means by which an expansion of money is achieved. Is it to be by increasing fiscal deficits or by central bank open-market operations? Where fiscal deficit spending raises sovereign debt (i.e., sovereign bonds plus banknotes and reserves), open-market operations do not.

7.4 A significant divide

With a greater inclination to intervene than in earlier times, there was a tendency for economists in the early-1930s to back deficit-financed public expenditure, primarily as the means to put base money directly into circulation. Only superficially does this have any bearing upon later Keynesian or Monetarist thinking. The superficial similarity with Monetarism is that open-market bond purchases puts base money into circulation. Although this might serve to dampen the cycle, the view held by the early Chicago School is that such action is a 'feeble, inadequate, and anomalous implementation of monetary policy' (Simons, 1942, p. 167). By contrast, a fiscal deficit (surplus) causes sovereign debt to increase (decrease). Unlike open-market operations, money-financed fiscal deficits directly increase the circulation of base money as it increases sovereign debt by the same magnitude.

As Simons persisted in arguing the relevance of raising fiscal deficits, many would confuse his presentation with the rationale propagated by Keynes. Simons's argument is that, because '[u]ltimate control over the value of money lies in fiscal practices' (Simons, 1936, p. 22; 1948, p. 175), price-level stabilisation should not be left to 'banking authorities'. It then follows 'that the whole argument of this [i.e., the seminal "Rules versus Authorities"] paper might properly be developed with primary emphasis upon problems of government finance' (*ibid.*, p. 24, fn. 21; p. 175, fn. 21).

From the 1990s, the argument for the predominance of fiscal policy, as elucidated by Simons, has been modelled formally and presented anew as the 'fiscal theory of the price level'.[13] Without doubt, it is a fair comment to say that Simons denigrated 'monetary powers narrowly conceived' (Friedman, 1967, p. 13). The alternative perspective that Simons takes is that of monetary powers (i.e., sovereign debt: both bonds and base money) broadly conceived.

Henceforth, as discussed as follows and in the next chapter, the core idea is referenced as Fiscal Monetarism.

Contrasting with those strands of monetary theory is the development of Keynes's *General Theory*, which couples a controversial bond-price theory of interest rate determination with a liquidity trap to render monetary policy ineffective. Fiscal deficit expenditure then takes centre stage as the trigger for the real income multiplier. However, where *The General Theory* provides a rationale for expenditure upon public works, Chicago economists had already produced a parallel case for expanding sovereign debt in the form of base money, where the income multiplier has no relevance. Rather, the goal is to secure price stability. In holding a firm grasp upon his Keynesian perspective, Robert Skidelsky argues that, without the multiplier concept, the Chicago case was simply lacking; but by his suggestion that 'on public works as a remedy for American unemployment' Chicago economists were 'more Keynesian than Keynes' (Skidelsky, 1992, p. 392), it is clear that fundamental differences are being overlooked.

7.5 Raise expenditure or cut taxation?

From among Simons's papers, there is an undated and 'unidentified statement on government expenditure and depression' (see Rockoff, 2015, p. 45, fn. 5), wherein Simons argues that the action that he believes is necessary to achieve price stability is best taken in 'the form of generous federal expenditures, financed without increase of taxes on commodities or transactions'. Another passage in *Personal Income Taxation* (1938) –

> Once a deflation has gotten under way … Only great government deficits can check the hoarding of lawful money and the destruction of money substitutes … the proper checks in this direction also are to be found in the taxing, borrowing and spending activities of the national government.
>
> (Simons, 1938, p. 222)

– is consistent with that earlier undated assessment. Although the previous citation elicits the comment – 'it appears that the founder of the Chicago School of Monetary Economics was a thoroughgoing Keynesian!' – 'appears' *is* the operative word, because further elaboration gives the true perspective:

> What is needed during depressions is deficits, not expenditures; and deficits may properly be obtained by tax reductions as well as through emergency outlays. … Adequate reflationary deficits could be obtained without tossing money recklessly in all directions, without reliance on the hurried schemes of bureaucrats, without the numerous disadvantages of "emergency public works," and without the awful prospect of fiscal reflation carried far beyond the time when it should be reversed.
>
> (Simons, 1938, p. 223)

By this second passage, Simons is clearly most firmly at odds with the core arguments of *The General Theory*.

When the objective is to lift a market economy out of deep recession, 'central bank action is a feeble, inadequate, and anomalous implementation of monetary policy' (Simons, 1942, p. 167). Unlike the bland force of open-market operations (aka quantitative easing), money-financed fiscal deficits (aka 'monetary financing') *is* the relevant intervention. As sovereign debt then rises, base money in circulation increases and commodity prices begin to rise, so reversing a general deflationary movement. Prosperity is restored as new private spending revitalises the confidence of business entrepreneurs.

7.6 Involuntary unemployment and make-work schemes

The concept of 'involuntary unemployment' is a core feature of *The General Theory* (there are thirteen citations in the index), but it rarely features in any modern presentation of macroeconomic policy. The analysis is straightforward. A conventional sketch of equilibrium between demand and supply in a competitive labour market gives the real wage and employment on the respective axes. In equilibrium, labour's productivity at the margin is equal to the real wage, which is defined as the 'money-wage' (W) divided by an index of 'the price of wage-goods' (P). Involuntary unemployment then exists when there is

> no expedient by which labour as a whole can reduce its real wage to a given figure by making revised money bargains with the entrepreneurs.... Men are involuntarily unemployed if, in the event of a small rise in the price of wage-goods relatively to the money-wage, both the aggregate supply of labour willing to work for the current money-wage and the aggregate demand for it at that wage would be greater than the existing volume of employment.
>
> (Keynes, 1936, p. 15)[14]

In the conventional labour-market diagram, the implication of that rise in 'the price of wage-goods' (from P_1 to P_2) 'relatively to the money-wage' (W) is that the respective quantities of the 'supply of labour' and 'the demand for it' both rise to levels that are above 'the existing volume of employment'. Labour is priced back into work because (the assumption of) diminishing returns to labour is commensurate with a falling real wage. However, if the higher price of 'wage-goods' is matched by a higher level of money wages, the stimulus to employment and output is lost.

By the assumed necessary absence of a prices-wages spiral, Keynes did not conflate 'a small rise in the price of wage goods' with persistent inflation. Any hint to the contrary is dispelled when it is recognised that the fall in real wages is a once and for all readjustment. That much can be inferred from the argument that

> an increase in the quantity of money will have no effect whatever on prices, so long as there is any unemployment, … whilst as soon as full employment is reached, it will thenceforward be the wage-unit and prices which will increase in exact proportion to the increase in effective demand.
>
> (Keynes, 1936, p. 295)

Although Keynes conceded possible make-work elements in the first round of increased public expenditure, the anticipation of a prolonged positive multiple impact is present:

> [i]f the consumption psychology of the community is such that they will chose to consume, *e.g.*, nine-tenths of an increment of income, then the multiplier *k* is 10: and the total employment caused by (*e.g.*) increased public works will be ten times the primary employment provided by the public works themselves, assuming no reduction of investment in other directions.
>
> (*ibid.*, pp. 116–17)

The relevant question here is, how long could this continue? The analysis is deficient in failing to address the necessity for Keynes's interventions to be repeated year-on-year in order to sustain a given level of aggregate expenditure. The practical accommodation of that necessity can only be in the form of an ever-rising volume of sovereign debt.

7.7 The concept of fiscal monetarism

Where there is a need to counter a deflationary process (in the form of a general liquidation of financial assets and a contraction of bank credit), Simons understood that this cannot be achieved merely by altering the composition of sovereign debt (through open-market operations). Rather, the whole counter-inflationary process must be undertaken by the fiscal authority.[15]

The core of Fiscal Monetarism is that ultimate control over the value of money lies in fiscal practices. In modifying Friedman's aphorism, inflation is always and everywhere a sovereign debt phenomenon, rather than a monetary phenomenon. In running a fiscal deficit, a sovereign meets its revenue shortfall by selling new-issue bonds; and if those bonds are purchased by a central bank, sovereign debt is 'monetized'.

The nominal value of sovereign bonds is measured in the same money unit as the sovereign currency (base money) in which maturing bonds are redeemed. As the nominal value of sovereign debt rises in relation to national income, so the willingness of market participants to hold that debt diminishes. The explanation is that coupon payments are financed from taxation and that an upper limit to the *real* value of sovereign debt exists at the level where future tax receipts are perceived to have become insufficient to repay the obligations to bondholders. As the former exceeds the latter, the real value of the money unit falls.

The erosion of market confidence in the real value of sovereign debt goes hand in hand with the falling purchasing power of the money unit in which sovereign bonds are denominated.[16] It follows that general price stability can be achieved only where fiscal deficits do not push the volume of debt against an upper limit that is set by financial market sentiment. By the view taken by Simons as the most appropriate policy for the 1930s, price deflation needed to be countered by allowing fiscal deficits to push the volume of sovereign debt beyond that upper limit. It was a radical measure to redress desperate circumstances.

Simons makes the pertinent observation that, whenever the responsibility for monetary stability is left to banking authorities, there is 'only vague recognition that reckless accumulation of federal indebtedness might give rise to difficulties' (Simons, 1936, p. 19; 1948, p. 173, fn. 21). The crux of Fiscal Monetarism is that (whether by an increase in base money or interest-bearing bonds) the use of that 'paper' to finance fiscal deficits is potentially inflationary[17]; and that is the basis for Simons's subsequent speculation that 'drastic measures for debt retirement… may soon become imperatively necessary to prevent a disastrous inflationary boom' (Simons, 1936, p. 19; 1948, p. 173).

7.8 Moneys, practical moneys and near moneys

Political instability is threatened when fractional reserve banking delivers 'a mass of ersatz moneys' that are supported by the illusion that they are then 'really convertible into the real thing'. Certainly, base money is 'highly amenable to democratic legislative control', but

> money is not easily manageable alongside a mass of private debt and private near-moneys whose aberrations fiscal policy must work against, or alongside a mountain of debt, short-term and long, which rises prodigiously in emergencies and is not reducible at other times.
>
> (Simons, 1942, p. 176)

Simons was emphatic that, while the 'miscellany' of different forms of sovereign debt serves no useful purpose, it introduces unnecessary confusion:

> [t]here is little hope for sound monetary-fiscal policy … if our representatives persist in confusing everybody, including especially themselves, by issuing moneys, practical moneys, and near moneys under other names.
>
> (Simons, 1944, p. 357)

Given that 'miscellany' of different moneys, any formal representation of the quantity theory of money would require a weighted composite for 'Money'. Indeed, 'when monetarism was in fashion it was the subject of much research by economists exploring Divisia indexes' where the typical assumption was 'that the properties of an asset that determine its moneyness are more or less permanent' (Rockoff, 2015, pp. 7–8). If that were so, money would present fewer problems for the real economy. However, the introduction of new forms, the demise of existing forms and cyclical variations in the acceptability of all forms undermine the practical coherence of monetary policy.

The purchase of €200bn of Eurozone sovereign debt by the European Central Bank (ECB) in 2010–2011 presents an example of the confusion (or else deliberate sleight of hand) that can arise. Payment for those bonds was effected by crediting banks with 'reserves' (i.e., claims upon the ECB) when it was argued that, by accepting one-week rolling deposits to the same value, the ECB had absorbed the additional liquidity. From that basis, the ECB asserted that no monetisation of debt had occurred. The claim is clearly disingenuous. Given that one-week bills could be used as collateral to obtain bank reserves, they are barely less liquid than the reserves they replaced. The practice ceased in June 2014.

To remove the potential for such confusion – and misleading statements by central bankers – Simons recommends that a single category of bonds be issued. These would be perpetual bonds, i.e., 'consols'. With no redemption date, these are 'the antithesis of money'; and with the achievement of that strict dichotomy between money and interest-bearing debt, both the demand for base money and the rate paid on bonds would rise. The practical question of the respective proportions held of consols and base money would be decided by experiment: '[t]he rule for policy as to consols and currency, i.e., for *composition* of the debt including money, is simply stabilization of the value of money' (Simons, 1944, p. 357). With that argument, Simons describes the Fiscal Monetarist concept of sovereign debt as comprising treasury bonds and central bank base money. Market-driven price adjustments then constrain the *real* value of sovereign debt (and the relative proportions of its components) at levels no higher than financial market participants are willing to hold.

The Fiscal Monetarist view is that, when the magnitude of sovereign debt is unchanged (as with quantitative easing), the purchasing power of the money unit is largely unaffected; i.e., the *composition* of sovereign debt has inflationary relevance only when it affects the willingness of market participants to hold that debt. As the sovereign-debt-to-GDP-ratio ('sovereign debt ratio') rises, it becomes ever more problematic to raise sufficient tax revenue to service and/or redeem sovereign debt. The implication is that it is a general unwillingness to hold sovereign debt that drives down its real value by creating an excess demand for goods and services. It is then that demand-pull inflation occurs.

In following Simons's recommendation for the elimination of all categories of sovereign bonds other than consols, clarity is brought to the administration of monetary policy. The implication of the *composition* of sovereign debt is also changed; and this explains an apparent contradiction where Simons laments an 'extreme perversity'. That perversity can exist during a cyclical upswing, when the expansion of commercial bank credit may coincide with the use of fiscal surpluses to retire long-term sovereign debt obligations. The latter increases base money, when the very opposite is required; i.e., in a cyclical upswing the sale of long-term debt, obligations needs to be 'increased to permit the impounding of currency' (Simons, 1936, p. 19; 1948, p. 173, fn. 21).

7.9 Concerns about Keynes

Governments must not undermine the 'confidence of their creditors in the future of fiscal policy'. Rather, they should 'carefully conserve their borrowing powers for inflationary emergencies (wars) and promptly amortize debts occurring on such occasions'. Both by the psychology that says that prices must sooner or later revert to pre-crisis levels and by the 'cheap-money movements' that it stirs, deflation is more readily countered than inflation. By contrast, 'once governments have squandered their borrowing powers and undermined confidence of their creditors in the future of fiscal policy', measures to curb inflation are undermined by the psychology of 'expectations endlessly aggravating' and a financial structure that delivers near-moneys. The crux of the fears that engage Simons is that Keynesian options promise 'a future of free spending with a minimum of political flexibility, of taxes near the limit of taxable capacity … and of huge debt, growing at an uneven rate but always growing' which then 'facilitates a dangerous muddling of monetary questions and questions of socialization' (Simons, 1942, pp. 177–78).

Sovereign borrowing becomes easier for the fiscal authority whenever market yields are lowered (say, by restrictive industrial practices), so inducing private investors to seek better returns from sovereign bonds. That diversion from the private to the public sector is more readily facilitated if the general ethos that builds from Keynesian actions fuels the idea that sovereign debt 'should rise indefinitely' and that 'the rate of increase should be adjusted to the degree of unemployment'. By implication, it may become routine for excessive wage increases to be accompanied by rising price levels:

> Presumably the private economy is to struggle along as best it can, whatever happens to wage rates, the unemployed being absorbed continuously into public employment, i.e., into an expanding socialized sector which, supported out of taxing and borrowing need not be seriously concerned about relations between wage rates and productivity.
>
> (*ibid.*, p. 180)

Indulgent sovereign spending leaves a damaging legacy for future legislatures, including that of political instability as 'taxpayers or claimants of government dispensations will revolt against deprivations in the name of bondholders'[18] (*ibid.*, p. 174).

Simons points to a collectivist bias in the Keynesian presumption that saving is excessive and consumption is inadequate in all phases of the business cycle. Indeed, that bias is explicit in Keynes's anticipation that 'a somewhat comprehensive socialisation of investment will prove the only means of securing an approximation to full employment' (Keynes, 1936, p. 378). Moreover, the emphasis that Keynesians place upon adjustments to spending, rather than adjustments to taxation, is to disregard the greater flexibility of the latter, given the resistance of pressure groups to expenditure cuts. To make spending the only variable carries the implication that a continuous expansion of government activities must follow as an implication of stabilization.

The consequences of Keynesian palliatives might be ameliorated if fiscal deficit-spending were redirected. Instead of supporting an ever-increasing level of spending, fiscal deficits might be used to remove excise taxes, when the outcome would be 'a less regressive system and one far more amenable to cyclical adjustment' (Simons, 1942, p. 188). Simons cites a reduction in tobacco and liquor taxes to raise general consumption. The objection, that income taxation involves significant lags between legislation and subsequent changes in tax revenue, could be addressed by modifying the taxation system so that revenues are more closely correlated with the business cycle.

In respect of economic growth, Simons accepts the expedient of wages rising in line with labour productivities, not least because the benchmark for fiscal policy is most readily stated in terms of a price index:

> in a political environment uncongenial if not hostile to owners of sunk investment, one may commend the total ordering of fiscal policy toward stabilization of a broad commodity-price index and provision of all the liquidity consistent with that norm.
>
> (*ibid.*, p. 181)

In conceding the value of 'the most expansive fiscal practices consistent with [price] index stability' (*ibid.*), Simons finds 'no basis for substantial disagreement' with Keynesians, except in the matter of implementation: 'monetary authorities must be bound by simple, definite rules (a price index) and … *their only real powers should be those of conducting operations in the public debt*' (*ibid.*, p. 182; italics in the original). If it were otherwise, then Simons fears that unlimited discretionary action would risk trading democracy for 'the managed state': '[t]he only real authority is the public; and the only possible rules are norms which the community … accepts and demands to be observed in government finance' (*ibid.*, p. 183).

7.10 A rules-based system

The severely limited role for a monetary authority would be to advise a legislature on whether any proposed course of action is in line 'with accepted norms of fiscal action'; and, to achieve that, the authority needs the support of rules to deliver legislative cooperation. Once a general expectation is established that the legislature has a commitment to abide by a set of definitive rules, 'anticipations would make them nearly self-implementing'. With no confusing array of money, near moneys and medium-term and long-term securities, monetary adjustments would be achieved 'by open-market operations replacing consols by demand obligations [reserves], or conversely'. The only overt action required would be 'that of giving publicity to index movements and some advance notice of its recommendations' (*ibid.*).

The core characteristic that provides the rationale for adopting a rules-based monetary system is that it provides 'a minimum of uncertainty for entrepreneurs and investors as to monetary conditions in the future' (Simons, 1936, p. 29; 1948, p. 181). Three decades later, that same sentiment would be echoed by Friedman in his conclusion to a seminal presidential address to the American Economic Association: 'steady monetary growth would provide a monetary climate of those basic forces of enterprise, ingenuity, hard work, and thrift that are the true springs of economic growth' (Friedman, 1968, p. 17) and subsequently: 'a monetary structure that fosters steadiness and predictability in the general price level is an essential precondition for healthy noninflationary growth' (Friedman, 1987, p. 362).

Similarly motivated to limit the damage from activist monetary policy, Friedman's preference for a fixed-percent growth rate rule for the money supply was originally advanced within the context of 100 percent reserve banking. Even then, however, it would be necessary to accommodate the distinction between deposits subject to the 100 percent requirement and deposits that are exempt. Given the possibility of converting covered deposits into higher yielding uncovered deposits, monetary policy would remain ill-defined. Although Hayek endorses the desirability of a rules-based system, he understands that the convertibility of near-money into base money might prove necessary to avoid severe liquidity crises or panics:

> As regards Professor Friedman's proposal of a legal limit on the rate at which a monopolistic issuer of money was to be allowed to increase the quantity in circulation, I can only say that I would not like to see what would happen if it ever became known that the amount of cash in circulation was approaching the upper limit and that therefore a need for increased liquidity could not be met.
>
> (Hayek, 1978, p. 81)

The key features that Simons believes are necessary to achieve the smoothest transition to a rules-based system are that the rules should be definitive and simple, expressive of strong popular sentiments and allowing the fullest stable employment. They should 'facilitate adjustment to such basic changes (especially technology) as are likely to occur … [and] … minimise inequities between debtors and creditors'; and they should set the objective of achieving constancy of 'an index of competitively produced commodities' (Simons, 1936, pp. 29–30; 1948, pp. 181–82). While those features are relevant to minimising 'problems of a transition period', Simons's baseline speculation is that, once a rules-based policy is 'well established and generally accepted as the basis for anticipations, any one of many different rules (or sets of rules) would probably serve about as well as another' (*ibid.*).

7.11 Monetary reform (2015/2016)

Although few academic economists are alert to the arguments that support Simons's agenda for reform, his work periodically takes the attention of practitioners. Recent examples are a report commissioned by the Icelandic Prime Minister (Sigurjonsson, 2015) and a book from a former Governor of the Bank of England (King, 2016).

In his forward to the Iceland report, Adair Turner (former chairman of the UK Financial Services Authority) writes that, while relevant reforms have been introduced by regulators and central banks, they fail to address the fundamental issue: the instability that is inherent in allowing banks to create endogenous money. The author of the report – Frosti Sigurjonsson (Member of the Parliament of Iceland and Chairman of the Committee for Economic Affairs and Trade) – reiterates that sentiment, as he notes that, over fifty years and more, Iceland has experienced 'inflation, hyperinflation, devaluations, an asset bubble and ultimately the collapse of its banking sector in 2008' (Sigurjonsson, 2015, p. 9). The purpose of his report is to fuel debate on how the money creation process might be reformed.

The End of Alchemy (2016) is an early fruit of Lord King's return to academia. He defines a modern form of alchemy as 'the belief that all paper money can be turned into an intrinsically valuable commodity' and that 'money kept in banks can be taken out whenever depositors ask for it' (King, 2016, p. 8). By that definition, alchemy is present whenever (endogenous) commercial bank money is recognised as a claim on (exogenous) central bank money. King's prime motivation is to find 'a way of retaining the attractive feature of the Chicago Plan – that it ends bank runs – while at the same time reducing alchemy in the wider banking system' (*ibid.*, p. 268).

With the creation of bank credit money, the deposits (liabilities) of commercial banks are not fully covered by reserves; but a bank remains solvent where the value of its assets equals the value of its liabilities. Yet, without sure means to identify solvent banks, a run on one bank undermines faith in others. If one bank then finds it necessary to sell assets at distressed 'fire-sale' prices, other banks may be forced to mark their own assets to the reduced market values. That, in turn, may incite further fire sales across many other institutions. To preclude such events, the Bank of England was urged by Bagehot (1873) to lend 'quickly, freely and readily' at a penalty rate to any bank that could offer 'good securities' as collateral. This 'lender of last resort' (LOLR) doctrine became the conventional wisdom for central bankers.

King argues that LOLR is outdated in three aspects: (i) banks have little incentive to avoid calling upon the LOLR; (ii) central bank lending absorbs good collateral that might otherwise support lending elsewhere and this deters loans being rolled over; (iii) in a crisis, a central bank may be pressured to lend against dubious collateral. Therefore, King advocates a new structure – a 'pawnbroker for all seasons' (PFAS) – to shield taxpayers from bank bailouts.

One element of PFAS is already in place. In the same spirit as the Basel III liquidity rules (Basel Committee, 2013) and as featured in the 'Red Book' (Bank of England, 2015), assets are 'pre-positioned' (PPA) as collateral, with the central bank deciding 'haircuts' for different categories of assets. Each bank then knows its borrowing limit, which, when added to its reserves, determines its 'effective liquid assets'. A companion aggregation of bank liabilities delivers a simple regulatory calculation: 'effective liquid assets should exceed their effective liquid liabilities'[19] (*ibid.*, p. 272). PFAS would then be applied to all financial intermediaries with the scheme implemented over a period of twenty years or so, during which time prudential regulation would remain. In summary, King's proposals embrace six elements:

1. a central bank supported by fiscally prudent government is the ultimate source of liquidity.
2. a gradual progression in raising the reserve ratio of banks.
3. competition between banks and financial intermediaries in structuring their balance sheets.
4. PPA haircuts to displace the moral hazard of LOLR.
5. recent market features support PFAS: (i) large amounts of bank reserves produced by quantitative easing; (ii) the assessment and management of collateral by the central bank.
6. PFAS regulation requiring: (i) effective liquid assets in excess of effective liquid liabilities; (ii) a maximum value for the leverage ratio (of bank equity to total assets).

To ensure that private money 'does not simply migrate outside the regulated sector, and end up benefiting from an implicit public subsidy' (*ibid.*, p. 274), legislation would need to keep pace with strategic gaming. More easily stated than achieved, 'who guards the guards' remains an unresolved problem that troubled Simons rather more than it appears to trouble King. By contrast, King argues that PFAS enhances market solutions by moving in the direction of a full internalisation of social cost; and he optimistically anticipates 'the gradual evolution of expectations towards the view that banks will not be bailed out' (*ibid.*, p. 280).

PPA haircuts are proposed as the means to make PFAS operational; i.e., this is the insurance that pays out when banks demand liquidity from the central bank. King explains the difference between the risk-weighting of bank assets (RWA) and haircuts to PPA:

> For one [RWA], the aim is to compute the overall risk of a portfolio of different bank assets which requires knowledge of all possible outcomes

> and the correlations of returns on different assets. For the other [PPA haircuts], the more limited aim is a rough and ready calculation of the discount at which an asset pledged as collateral could be sold when a bank could not repay the central bank.
>
> (*ibid.*, p. 277)

Although PPA should be of superior quality, a central bank must be mindful of its capacity to absorb losses. When financial markets are in crisis, banks may be forced to engage with fire sales of risky assets; but a central bank can defer the liquidation of PPA until an opportune moment of its own choosing. Yet, this might prove more difficult that King allows: value is time dependent; there are no risk-free assets; and asset values may not recover. Even so, there is a belief that

> [b]ank resolution - a special bankruptcy regime for banks - would be simpler than it is today because deposits (liabilities) and the collateral lodged with a central bank (assets) could be lifted out of the failed bank, and then deposits transferred to another bank together with the liquid reserves for which the collateral was pledged ... without serious disruption to its depositors.
>
> (*ibid.*, p. 279)

The infrequency with which central banks resort to bank resolution in liquidating collateral raises some curiosity. The explanation may rest with the status of those resolution schemes as legal enactments, which are largely national in character. The implication is that '[t]he prospective failure of a large cross-border bank ... would prompt telephone calls between political leaders to override regulators and prevent the closure of a well-known institution' (*ibid.*, p. 390, fn. 30).

Although crisis measures rescued the banking system in 2008, deep structural problems remain to be addressed across the world economy, among which are China's growing debt, Japan's chronic stagnation and the dysfunctional structure of the Eurozone. Whatever new policy initiatives might be implemented, the spontaneous order of continuous market readjustments must allow entrepreneurs to succeed or fail by their uniquely speculative initiatives. The alternative of macroeconomic palliatives simply protects failing projects as it distracts attention from meaningful reform.

At the core of the easy to state and hard to achieve options for reform are greater competition, the elimination of distortions both to the tax system and to saving and spending, greater efficiency in providing public services, less regulation in the private sector, general improvements to public infrastructure, the removal of impediments to free trade and the restoration of flexible exchange rates. All of which are redolent of Simons's drive for simplicity, flexibility and consensus.

Notes

1 The initial statement of a Chicago preference for rules over discretion is attributed to Douglas and Director (1931); see Tavlas (1997) pp. 160–61.
2 See Chapter 9 (the section, 'Austrian business cycle theory').
3 'When the definitive history of economic analysis during the nineteen thirties comes to be written, a leading character in the drama (it was quite a drama) will be Professor Hayek. ... Hayek's economic writings ... are almost unknown to the modern student; it is hardly remembered that there was a time when the new theories of Hayek were the principal rival of the new theories of Keynes. Which was right, Keynes or Hayek?' (Hicks, 1967, p. 203).
4 Although Knut Wicksell (1851–1926) originated the description of neutral money as 'an interesting case of a concept's rendering valuable service by proving unworkable' (Schumpeter, 1954, p. 1088), Hayek is given credit for deploying the concept 'as a means to contrast his own view of money with the more aggregative views' according to which 'money is neutral so long as the value of money (as measured by the general level of prices) remains unchanged' (Garrison and Kirzner, 1987, p. 611).
5 See Chapter 8 (the section, 'The Treasury view').
6 That practical measures might prove elusive is confirmed by Hayek having repeatedly returned to the task (Hayek, 1960, 1976, 1978, 1986). Though conceding 'intellectual priority' (Hayek, 1978, p. 23, fn. 1) to others, Hayek's final position favours the use of private currencies.
7 With the working assumption of a constant income velocity, Simons notes that, assuming 'physical production' is on a rising trend (which implies a rising transactions demand for money), chronic fiscal deficits ('not accompanied by corresponding growth of the interest bearing debt') are required to meet a price-index target. In short, fiscal deficits must be financed by growth in base money. With the presumption that low interest rates induce price rises and vice versa, if a price-index target is to be met through each cyclical phase, the fiscal authority would need 'consistently to make open-market purchases of its obligations when their prices were highest and sell them when their prices were abnormally low' (Simons, 1936, p. 23, fn. 20; 1948, p. 176; fn. 20). Upon the supposition that this might 'induce widespread financial insanity' (ibid.), Simons finds further reason why (given the elimination of near-moneys) 'the rule of a fixed quantity of money was fundamentally correct', but that it would require the ideal conditions of 'a flexible price structure' (ibid., pp. 15–16; 1948, p. 170).
8 The willingness to hold broad money increases if competition for market share raises interest payments on sight deposits; and that willingness rises as tightened monetary policy raises rates in general. That this was so in the UK is indicated by the retrospective appraisal of its finance minister: '[f]or broad money it has been clear since the autumn that the range was set too low. Throughout the 1980s – and in sharp contrast to the 1970s – broad money has grown far faster than money GDP. Experience has demonstrated that this has not posed a threat to inflation. This rapid growth largely reflects the increased attractions of holding interest-bearing deposits, at a time both of low inflation and high real interest rates, and of innovation and liberalisation in the financial system' (Lawson, 1986).
9 See Chapter 9 (the section, 'Shadow banking').
10 The existence of 'shadow' banks can often be traced to state regulation. For example, US money market funds were a means to avoid the prohibition on demand deposit interest. Simons's concern, that a regulation or a rule has the potential to incite institutional adaptations, is articulated in 'what we nowadays call

the "Lucas critique" or "Goodhart's law"' (Laidler, 1993, p. 1098). Generic to all regulation (as to central planning generally) is that it removes the market's way of moderating risk as it undermines the expectation of self-responsibility. Yet, there are many who would believe that regulators have the know-how and capability to act in the public interest. Even in applying modest constraints, effective regulation must be able to counter all the unforeseen reactions and error-learning adjustments that typically follow.

11 Those holding undated interest-bearing debt ('contracts in perpetuity') find that their wealth is eroded by inflation as readily as the wealth of those holding base money; but the impact upon the wealth of those holding time-dated debt is weakened because, as their debt is rolled over, they benefit from inflation having raised nominal rates.

12 Under the Federal Reserve Act, the lender of last resort facility was constrained by the gold standard; i.e., '[t]he reserve banks were required to maintain minimum gold reserve ratios against their note and deposit liabilities as well as collateral in the form of eligible commercial paper against their note issues' (Carlson and Wheelock, 2012, p. 13).

13 See Chapter 8, fn. 6.

14 The concept of involuntary unemployment was put to the test on Keynes's estate at Tilton: 'The farm was less amused when he gave everyone a rise and at the same time announced that free milk, which was one of the labourers' perquisites, would henceforth be delivered in pint bottles. On the face of it nobody could possibly complain of this, but it fact everyone knew that when the milk was taken home in a can much more that the allotted pint would go home each evening with the labourer and that in fact Maynard would more than recoup the advances in wages. It was an arguably unjust measure … but the workers … felt more bitterly about it than they would if he had reduced their wages outright' (Bell, 1980, pp. 82–83).

15 Quantitative easing by a central bank is essentially a form of sovereign debt management. Where interventions are made by the fiscal authority, 'obligations more or less serviceable as money' are sold and the proceeds used to purchase undated bonds. By such means, a monetary initiative becomes a 'debt-management operation in form as well as in substance' (Allen, 2012, p. 832). Short-term yields then rise, long-term yields fall, the yield curve twists, but sovereign debt remains unchanged. Given the long legacy of Keynes's analysis, it is important to note that, in recognising the equivalence of fiscal/monetary routes to that same end, the representation of fiscal and monetary interventions as independent policy options (familiar to students of economics as ISLM analysis) is more limited than is generally appreciated.

16 Conversely, when open-market quantitative easing is undertaken by a central bank, sovereign debt remains constant and backed by an unchanged capitalised value of expected primary fiscal surpluses.

17 A clear difference between sovereign debt and corporate debt is that the latter must generate market returns sufficient to pay interest on the loan and to repay the principal. With sovereign debt, taxation must be levied to repay creditors.

18 A clear illustration of that instability is the 'anti-austerity' repackaging of Keynesian panaceas and the political pressures with which this was accompanied, once the sub-prime Credit Crunch crisis of 2008 had exposed the inherent indiscipline that exists within the Eurozone, where numerous fiscal authorities are constitutionally independent of a single monetary authority.

19 As proposed by Basel III, the Liquidity Coverage Ratio is a key reform to ensure 'that banks have an adequate stock of unencumbered high quality liquid assets (HQLA) that can be converted easily and immediately into in private markets into cash to meet the liquidity needs for a 30 calendar day liquidity stress scenario' (Basel Committee on Banking Reform, 2013, p. 4).

Bibliography

Allen, W. A. (2012) 'Quantitative Monetary Policy and Government Debt Management in Britain since 1919', *Oxford Review of Economic Policy*, vol. 28, no. 4, 804–36.

Bank of England (2015) 'One Bank Research Agenda', February; www.bankofengland.co.uk/research/Documents/onebank/discussion.pdf (accessed 1 April 2015).

Basil Committee on Banking Supervision (2013) *Basel III: The Liquidity Coverage Ratio and Liquidity Risk Monitoring Tools,* January; www.bis.org/publ/bcbs238.pdf (accessed 15 July 2015).

Bell, Q. (1980) 'Recollections and Reflections on Maynard Keynes', in Crabtree and Thirlwell, 1980, pp. 82–83.

Carlson, M. A. and D. C. Wheelock (2012) 'Lender of Last Resort. Lessons from the Fed's First 100 years', Federal Reserve Bank of St. Louis, Research Division, Working Paper 2012–056B.

Crabtree, D. and A. P. Thirlwell (1980) (eds.) *Keynes and the Bloomsbury* (London: MacMillan).

Dorn, J. A. (ed) (1987) *The Search for Stable Money: Essays on Monetary Reform* (Chicago and London: University of Chicago Press; Washington: Cato Institute).

Douglas, P. H., and A. Director (1931) *The Problem of Unemployment* (New York: MacMillan).

Eatwell, J., M. Milgate and P. Newman (eds.) (1987) *The New Palgrave: A Dictionary of Economics* (London: Macmillan Press Ltd.).

Friedman, M. (1967) 'The Monetary Theory and Policy of Henry Simons', *The Journal of Law and Economics*, vol. 10, October, 1–13; reprinted in Friedman, 1969, pp. 81–93.

Friedman, M. (1968) 'The Role of Monetary Policy', *The American Economic Review*, vol. LVII, no. 1, March, 1–17.

Friedman, M. (1969) *The Optimum Quantity of Money and Other Essays* (Chicago: Chicago, Aldine Publishing Co.).

Friedman, M. (1987) 'Monetary Policy: Tactics versus Strategy', in Dorn, 1987, pp. 361–82.

Friedman, M. and A. Schwartz, (1963) *A Monetary History of the United States, 1867–1960* (Princeton: Princeton University Press).

Garrison, R. W. (1996) 'Friedman's Plucking Model: Comment', *Economic Inquiry*, vol. 24, 799–802.

Garrison R. W. and I. Kirzner (1987) 'Friedrich August von Hayek', in Eatwell, Milgate and Newman, 1987, pp. 609–14.

Hawtrey, R. G. (1925) 'Public Expenditure and the Demand for Labour', *Economica*, vol. 5, March, 38–48.

Hawtrey, R. G. (1932) *The Art of Central Banking* (London, New York & Toronto: Longmans, Green and Co.).

Hayek, F. A. (1935) *Prices and Production*, 2nd ed., revised and enlarged (London: Routledge and Kegan Paul); 1st ed., 1931 (London: George Routledge and Sons); originally published in German as *Preise und Produktion* (Wien-Leipzig: Hölder-Pichler-Tempsky A.G.).

Hayek, F. A. (1939) *Monetary Nationalism and International Stability*, Institut Universitaire de Hautes Etudes Internationales, Genève, Suisse; no. 18, 2nd ed. (London: Longmans, Green and Co).

Hayek, F. A. (1960) *The Constitution of Liberty* (London and Henley: Routledge and Kegan Paul).

Hayek, F. A. (1976) *Choice in Currency*, Occasional Paper 48 (London: Institute of Economic Affairs).

Hayek, F. A. (1978) *Denationalisation of Money*, 2nd edition, Hobart Special paper 70 (London: Institute of Economic Affairs).

Hayek, F. A. (1986) 'Market Standards for Money', *Economic Affairs*, vol. 6, no. 4, 8–10.

Hicks, J. R. (1967) *Critical Essays in Monetary Theory* (Oxford: Oxford University Press).

Keynes, J. M. (1936) *The General Theory of Employment Interest and Money* (London: Macmillan).

King, M. A. (2016) *The End of Alchemy: Banking, the Global Economy and the Future of Money* (London: Little, Brown Book Group).

Laidler, D. (1993) 'Hawtrey, Harvard, and the Origins of the Chicago Tradition', *Journal of Political Economy*, vol. 101, no. 6, December, 1068–1103.

Lawson, N. (1986) Budget Speech, 18 March, Hansard HC [94/166–184], cited from The Thatcher Foundation; www.margaretthatcher.org/document/109503 (accessed 24 May 2016).

Rockoff, H. (2015) 'Henry Calvert Simons and the Quantity Theory of Money' *mimeo* 27 September; https://bfi.uchicago.edu/research/working-paper/henry-simons-and-quantity-theory-money (accessed 24 September 2016).

Schumpeter, J. A. (1954) *History of Economic Analysis* (Oxford: Oxford University Press).

Sigurjonsson, F. (2015) 'Monetary Reform, A Better Monetary System for Iceland', a report commissioned by Prime Minister Sigmundur David Gunnlaugsson. Reykjavik; www.forsaetisraduneyti.is/media/Skyrslur/monetary-reform.pdf (accessed 28 June 2016).

Simons, H. C. (1936) 'Rules versus Authorities in Monetary Policy', *Journal of Political Economy*, vol. 44, no.1, February, 1–30; reprinted in Simons, 1948, pp. 160–83.

Simons, H. C. (1938) *Personal Income Taxation: The Definition of Income as a Problem of Fiscal Policy* (Chicago: University of Chicago Press).

Simons, H. C. (1942) 'Hansen on Fiscal Policy', *Journal of Political Economy*, vol. 50, no. 2, April, 161–96.

Simons, H. C. (1944) 'On Debt Policy', *Journal of Political Economy*, vol. 52, no. 4, April, 356–61; reprinted in Simons, 1948, pp. 220–30.

Simons, H. C. (1948) *Economic Policy for a Free Society* (Chicago: University of Chicago Press).

Skidelsky, R. (1992) *John Maynard Keynes. vol. 2. The Economist as Saviour, 1920–1937* (London: Macmillan).

Tavlas, G. S. (1997) 'Chicago, Harvard, and the Doctrinal Foundations of Monetary Economics', *Journal of Political Economy*, vol. 105, no. 1, February, 153–77.

8 Monetarism and Fiscal Monetarism

8.1 Revolution in economics

A revolution within the social sciences presumes the 'existence of an established orthodoxy'; and it is further marked by an 'unexpected speed of change' (Johnson, 1971, pp. 1–3). The orthodoxy that grew to represent Keynes's *General Theory* is that equilibrium at less than full employment is a normal state of affairs that calls for persistent remedial action by the state. The Keynesian orthodoxy is that fiscal interventions are necessary to maintain full employment, not least because the impact of monetary policy is indirect, affecting bond prices only. When there is an excess in the supply of money, there is an increase in the demand to hold bonds. However, that willingness to purchase bonds is limited by the presence of a liquidity trap.

The liquidity trap can be examined in the context of the systematic management of a portfolio of financial assets. When money is supplied in excess, portfolio managers adjust the proportions of less liquid and more liquid assets within their asset portfolios. In the stylised choice between liquid money and illiquid bonds, money holdings fall/rise as bonds are purchased/sold; and, as bond prices rise/fall, bond yields fall/rise. Across competitive financial markets, bond yields and interest rates generally adjust until eventually bond prices reach levels that are commensurate with liquidity preferences.

However, a situation may arise where the general belief is that bond prices can go no higher and that interest rates can fall no lower. It is then that interest rates are described as having reached the zero lower bound. If the authorities were then to issue still more money, that new 'liquidity' would remain 'trapped' within asset portfolios because of a general reluctance to buy bonds now priced at their maximum level.

The 'liquidity preference theory' (of interest rate determination) is one of the novel features of *The General Theory*. It was necessary for Keynes to devise an alternative theory, because the classical loanable funds theory of interest rate determination is incompatible with Keynes's income multiplier. However, if business confidence is low, Keynes argues that monetary policy (as the means to lower interest rates) has little relevance to reducing unemployment and no relevance at all to general price inflation. In regard to the latter, fixed-price models are a core feature of the Keynesian orthodoxy: 'an increase in the quantity of money will have no effect whatever on prices, so long as there is any unemployment' (Keynes, 1936, p. 295). By the presentation of *The General Theory*, price inflation becomes an issue only as full employment is reached, because it is only then that unit costs of production begin to rise. Hence the notion of 'cost-push' inflation[1] which, taken together with liquidity preference and the income multiplier, are core elements of the Keynesian paradigm. That inflation can only emerge as the economy is near to full employment is a proposition that would be challenged by the Monetarist counter-revolution.

Prior to the publication of Keynes's *General Theory*, monetary policy had been 'the single established instrument of aggregative economic policy, and price stability was its established objective' (Johnson, 1962, p. 367). Thereafter, the mainstream followed Keynes's presentations in discounting both the impact of monetary policy upon prices and the relevance of monetary intervention to lift an economy from depression. By the rapidity and extent by which the Keynesian orthodoxy emerged and was accepted by academics and policymakers, attempts to refute the general idea that 'money does not matter' tended to be ignored. It was necessary to wait. In retrospect, it needed price inflation to occur in conditions of less than full employment and then to become recognised as a persistent problem. In an epoch of fixed exchange rates, that 'event' was triggered by fiscal deficit spending in the US to meet high-cost welfare reforms at home and escalating military expenditures overseas. Put bluntly, 'the appearance of monetarism … had to wait until the aftermath of the escalation of the war in Viet Nam in 1965' (Johnson, 1971, p. 7).

Towards the end of the 1960s, US sovereign debt began to rise rapidly. Within the context of the international currency parities that had been fixed to the US dollar at Bretton Woods in 1944, the inevitable result was that price inflation – so obviously initiated by policy in the US – became a general feature across Western economies. The empirical Phillips curve trade-off (of a stable inverse relationship between percentage wage increases and unemployment) vanished, exactly as Milton Friedman (1968) and Edmund Phelps (1967) had anticipated. Freidman's reputation soared:

> What was new was his statement that there is a direct link between monetary growth and inflation through the medium of inflation expectations in the labour market. This statement was so distinct from Keynesianism that it became necessary to invent a new label for such an idea. In 1968, Karl Brunner called it 'monetarism' and the name stuck.
>
> (Foster, 1987, p. 42)

It was only then that the Keynesian orthodoxy encountered the full force of the Monetarist counter-revolution.

8.2 The quantity theory of money

Monetarism: the novelty of a new name tends to obscure its relevant antecedents. The basic idea is that price inflation is determined by the prior excessive growth of money. Alternatively stated, inflation *is* currency debasement. However, the quantity theory of money has invited considerable inventiveness and embellishment since attention was first taken by the impact of money upon trade and industry. Which are the key transmission mechanisms between money and prices? Friedman's 'The Quantity Theory of Money. A Restatement' (Friedman, 1956) describes a transmission based upon adjustments to portfolios of financial assets – i.e., the exact same mechanism upon which Keynes bases his liquidity preference theory of interest rate determination. By Keynes's presentation, with an economy at under-full employment, the liquidity preference theory of interest rate determination is held to be more plausible than the classical loanable funds theory.[2]

Although the basic idea of the quantity theory of money is traceable to ancient times, an early 'theoretically satisfactory presentation' (Schumpeter, 1954, p. 311) is credited to Jean Bodin (1568); but it was John Stuart Mill (1848) who brought precision to the idea:

> If we assume the quantity of goods on sale, and the number of times these goods are resold, to be fixed quantities [T] the value of money [$1/P$] will depend upon its quantity [M], together with the average number of times that each piece changes hands in the process [V]'.
>
> (Mill, 1848; cited from Kahn, 1984, p. 39; M, V, P, T added, where $MV \equiv PT$)

Thereafter, Mill's presentation mutated successively into Irving Fisher's 'equation of exchange' (1911), Alfred Marshall's 'Cambridge equation' (1923), Milton Friedman's 'restatement' of the quantity theory of money (1956) and 'Monetarism' (1968) and the 'Fiscal Monetarism' of Karl Brunner and Alan Meltzer (1972a, 1972b). As is examined later, Fiscal Monetarism derives from ideas that originate with David Ricardo (1817) and were extended by Robert Barro (1974).

8.3 A Chicago monetary traditon

Prior to the Western experince of inflation from the mid 1960s, Friedman's embellishment of the quantity theory of money a decade earlier had attracted relatively little attention. Thereafter, the context in which presentational claims were then made by Friedman is disputed:

> At Chicago, Henry Simons and Lloyd Mints directly, Frank Knight and Jacob Viner at one remove, taught and developed a more subtle and relevant version, one in which the quantity theory was connected and

> integrated with general price theory and became a flexible and sensitive tool for interpreting movements in aggregate economic activity and for developing relevant policy prescriptions.
>
> (Friedman, 1956, p. 3)

By the recollection of his first-hand exposure and from the evidence of his student notes, Don Patinkin insists that the work of Chicago monetary economists in the 1930s and the 1940s 'lacked some of the basic ingredients of the flavour of the model which Freidman has presented of it' (Patinkin, 1969, p. 53). Upon that basis, Patinkin argues that the presentation is one in which Friedman draws heavily from Keynes:

> Friedman is primarily concerned with the optimal relationship between the stock of money and the stocks of other assets, whereas the quantity theorists were primarily concerned with the relationship between the stock of money and the flow of spending on goods and services.
>
> (Patinkin, 1969, pp. 60–61)

Although Patinkin is content to describe the early 1930s as a period in which 'the Chicago School was independently developing the traditional $MV = PT$ quantity-theory approach' (Patinkin, 1979, p. 221), he objects to Friedman's persistence 'in presenting his exposition of the demand for money function as a "reformulation of the quantity theory of money"' (Patinkin, 1969, p. 62). Patinkin is emphatic and insistent in viewing Friedman's Monetarist counter-revolution 'as a continuation of the Keynesian theory of liquidity preference' (Patinkin, 1969, p. 47).

Friedman's response is to refocus the argument and to criticise Patinkin for ignoring pertinent details of the Chicago tradition – i.e., 'short-run movements, the reasons for the great depression, and the role of monetary and fiscal policies' (Friedman, 1972, p. 933). Among the details of Friedman's counterclaims are: (i) the existence of a Chicago oral tradition as evidenced by the differential impact of *The General Theory* upon economics at Chicago and economics elsewhere; and (ii) a general failure to acknowledge the influence of the quantity theory on Keynes's writing: 'Keynes was a quantity theorist long before he became a Keynesian' (*ibid.*).

The counterclaim by Friedman is that the parallels that exist between his own monetary theory and monetary aspects of *The General Theory* do not *per se* constitute evidence against the existence of a Chicago monetary tradition. And so, the argument remains unresolved and, to an impartial audience, the obvious suspicion is that the two economists – Friedman and Patinkin – are engaged in trying to unscramble eggs. The telling point is that where Keynes insists that inflation cannot exist below full employment, Friedman knew that to be wrong.

Friedman describes Keynes's *A Tract on Monetary Reform Tract* (1923) as 'the most explicitly monetarist work amongst the writings of the Cambridge

School (letter, 5.8.85)' (Presley, 1986, p. 192). As is also true of the Chicago School, a central theme of *A Tract* is that stability in the value of money is essential to a sound economy. *A Tract* also points (somewhat narrowly) to some of the implications of fractional reserve banking: given the composition of commercial bank reserve assets (banknotes and reserves), the capacity for bank credit creation 'is mainly governed by the policies and actions of the Bank of England and the Treasury' (Keynes, 1923, p. 182). With broad money in circulation comprising banknotes and commercial bank deposits, Keynes suggests that an index of prices might be used as a benchmark to guide monetary policy:

> it would promote confidence and furnish an objective standard of value, if, an official index number having been compiled of such a character as to register the price of a standard composite commodity, the authorities were to adopt this composite commodity as their standard of value in the sense that they would employ all their resources to prevent a movement of its price.
>
> (Keynes, 1923, p. 187)

Whatever the relative strengths of views taken on the tradition that held in Chicago, neither Friedman nor Patinkin denies that the 'reformulation of the quantity theory' was

> strongly affected by the Keynesian analysis of liquidity preference ... [that] ... emphasizes the role of money as part of capital or wealth theory concerned with the composition of the balance sheet or portfolio of assets.
>
> (Friedman, 1968, pp. 439–40)

By Friedman's account, the difference between the rival propositions lies with the relevant variables to which attention is directed and the process of adjustments to monetary disequilibrium. He points to the spontaneous remedial action that might be expected when there is 'a difference between actual and desired stocks of money'. Respectively, the emphasis given by

1 quantity theorists is upon 'the use of current flows of income and expenditure to add to or subtract from some assets and liabilities'
2 Keynesian analysis is upon 'a rearrangement of assets and liabilities through purchase, sale, borrowing, and lending'.

Where there is an excess supply of money, quantity theorists anticipate ever-extending sequences in terms of rising prices over a period of time; but Keynesian analysis is focused upon a single adjustment to bond prices and, by implication, to interest rates. Yet, Friedman concedes that these are not mutually exclusive, and he insists that the reformulation of the quantity theory 'enforces consideration of both' (Friedman, 1968, p. 441). Nevertheless, the most prominent feature of Monetarist analysis – which is lacking in presentations from Chicago economists in the 1930s – is the emphasis placed by Friedman upon on the stability of the demand to hold money.

Setting that important detail to one side, David Laidler presents a compelling argument that only one of 'the three distinctive characteristics that Friedman attributes to 1930s Chicago monetary economics' (Laidler, 1993, p. 1069) is a uniquely Chicago trait. Of the two whose antecedents lie elsewhere, both the general power of monetary policy (so emphatically downplayed by Keynes) and Friedman's monetary interpretation of the Great Depression either predate, or are contemporaneous with, work undertaken by Lauchlin Curry and Allyn Young at Harvard. That work follows earlier lines of thought (Hawtrey, 1913, 1919), where emphasis is placed upon the importance of monetary policy in stabilising business fluctuations. It was Young who made the arrangements for Hawtrey's year as a Harvard visiting professor in 1928–1929.[3]

By Laidler's assessment of likely influences, the unique feature of Chicago analysis in the 1930s was 'to forge a link between a monetary explanation of the cycle and a liberal political agenda' (Laidler, 1993, p. 1070). By that appraisal, emphasis is given to Simons as having provided a 'lucid blue print of classical liberalism' (Stigler, 1988, p. 139); and that broad perspective is complemented by the insistence of Simons, that taxation alone must fund fiscal expenditure. To that end, sovereign debt should be reshaped, both in respect of its particular form and its use. Only undated bonds should be sold, so that short-term sovereign debt would no longer be available to serve either directly as 'near moneys' or indirectly as collateral for new bank credit money. Equally firm is the conclusion that the only justification for raising sovereign debt is to check incipient inflation, pending a staged permanent rise in taxation: 'there is never any excuse for borrowing save to *prevent* expansion. Borrowing is a means for displacing money (deposits) with less effective money substitutes (consols)' (Simons, 1942, p. 174). With the insistence that current taxation should provide the resource for current fiscal expenditure, Simons implicitly aligns the principle of Ricardian equivalence (between taxation and sovereign borrowing) with the liberal political agenda:

> [g]iven real consensus of fiscal norms (a monetary constitution) and given a private economy free enough to benefit from monetary stabilization, the government could easily implement such stabilization by proper use of taxation, spending and issuing powers without extending for that purpose, the range or magnitude of its total activities
>
> (*ibid.*, p. 178)

8.4 Fiscal Monetarism

In Friedman's Monetarist presentation, great store is placed upon the alternative financial assets that are traded, either generally or within the open market operations conducted by a central bank. By those adjustments, the magnitude of sovereign debt (i.e., the aggregate value of base money and treasury bonds) remains unchanged. That outcome is in line with Keynes's somewhat theatrical recommendation:

> If the Treasury were to fill old bottles with bank-notes, bury them at suitable depths in disused coal-mines which are then filled to the surface with town rubbish, and leave it to private enterprise on the well tried principle of *laissez-faire*, to dig the notes up (the right to do so being obtained, of course, by tendering for leases of the note-bearing territory) there need be no more unemployment.
>
> (Keynes, 1936, p. 129)

The awkward phrase that Keynes sets in parenthesis ensures that, by the payments collected from those who obtain the 'leases of the note-bearing territory', there is no net addition to sovereign debt.

Where Milton Friedman points to policy of that same ilk, it is to argue that Keynes's remedy would not be effective. Friedman first draws attention to 'the continued widespread acceptance… that fiscal policy is the key to control the level of money income', which he counters as follows:

> The quantity theory implies that the effect of government deficits or surpluses depends critically on how they are financed. If a deficit is financed by borrowing from the public without an increase in the quantity of money, the direct expansion effect of the excess of government spending over receipts will be offset to some extent and possibly to a very great extent, by the indirect contractionary effect of the transfer of funds to the government through borrowing.
>
> (Friedman, *Encyclopedia Britannica* entry cited from Werner, 2007)

In Friedman's presentation, when government borrowing is financed by a transfer of funds from other parts of the economy, the net effect is, at best, negligible. Thus, Keynes and Friedman both describe adjustments that parallel the impact of open-market operations, where the level of sovereign debt remains unchanged. Yet, where Keynes envisages a major macroeconomic stimulus, Friedman sees little of substance, when there is merely a substitution between interest-bearing and non-interest-bearing components of sovereign debt.[4]

The general feature that is present in all three of these outcomes – banknotes in bottles, the transfer of borrowed funds away from private and into government schemes, and open-market operations – is one that is contrasted by Simons's focus upon the *magnitude* of sovereign debt. From among Simons's papers, there is an undated and 'unidentified statement on government expenditure and depression',[5] wherein Simons argues that the action necessary to raise prices is best taken in 'the form of generous federal expenditures, financed without increase of taxes on commodities or transactions'. A passage in *Personal Income Taxation* (1938) reinforces that undated assessment:

> Once a deflation has gotten under way ... Only great government deficits can check the hoarding of lawful money and the destruction of money substitutes ... the proper checks in this direction also are to be found in the taxing, borrowing and spending activities of the national government.
>
> (Simons, 1938, p. 222)

The tenet of (original) Monetarism is that inflation is caused by an excess supply of money, the corollary of which is an excess demand for goods and services. If individuals hold too much of one thing, they must hold too little of another. Fiscal Monetarism is a derivative of Monetarism. The conceptual change is both minimal and fundamental. The tenet of Fiscal Monetarism is that inflation is caused by an excess supply of sovereign debt. The recurring theme of Monetarism is that 'inflation is always and everywhere a monetary phenomenon'; but with Fiscal Monetarism, that becomes 'inflation is always and everywhere a sovereign debt phenomenon.'

In reiterating key features from Chapter 7, it is revealing and practically relevant to consider a national central bank and a national sovereign treasury as 'two-in-one' – i.e., for the interrelated decisions taken by a central bank and a treasury to be analysed as those from a single authority (referenced as the 'sovereign'). From that perspective, sovereign debt consists of money and bonds. Respectively, these are: (i) short-term base money (banknotes and bank reserves, i.e., claims on the central bank); and (ii) longer-term debt (sovereign bonds, i.e., claims on the treasury). Base money (banknotes and reserves) and sovereign bonds are valued in the same currency unit; and a maturing sovereign bond is redeemed in base money. It runs close to stating the obvious to say that the nominal unit value of both base money and maturing sovereign bonds is identical. It is by that simple point that the focus broadens from Monetarism to Fiscal Monetarism.

There is an important difference between *sovereign* debt and *corporate* debt. Upon maturity, those holding sovereign bonds and corporate bills expect to be repaid in base money. The options then denied in financing the repayment of corporate bonds are increased taxation and/or the issue of new base money; so corporate debt falls. With the redemption of sovereign bonds, those options remain open. If taxation is unchanged, the volume of sovereign debt remains unchanged; i.e., the repayment of sovereign debt reduces long-term debt (bonds) as it increases short-term debt (base money). It then follows that the idea that bond-financed sovereign borrowing competes against – and thereby 'crowds out' – corporate borrowing is too simplistic. Unlike corporate borrowing, sovereign borrowing is *not* constrained by finite resources as determined by the willingness of individuals to redirect income from consumption to saving.

The capacity of a sovereign to raise tax revenue is determined by the wealth and income (i.e., the 'tax base') of the citizens within a sovereign nation. As an approximation, gross domestic product (GDP) is the source of tax revenue. It then follows that the sovereign-debt-to-GDP-ratio ('sovereign debt ratio') is an indicator of solvency – i.e., the capacity to reduce sovereign debt with revenue that accrues from taxation. As the sovereign debt ratio rises, the likelihood increases of the sovereign being unable to raise sufficient revenue from taxation to service and/or to redeem sovereign debt.

Although there is no upper limit to the magnitude of nominal sovereign debt, market-driven price adjustments do constrain the *real* value of sovereign debt, holding it at a level no higher than market participants will countenance. As that level is breached, there is an excess supply of (and a reluctance to hold) sovereign debt. This simultaneously creates an excess demand for other items and, as the nominal prices of those items then rise, the real value of sovereign debt must fall; i.e., there is demand pull inflation.

Whenever there is an excess supply of sovereign debt (as base money or bonds), there is the corollary of an excess demand for goods and services (and non-sovereign financial assets). By the joint (exchange rate) devaluation of base money and sovereign bonds, sovereign debt falls to a level (in real terms) that is acceptable to individuals and agencies. The general conclusion that emerges is that general price stability can be achieved only by market credibility; i.e., only if the sovereign's commitment and capacity to deliver future primary fiscal surpluses is perceived to be sufficient to service and/or to redeem sovereign debt can its real value be expected to remain unchanged.

Where a sovereign currency exists, sovereign debt can always be monetised; i.e., new base money can be issued to redeem maturing sovereign bonds. Even if that 'swap' of base money for bonds leaves total debt unchanged, the Monetarist view is that this would incite inflation expectations, with the effect of causing the real value of the money unit to fall. The Fiscal Monetarist view is that, if monetisation changes the composition of sovereign debt (as it leaves total debt unchanged), the real value of the money unit would be largely unaffected. The adjective 'largely' demands an explanation. Any single act that alters the composition of a portfolio of assets may set in train comprehensive readjustments. Yet, where the level of sovereign debt remains unchanged, any impact upon the nominal value of real goods and services is from an adjustment of preferences. In general, price stability requires the sovereign to recognise that general market sentiment sets an upper limit to the real value of sovereign debt, where the relative proportions of base money and sovereign bonds have little consequence. The *composition* of sovereign debt has inflationary relevance only if it affects the willingness of market participants to hold that debt.[6]

8.5 Ricardian equivalence

Although it is a derivative of Monetarism, Fiscal Monetarism finds antecedents that are uniquely its own, in the arguments presented by David Ricardo.

The foundation of Ricardian equivalence is that a loan merely defers a payment and that borrowing rests upon the perceived capacity of the borrower to repay the loan. The greater the perceived default risk, the less likely (or the more expensive) it is to borrow. Although default risk generally rises with the real value of outstanding debt, as explained before, this does not hold in respect of sovereign debt, because the sovereign has unique powers to raise taxation and/or to create base money.

The nub of Ricardian equivalence is that sovereign borrowing is equivalent to taxation and that the timing of taxation (whether immediate or deferred by borrowing) is irrelevant if prospective taxpayers are rational. The details were first examined in David Ricardo's *On the Principles of Political Economy and Taxation* (1817)[7] with the illustration of a requirement to raise £20 million in order to take the nation to war. The alternatives are for the state to raise the full amount either in taxation or as a loan at £1 million annual interest. If taxes are raised, taxpayers have the option of either paying the full amount from their own funds or obtaining private loans at interest. Whatever are the means by which the £20 million is raised, the nature of the transaction is unchanged: resources are diverted to war and taxpayers have less for themselves.

Ricardo comments further upon an adjacent issue – i.e., the relative ease by which government and individuals can obtain loans to smooth transitory spikes in spending and/or taxation. Capital markets are less than perfect and it is arguable that the 'frictions' relating to sovereign borrowing are less than those that relate to a myriad of small loans to individuals. It then follows that it is less costly for the state to borrow and for those loans to be repaid from taxation raised over successive periods.

Against this, Ricardo sounds a note of caution. From his experience as a successful entrepreneur, Ricardo is alert to the imperfections of the real world, and he warns that state borrowing can 'blind us to our real situation' and 'make us less thrifty'. Where a taxpayer endeavours 'to save speedily … from his income', borrowing fosters the delusion of being 'as rich as before'. In the epoch of Keynesian aggregate demand management, governments became especially susceptible to that delusion not least when, as a crisis measure, quantitative easing has been deployed to drive long-term interest rates below levels that reflect the thriftiness of individuals and the productivity of entrepreneurship.

8.6 The Treasury view

The core principles of Ricardian equivalence are that an 'economy' contains (tautologically) only scarce resources and that it is only when entrepreneurial initiative succeeds in realising genuinely productive activities that previously idle 'factors' have their status raised to that of scarce (i.e., economic) resources. The further implication is that, for resources to be optimally allocated, it is necessary for inputs to be continuously adjusted between alternative uses. That dynamic is necessary to meet changes both in consumers' tastes and producers' efficiencies. Thus, in order to expand 'option A', resources must be taken from 'option B'. The association of those basic economic principles with the UK Treasury derives from Winston Churchill's budget speech of 1929, in which he articulated

> the orthodox Treasury doctrine which has steadfastly held that, whatever might be the political and social advantages, very little additional employment, and no permanent additional employment can, in fact, and as a general rule, be created by state borrowing and state expenditure.
>
> (House of Commons, 1929, p. 54)

Churchill's citation of an academic paper (Hawtrey, 1925) was viewed as political improvisation to bolster opposition to the clamour from the Liberal Party for increased spending on public works. The person most closely associated with the 'Treasury view' is Ralph Hawtrey, who was a Treasury civil servant from 1904 until his retirement in 1945. As part of the British delegation to the intergovernmental International Economics Conference at Genoa in 1922, Hawtrey had promoted the retention of a gold exchange standard – i.e., the use of gold-based currency. He recognised the importance of limiting the quantity of paper money that is not backed by gold. With bank credit as the principal means to finance business transactions, he also understood that, for an effective system to flourish, it is necessary to constrain credit. Such general concerns would eventually focus and become a principal driver of the Chicago Plan for 100% reserve banking.

The case presented by Hawtrey is that sovereign expenditure crowds out private expenditure, because the resources necessary for sovereign activity must be drawn 'from genuine saving' (Hawtrey, 1925, p. 40). So, when the resources from saving are merely transferred from one activity to another, that redistribution can have no relevance to employment. For sovereign expenditure on public works to generate additional employment, it would need to be financed by non-saving – i.e., either by the provision of additional base money or additional bank credit money:

> What has been shown is that the expansion of public works, if accompanied by the creation of credit, will give employment. But the same reasoning shows that the creation of credit, unaccompanied by any expenditure on public works would be equally effective in giving employment.
>
> The public works are merely a piece of ritual, convenient to people who want to be able to say that they are doing something, but otherwise irrelevant.
>
> (Hawtrey, 1925, p. 44)

In contradicting that argument, Keynes underlines the key emphasis placed by *The General Theory* upon the necessity for fiscal action to create employment opportunities directly. Thus, from Keynes came the illustration (previously cited) that unemployment could be vanquished by the Treasury using mineshafts to bury banknotes in bottles, allowing private enterprise to disinter them. In following Hawtrey, the bottles and the mineshafts would be an irrelevance: there is nothing that entrepreneurs can do with their exhumed banknotes that could not be done if they were to receive tax rebates financed by fiscal deficits. However, for such a measure to deliver new employment that can be sustained, it must be repeated in successive periods. The necessity for an ever-escalating level of sovereign debt is a detail that is seldom mentioned by those who follow the Keynesian orthodoxy.

In later contributions from Robert Barro, Ricardian equivalence is set within the context of New Classical Economics, where Keynesian interventions are thwarted by the theoretical behaviour of rational individuals, who save to provide cover for their future obligations (as taxpayers). In a presentation that is redolent of Fiscal Monetarism, it is argued that sovereign bonds purchased by taxpayers are 'perceived as net wealth only if their value exceeds the capitalized value of the implied stream of future tax liabilities' (Barro, 1974, p. 1095). Otherwise, the bond-financed sovereign expenditure that is intended to promote growth becomes crowded out by the higher saving of rational taxpayers. In the presence of rational expectations and where wages and prices are perfectly flexible, New Classical Economics shows that Keynesian interventions are irrelevant.

The refinements introduced by Robert Barro have been countered by the formulation of New Keynesian models that throw metaphorical spanners into New Classical works. By invoking a variety of market failures – externalities, imperfect wage and price setting, information asymmetries, principal-agent problems, time-inconsistent preferences, non-competitive markets – New Keynesian Economics delivers a variety of circumstances in which public policy interventions might be relevant; but (a big 'but'), they only become relevant if they are able to redress the market failures that are at the core of New Keynesian concerns.

8.7 Broad money and its credit counterparts

Through the exercise of Keynes's powers of persuasion, politicians were drawn to the idea of controlling aggregate demand by the near-exclusive application of fiscal policy: to stabilise employment and to address levels of sovereign debt that had become bloated by war. By 1941, national income identities had become sufficiently developed to inform attempts to manage aggregate demand:

> *An Analysis of the Sources of War Finance and an Estimate of the National Income and Expenditure for 1938 and 1940* (1941, Cmd. 6261) … was published in time for the 1941 Budget …. the use of national income and expenditure estimates in relation to the formulation of the budget was a major event in the history of the application of economics to policy formation.
>
> (Gilbert, 1982, p. 31)

Contemporaneous with those changes, the Bretton Woods Agreements of 1944 obliged sovereign nations to hold their respective currencies within a one percent margin of a value fixed to the US dollar. Also emanating from the Bretton Woods Agreements, the International Monetary Fund (IMF) came into formal existence in 1945 with the goal of reconstructing the international payments system.

Only subsequently did the IMF seek to redress what it regarded as a deficiency in the Keynesian perspective. This was the omission both of data relating to inter-sector finance and of an analysis of liquidity (see Hicks, 1957). The remedial presentation that then emerged was to dichotomise the growth of broad money (ΔM – central and commercial bank lending) into 'money of foreign origin' (ΔR – money issued to acquire foreign exchange reserves) and 'money of domestic origin' (*DCE* – domestic credit expansion). *DCE* is then divided between net central bank credit to the sovereign (DCE^S) and net commercial bank credit to private agencies (DCE^P)

$$\Delta M \equiv DCE^S + DCE^P + \Delta R \tag{8.1}$$

In this presentation, fiscal deficits ($G - T$) are financed by bond sales to the private sector (ΔB^P) and/or borrowing from the central bank (DCE^S):

$$(G - T) \equiv \Delta B^P + DCE^S \tag{8.2}$$

so that

$$\Delta M \equiv (G - T) - \Delta B^P + DCE^P + \Delta R \tag{8.3}$$

The representation in line (8.2) shows how a central bank and its sovereign treasury are a single entity: a fiscal deficit is necessarily equivalent to net bonds sales plus net central bank credit to the sovereign. It is a representation that sheds light upon the forlorn attempt of the Eurozone project to integrate a single monetary authority with diverse fiscal authorities. On that attempt, Henry Simons delivers a prescient verdict:

> The plain fact is that the ultimate monetary powers and the ultimate legislative powers are those of taxing and spending. This suggests a fatal weakness of schemes for supra-national currencies or world-currencies.
> (Simons, 1942, p. 182, and fn. 14)

Clearly, the enactment of decisions ('legislative powers') on 'taxing and spending' ($G - T$) is logically equivalent to changes in the size of sovereign debt ($\Delta B^P + DCE^S$); and it is the determination of sovereign indebtedness that decides ('monetary powers') the unit value of sovereign currency. Simons's verdict would be echoed by Friedman, who expressed similar sentiments during the halcyon days of the Eurozone project: '[The euro's] real Achilles heel will prove to be political; that a system under which the political and currency boundaries do not match is bound to prove unstable' (Friedman and Mundell, 2001, p. 11). The delegation of responsibility for a 'supra-national currency' to the European Central Bank (ECB) is compromised by 'the ultimate legislative powers ... of taxing and spending' that have remained the prerogative of sovereign legislatures across the Eurozone. Thereby, a unitary authority was constitutionally split, with the implication that the 'real Achilles heel' became exposed to baseline political protest: street demonstrations and riots.

In setting line (8.2) within the definition of broad money growth, it is the configuration of line (8.3) that was put to early use by De Nederland Bank (see Holtrop, 1957, p. 314). Of the five interdependent components there represented, four are referred to as the 'credit counterparts' of broad money growth (ΔM), each one of which is associated with a policy concern:

$G - T$	budget deficit/surplus	*fiscal stance*
ΔB^P	sovereign debt bought by private agencies	*interest rate control*
ΔDCE^P	commercial bank lending	*bank credit control*
ΔR	foreign exchange reserves, rise/fall	*exchange rate target*

It would be wrong to seek to identify any one (or more) item(s) within this tautological structure as separately representing the prerogative of either a fiscal authority or a monetary authority. Even though constitutional arrangements might delegate certain decisions (say, to a monetary policy committee of a central bank) such 'authorisation' cannot disturb the integrity of a unitary authority. Indeed, the five interrelated perspectives expose the pretence that a monetary authority (whether the Bank of England or the ECB) can operate independently of a fiscal authority (whether within the UK or dissipated across the Eurozone).

A related presentation incorporates international trading aspects in a manner that is consistent with the prior exposition. This is the 'impossible trinity' that is credited to Robert Mundell (see Krugman, 1999). Only two of three options exist: a fixed exchange rate, national monetary independence and free international capital movements. Set within the context of the Eurozone, any sovereign that steps out of line, most obviously by engaging in chronic fiscal deficit spending (which adherence to the *Stability and Growth Pact*, 1997 would have prevented), is confronted by an analogous trinity: no bailout, no exit and no default. The possibilities within this 'trilemma' are

1 no bailout nor exit, so that (without an independent monetary policy to address reserve losses) default becomes necessary
2 no bailout nor default, so that exit becomes necessary (July 2015: Greece option 1)
3 no exit nor default, so that a bailout transfer becomes necessary (July 2015: Greece option 2)

As demonstrated in Athens 2015, the humiliation of *hoi polio* within a sovereign autarky is an inherent risk when decisions are constrained by a supranational currency. The fatal weakness is a legislature (the Hellenic Parliament) that lacks an option that would attract a democratic mandate. The implication is the imposition of remedial action by a colonial power: the 'troika' of the European Commission, the ECB and the IMF.

Notes

1 See endnote 2.
2 If monetary expansion caused only bond prices to rise, the quantity theory of money would have no relevance to price inflation; but see Chapter 3, the section, 'Keynes's economics (interest rate determination)' and Chapter 4, endnote 7.
3 Hawtrey engages further historical interest in that, even though he is one of a select group of four who receives acknowledgement from Keynes in the preface to *The General Theory*, he bears responsibility for providing the contra-Keynes exposition of fiscal expenditure, which became known as the Treasury view.
4 Although the magnitude of sovereign debt remains constant, some minor impact might follow from the change in the interest-bearing portion.
5 See Rockoff (2015, p. 45, fn. 5).
6 An early enunciation of the core idea of Fiscal Monetarism is in Simons (1936) (see the citation in Chapter 7). Having been rediscovered and attributed to Leeper (1991) and others, the idea is referenced as 'the fiscal theory of inflation' or 'the fiscal theory of the price level'. As it switches traditional roles, this modern engagement with mathematical modelling gives definitive direction to transmission mechanisms. Inflation is a consequence of fiscal policy, not monetary policy: '[n]ew research has discovered that assignments can be reversed with monetary policy stabilizing debt and fiscal policy determining the price level' (Leeper, 2015). In passing, one might question the claim that a mathematical model *per se* constitutes a research finding on policy options; after all, it is entirely feasible for a mathematical model to show that flight is a consequence of negative gravity. The alternative is to invoke core economic principles: where there are disparate scarcities, choice determines relative values. Therefore, as sovereign debt grows (in relation to the capacity to repay debt from national income), its real value falls.
7 See: www.marxists.org/reference/subject/economics/ricardo/tax/ch17.htm, for the citations.

Bibliography

Barro, R. (1974) 'Are Government Bonds Net Wealth?', *Journal of Political Economy*, vol. 82, no. 6, 1095–175.

Bilow, J. and A. Terzi (eds) (2017) *Euroland and the World Economy. Global Player or Global Drag*' (Basingstoke: Palgrave Macmillan).

Brunner, K. and A. H. Meltzer (1972a) 'Friedman's Monetary Theory', *Journal of Political Economy*, vol. 80, no. 5, 837–51.

Brunner, K. and A. H. Meltzer (1972b) 'Money, Debt and Economic Activity', *Journal of Political Economy*, vol. 80, no. 5, Sept-Oct, 951–77.

Collison-Black, R. D. (1986) (ed) *Ideas in Economics* (New Jersey: Barnes and Nobel Books).

Fisher I. (1911) *The Purchasing Power of Money. Its Determination and Relation to Credit, Interest and Crises* (New York: The Macmillan Co.).

Foster, J. (1987) *Evolutionary Macroeconomics* (London: Routledge).
Friedman, M. (1956) 'The Quantity Theory of Money - A Restatement', in Friedman, *et al.* (eds), 1956, pp. 3–21.
Friedman, M. (1968) 'The Role of Monetary Policy', *The American Economic Review*, vol. 52, no. 1, March, 1–17.
Friedman, M. (1972) 'Comments on the Critics' *Journal of Political Economy*, vol. 80, no. 5, Sept–Oct, 906–50.
Friedman, M., P. Cagan, J. J. Klein, E. M. Lerner and R. T. Selden (1956), *Studies in the Quantity Theory of Money* (Chicago: University of Chicago Press).
Friedman, M. and R. Mundell (2001) 'One World, One Money', *Options Politique*, May 10–28; http://web.ntpu.edu.tw/~guan/courses/Friedman-Mundell.pdf (accessed 17 June 2015).
Gilbert, J. C. (1982) *Keynes's Impact on Monetary Economics* (London: Butterworths).
Johnson, H. G. (1962) 'Monetary Theory and Policy', *The American Economic Review*, vol. 52, no. 3, June, 335–84.
Hawtrey, R. G. (1913) *Good and Bad Trade. An Inquiry into the Causes of Trade Fluctuations* (London: Constable and Co. Ld.).
Hawtrey, R. G. (1919) *Currency and Credit* (London, Longmans, Green and Co.).
Hawtrey, R. G. (1925) 'Public Expenditure and the Demand for Labour', *Economica*, vol. 5, March, 38–48.
Hicks, E. (1957) 'Monetary Analyses', *International Monetary Fund Staff Papers*, vol. 5, no. 3, February, p. 342.
Holtrop, M. W. (1957) 'Method of Monetary Analysis Used by De Nederlandshe Bank, *International Monetary Fund Staff Papers*, vol. 5, no. 3 (February) pp. 303–16.
House of Commons (1929) *Memoranda on Certain Proposals Relating to Unemployment*, Cmd 3331. London: HMSO (His Majesty's Stationery Office).
Johnson, H. G. (1971), 'The Keynesian Revolution and the Monetarist Counter-Revolution', *The American Economic Review, Papers and Proceedings,* vol. 61, no. 2, May, 1–14.
Kahn, R. (1984) *The Making of Keynes's General Theory* (Cambridge: Cambridge University Press).
Keynes, J. M. (1923) *A Tract on Monetary Reform* (London: Macmillan).
Keynes, J. M. (1936) *The General Theory of Employment Interest and Money* (London: Macmillan).
Krugman, P. (1999) 'O Canada. A neglected nation gets its Nobel'; www.slate.com/articles/business/the_dismal_science/1999/10/o_canada.html (accessed March 2012).
Laidler, D. (1993) 'Hawtrey, Harvard, and the Origins of the Chicago Tradition', *Journal of Political Economy*, vol. 101, no. 6, December, 1068–103.
Leeper, E. M. (1991) 'Equilibria under 'Active' and 'Passive' Monetary and Fiscal Policies'," *Journal of Monetary Economics*, vol. 27, no. 1, pp. 129–47.
Leeper, E. M. (2015) 'Real theory of the price level', Briefing, 21 September 2015; https://bfi.uchicago.edu/sites/default/files/file_uploads/Leeper_Background_3%20copy.pdf (accessed 8 August 2017).
Marshall, A. (1923) *Money, Credit and Commerce* (London: Macmillan).
Patinkin, D. (1969) 'The Chicago Tradition, The Quantity Theory, and Friedman', *Journal of Money, Credit and Banking*, vol. 1, no. 1, February, 46–70.

Patinkin, D, (1979) 'Keynes and Chicago', *Journal of Law and Economics*, vol. 22, no. 2, October, 213–32.

Phelps, E. S. (1967) 'Phillips Curves, Expectations of Inflation and Optimal Employment over Time', *Economica,* New Series, vol. 34, no. 3, August, 254–81.

Presley, J. R. (1986) 'Modern Monetarist Ideas: A British Connection?', in Collison-Black, R. D. (ed) 1986, pp. 192–210.

Ricardo, D. (1817) *On the Principles of Political Economy and Taxation* (London: John Murray).

Rockoff, H. (2015) 'Henry Simons and the Quantity Theory of Money', Becker Friedman Institute for Economics at the University of Chicago, September 27; https://bfi.uchicago.edu/research/working-paper/henry-simons-and-quantity-theory-money (accessed 5 January 2016).

Schumpeter, J. A. (1954) *History of Economic Analysis* (Oxford: Oxford University Press).

Simons, H. C. (1938) *Personal Income Taxation: The Definition of Income as a Problem of Fiscal Policy* (Chicago: University of Chicago Press).

Simons, H. C. (1942) 'Hansen on Fiscal Policy', *Journal of Political Economy*, vol. 50, no. 2, April, 161–96.

Stigler, G. J. (1988) *Memoirs of an Unregulated Economist* (New York: Basic Books).

Werner, R. (2007) 'Germany's Choice and Lessons from Japan: Supply vs. Demand Policy', in Bilow and Terzi, 2007, pp. 184–214.

9 Business, bankers and bubbles

9.1 Mainstream economics

The provision of finance for business has inherent risks and uncertainties. Yet, financial instability has had no prominence within the mainstream of economics as taught over the last eighty years or so. Often cited as the neoclassical synthesis, that mainstream combines the constrained optimisation of late nineteenth-century microeconomic theory with the core argument of twentieth-century macroeconomics, which is that fiscal intervention can be used to manage aggregate demand:

> In recent years 90 per cent of American Economists have stopped being 'Keynesian economists' or 'anti-Keynesian economists'. Instead, they have worked toward a synthesis of whatever is valuable in older economics and in modern theories of income determination. The result might be called neo-classical economics and is accepted in its broad outlines by all but about 5 per cent of extreme left wing and right wing writers.
>
> (Samuelson, 1955, p. 212)

Credit falls to John Hicks and Alvin Hansen for having reshaped Keynes's *General Theory* into the familiar geometry of textbook presentations. In stage one – that of 'the 45 degree diagram' – equilibrium exists where the goods that are produced match the goods that are purchased. In stage two, the addition of a rudimentary financial sector takes the twin forms of a sovereign treasury and a central bank. With consideration given to only two financial assets – sovereign bonds and central bank base money – an interest rate is set by the relative demand/supply of bonds and money; i.e., by Keynes's liquidity preference analysis. The absence of commercial banking[1] is a serious omission. The geometry of stage two is that of ISLM analysis: a unique pair of values for real income/output – where investment (I) equals saving (S) – and the interest rate – where liquidity preference (L) equals the supply of base money (M) – indicate equilibrium in both sectors.

In stage three, the assumption of fixed commodity prices is relaxed, which allows ISLM to be remapped to form an aggregate demand schedule (negatively sloped). The respective axes show the general level of prices and real income/output. An aggregate supply schedule (positively sloped) is introduced, for which the nominal wage is assumed to remain constant. At the intersection of aggregate demand and aggregate supply, a unique pair of values, for the general level of prices and real income/output, indicates full equilibrium. This presentation invites discussion of a possible trade-off between price inflation and the level of real income/output.

When a fiscal stimulus raises aggregate demand, real income/output can rise *only if* more labour is employed. This requires the nominal wage to remain unchanged[2] because, if the rise in the general level of prices were to trigger a rise in the nominal wage (i.e., if there were an upward shift in the aggregate supply schedule), that prices-wages interaction would leave the real wage and the levels of real income/output and employment unchanged. It is the latter scenario that Keynes describes as 'one of true inflation' (Keynes, 1936, p. 303).

Beyond stage three, there is a paradigm shift from static to dynamic analysis. In bringing 'microeconomic foundations' to the Keynesian paradigm, the neoclassical synthesis takes the form of dynamic stochastic general equilibrium (DSGE) analysis. A set of microeconomic agents is included where each agent (i.e., a consumer, a firm, a worker, etc.) is a utility-maximising representative whose rationally formed expectations guide all the decisions.[3] With DSGE analysis, the means to preclude spiraling inflation is achieved by the application of the Taylor rule (Taylor, 1993), which allows the 'authorities' to set an interest rate that is targeted upon an objective function containing a 'desired' inflation rate and an 'output gap' of zero (i.e., there is full employment).

One general conclusion that is drawn from the neoclassical synthesis is that, where adjustments to nominal wages are 'sticky', opportunities may exist for an astute policymaker to intervene to raise real income/output towards the full employment level. In that aspect, the original Phillips curve (Phillips, 1958) had appeared to provide empirical support to Keynes's insistence that, whatever the nature of policy interventions, 'cost-push' inflation occurs only as full employment is approached.[4] As a mainstream idea, that notion of a stable Phillips curve trade-off between inflation and real income/output held for but a brief interlude, until it was undermined by the experience of classical demand-pull inflation.[5]

With the breakdown of the original Phillips curve, a revised concept entered the mainstream: the expectations-augmented Phillips curve (Friedman, 1968; Phelps, 1967) catches the experience of 'stagflation', which is the coexistence of persistent inflation and chronic unemployment. This phenomenon gave a fillip to the Monetarist counter-revolution[6] and, as greater scrutiny bore down upon Keynesian economics, new attention was given to Friedman's restatement of the quantity theory of money (Friedman, 1956).

As policymakers (and the public at large) recognised that price instability is inimical to sound macroeconomic performance, attempts to manage aggregate demand gave ground to the classical idea of a causal relationship between base money and prices and to a policy of setting growth targets for broad money aggregates. When attempted in the UK in the early 1980s, the serial failure to hit the money supply targets as set by a Medium Term Financial Strategy[7] brought a greater appreciation of the relevance and complexity of behavioural, institutional and technological changes within banking and finance. Thereafter, money supply targeting was displaced by a focus upon exchange rates. The mutual convergence and the stability of currency rates were among criteria that were set, as the UK and other member states of the European Union prepared for the introduction of a common currency and the status of the ECB as the single monetary authority.

Concerns over the performance of Western economies in the 1930s, as first expressed by Keynes, are now less prominent than the concerns that had been expressed contemporaneously by Simons. Keynes's proposals for securing full employment have given ground to measures that might deliver greater financial stability. That the term 'macro-prudential' is now in prominent use reflects the potential for 'contagion' to wreak havoc across an entire financial system. Clearly, the desire to 'build and strengthen the constituency for financial stability' (House of Commons Committee on H. M. Treasury, 2012, p. 40) is a sensible goal. Where financial regulation was previously couched in general terms of capital requirements and leverage ratios, new arguments reflect the idea that constraints should be tailored to the finer detail of different asset markets. Beginning with the 1988 Basel Accord, central bankers are now engaged in seeking a definitive set of minimum capital requirements for banks, where an evolving framework is evident with Basel I, Basel II and Basel III.[8] In broad terms, utopian regulatory strategies require rules to deflate financial bubbles at an early stage, where there are inherent difficulties, not only with the identification of such rules, but also in recognising that the pace and the extent of contagion are set by a diversity of institutions and their ever-evolving and complex interdependencies.

9.2 Minsky moments

A recent entry into the economics lexicon describes the onset of a financial crisis as a 'Minsky moment'. Following an extended period of credit-led growth, a sudden major collapse of asset values marks such a moment. That occurrence bears the name of Hyman Minsky, who was both a student and an associate[9] of Simons. Both economists placed great emphasis upon social systems and the institutional structures of an industrial economy, from which it can be inferred that neither was caught by any mainstream of economics. Neither Minsky nor Simons is readily categorised. Although Minsky would not be out of place under the broad umbrella of post-Keynesian economics, Simons is far removed from that categorisation. Yet, by their shared concerns, there was mutual attraction: where Minsky saw himself as 'radical and optimistic', he describes Simons as 'becoming increasingly disillusioned and conservative'; and while 'there was an agreement on objectives', they 'differed on what was deemed possible' (Minsky, 2009, p. 201).

The close similarities between the analysis that delivers a Minsky moment and the ideas that are central to the work of Simons should cause no surprise. Simons had taught Minsky through to 1942, when Minsky left for graduate work at Harvard (which was halted by military service). After World War II ended, Minsky turned down the offer in 1946 of a fellowship from Chicago because – of his two key mentors – Simons was dead and Jacob Viner had left for Princeton.

Soon after Minsky's death in 1996, a decade of financial crises, in Asia, Russia, dot.com stocks and mortgage debt, added force to the idea that an investment financed by bank credit is inherently unsustainable.[10] The citation of a comment made by Paul McCulley (managing director of the Pacific Investment Management Company) – 'We are in the midst of Minsky moment' – on the cover of the *Wall Street Journal* (8 August, 2007; see Lahart 2007) caught the attention. A senior economist at the UBS investment bank was quick to add the detail. Following 'a prolonged period of rapid acceleration of debt' in which benign borrowing is replaced by borrowing to repay existing loans, there comes a moment 'when lenders become increasingly cautious or restrictive, and when it isn't only overleveraged structures that encounter financing difficulties. At this juncture, the risks of systemic economic contraction and asset depreciation become all too vivid' (Magnus, 2007, p. 7).

As asset prices begin to fall so that lenders become increasingly reluctant to roll over loans, investors may engage in 'bargain-basement' fire sales of even their less-speculative positions. Insolvencies become more likely. From that general scenario, Minsky's posthumous reputation builds upon two perceptions: (i) that the overextension of bank credit undermines financial stability; and (ii) that periodic bouts of business speculation tend to end in crises.

The decisions of established bankers are necessarily problematic, but the value of an accumulation of experience should not be discounted. Where a bank's loan commitments are likely to be written down by business foreclosure, an experienced banker is well placed to judge if a further extension of credit is the better option. As the availability of central bank refinancing is a factor within that calculation, acts of judgement are required. These are not to be confused with the palliative of easing credit whenever recession looms, for there lies the moral hazard of further affliction rather than the delivery of a salutatory lesson. Yet, as time-tested practices have given ground to rapidly evolving banking activities, new structures have a greater potential to trigger a contagion of damaging consequences. With that redundancy of seasoned judgement, successive layers of statutory and other regulatory practices appear not to have delivered much reassurance or stability to the business of banking and finance.

Across two decades to the mid-1960s, the achievement of economic growth with stable prices is viewed by Minsky as a special case. It was then, he argues, that unique opportunities for post-war reconstruction were gradually transformed into sustainable spending. Minsky contrasts this with both the deep recession of the 1930s and the 'intermittent stagflation of 1966–1979'. In Minsky's view, both epochs serve to represent 'the underlying instability of capitalism' (Minsky, 1980, p. 520).

Minsky is critical of the neoclassical synthesis for its failure 'to assimilate capital assets and money of the kind ... which is created by banks as they finance capital asset production and ownership' (Minsky, 1982, p. 91). The instability of capitalism that Minsky attempts to explain derives from the manner in which capital accumulation and asset holdings are financed:

> Simons was correct: Banking, that is, the financing of capital asset ownership and investment, is the critical destabilizing phenomenon. But, as Simons realized, control of banking - money, if you wish - is not enough; the liability structures available to units that own the massive capital assets of the economy must be constrained.
>
> (Minsky, 1980, p. 520)

As Minsky endorses many of the concerns expressed by Simons, he also falls short of having a solution for the expectation of regulation being thwarted as prohibited practices (or institutions) reappear in new and unregulated forms (see the section, 'Shadow banking' as follows).

By their 'responses to the same world situation', Minsky finds 'much in common' between the economics of Simons and Keynes. Yet, where Simons works with 'inherited economic theory', Keynes had presented radical policy options; coupled, it might be added, with Keynes's belief that, by following 'a right analysis of the problem ... nations can learn to provide themselves with full employment by their domestic policy' (Keynes, 1936, pp. 380–82). Minsky is less sanguine than Keynes. Where sovereign spending is small in relation to investment, and where the *monetary authority takes a narrow view of its responsibilities*, Minsky argues that recurring financial crises are likely to be followed by debt deflation[11] and deep depression; and where international financial relations inhibit government action, a slump is likely to be prolonged. Where Keynes had sensed that 'a comprehensive socialisation of investment' (Keynes, 1936, p. 378) might prove necessary as long-term remedial action, Minsky shows little confidence in that outcome. Where sovereign expenditure is large and where the *monetary authority takes a broad view of its responsibilities*, accelerating inflation is likely to be a feature of economic recession. By either outcome, there is confirmation of Minsky's pessimistic view of capitalism.

Setting aside that difference with Keynes, the common theme that Minsky finds, in Simons's 'Rules versus Authorities' and in Keynes's *General Theory*, is that 'the control of systemic instability is the critical problem in performance and policy' (Minsky, 1980, p. 521). Here, there is a need to avoid a confusion of instabilities – i.e., employment instability, prices instability and financial instability. With his single focus upon the general level of employment,

Keynes ignores financial instability and defers consideration of potential inflationary pressures at full employment. Keynes's hopeful trust in the role of 'statesmanship' fell short of its task, as indicated by an oft-cited retrospect from a UK prime minister:

> We used to think that you could spend your way out of a recession, and increase employment by cutting taxes and boosting Government spending. I tell you in all candour that that option no longer exists, and that in so far as it ever did exist, it only worked on each occasion since the war by injecting a bigger dose of inflation into the economy, followed by a higher level of unemployment as the next step. Higher inflation followed by higher unemployment. We have just escaped from the highest rate of inflation this country has known; we have not yet escaped from the consequences: high unemployment. That is the history of the last 20 years.
>
> (Callaghan, 1976)

Simons had been on an entirely different track to Keynes. Consistent with his rejection of bond-financed fiscal expenditures as a means to sustain aggregate demand, Simons believed that 100 percent reserve banking and an adherence to predetermined rules by a monetary authority would deliver a big step towards achieving monetary and financial stability. Yet, like Keynes, Simons left a crucial element for others to resolve – i.e., an ever-present incentive for 'regulatory arbitrage' and the consequences that follow. Although that problem has long been recognised –

> tradition and standards may be absent to such a degree that practically anyone, however lacking in aptitude and training, can drift into the banking business, find customers and deal with them according to his own ideas. In such countries or times, wildcat banking ... develops. This in itself - whatever the legal rules about collateral and so on may be - is sufficient to turn the history of capitalist evolution into a history of catastrophes.
>
> (Schumpeter, 1939, p. 117)

– it is regulation that is likely to deliver the ultimate moral hazard. Since an imposed regulation is no substitute for the spontaneity of behavioural integrity, adherence to a checklist of constraints is more likely to prove the means by which decision makers can absolve themselves from further action. Since the imposition of regulations tends to undermine tacit rules and individual responsibility, a general adherence to moral discipline may be more effective in achieving social stability: 'people who want to skirt the rules will always find creative ways of doing so. ...To restore trust, we need a shift toward greater integrity and accountability' (Lagarde, 2014). That takes time.

9.3 The Great Moderation

The relative stability experienced during a twenty-year period through to 2007 is referred to as the Great Moderation. Modern siren voices then lulled the senses, to the extent that another UK prime minister would be unkindly lampooned for having extolled the virtues of his earlier stewardship as finance minister: 'No return to boom and bust'. Gordon Brown was so proud of that boast that he repeated it more than 100 times in the House of Commons (see Rawnsley, 2010).

The Great Moderation is associated with the independent status that was afforded to central banks in North America and Europe, when decision-making was reassigned from sovereign treasuries to central banks that were allegedly (and, in the case of the ECB, constitutionally) independent of the fiscal authority.[12] Within the Eurozone, the Maastricht Treaty had bestowed that same independence upon all domestic central banks. With that attempt to neutralise the impropriety of political opportunism, the ECB was tasked to deliver price stability.

A key element of sustained growth during the Great Moderation was the international demand for US dollar assets, as supported by a flow of real saving, most notably from China. Low interest rates were then the driver for rising levels of sovereign and personal debt in the US. Dating from 1977, a second key element was that US federal law 'encouraged' commercial banks and savings associations to support a policy of home ownership across low-income households. As this led to the sub-prime mortgage fiasco, the Great Moderation gave way to the Credit Crunch of 2008.

When commercial banks finance a growing asset bubble, the potential contagion of a financial downturn is not an appealing prospect for the monetary authorities. When the credit bubble bursts, 'too big to fail' may then show in political action to sustain demand generally and, thereby, to allow the retention of workers in overexpanded sectors. Thus did the term 'zombie company' emerge in 1992, after the collapse of inflated Japanese real estate and stock market prices.

The proximate cause of the 2008 debacle rests with the bursting of an asset bubble in the US and the immediate cautionary contraction of inter-bank lending. Yet, business and banking activity does not ordinarily cause the degree of mayhem that then followed. A new and relevant feature was the greater distance between – and the greater anonymity of – borrowers and lenders; i.e., in the financial engineering by which subprime mortgages were financed.

As hundreds of loans are pooled together, a process of securitisation creates an asset-backed security. After the division of that pool into several *tranches*, there is a prescribed priority order of seniority in the event that some of the underlying loans default. The senior *tranche* only becomes impaired when the value of losses exceeds the value of all other *tranches*, making it more secure than the original pool. This process enabled banks to turn risky illiquid loans into assets that were attractive to investors because of the appearance of a diminished exposure to risk without commensurately diminished yields. With the sale of asset-backed securities to investors, those issuing the securities obtained new resources for additional lending.

Experienced heads (including that of the Chairman of the Federal Reserve) believed that securitisation brought great advantages: '[t]hese increasingly complex financial instruments have been especial contributors, particularly over the past couple of stressful years, to the development of a far more flexible, efficient, and resilient financial system than existed just a quarter-century ago' (Greenspan, 2002).

The professional judgement of credit-rating agencies attested the quality of the tranched securities; however, there was a conflict of interest in that their advice was also used in the design of the tranching structure. By the complacency that was a feature of the Great Moderation, rating agencies prospered: first as they were hired as consultants to those issuing the new securities; and second as financial regulators embedded their credit ratings within a risk-weighting regime of international standards for levels of bank capital, as codified in the Basel II Accord (June 2002). As perceived risks declined, the balance sheets of banks and other lenders acquired ever-larger volumes of 'low-risk' assets.

As the rise in house prices began to outstrip the reach of would-be occupants, the US housing market had peaked towards the end of 2005. By the following summer, prices were beginning to fall and mortgage defaults were rising. In May 2007, the then President of the Federal Reserve gave reassurance:

> given the fundamental factors in place that should support the demand for housing, we believe the effect of the troubles in the subprime sector on the broader housing market will likely be limited, and we do not expect significant spillovers from the subprime market to the rest of the economy or to the financial system.
>
> (Bernanke, 2007)[13]

In March 2008, after having posted a fourth-quarter loss of $854 million on massive mortgage-related write-downs, the US investment bank *Bear Stearns* secured an emergency agreement with *J. P. Morgan* and the Federal Reserve Bank of New York, in the largest-ever bailout of a US securities firm. The bubble had burst, with contagion in evidence as *Lehman Brothers*, the fourth-largest US investment bank, filed for bankruptcy protection in September 2008.

The losses on sub-prime lending lit the touchpaper on a powder keg of multilayered asset-backed securities. With those assets increasingly written down as 'toxic', the perceived solvency of many banks was undermined. As banks more generally became reluctant to lend, other banks found it necessary to seek support from their central bank: to provide liquidity for longer periods and against lower quality collateral. The alternative would have been to imperil the payments system.

The Great Contraction is attributable to more than the imprudent lending to low income households. The fundamentals – the 'soul' – of banking practice had changed. In a situation where loans are typically repaid over long periods, reputations build and the perceived risk of lending falls. This attracts new capital. Banks are fallible, but the tested structure of traditional banking was such that losses were commensurate with long-term viability. Yet, when structures evolve too rapidly for reputations to build, the consequence is that risks and bubbles are more likely to grow in unison. Solid reputations are established only with the passing of time, where time is of the essence. Therefore, the better option might be 'a move back to unregulated banking with "buyer beware" as the guiding rule rather than the artificial confidence that is derived from state regulation and the "too big to fail" guarantee of a state (and taxpayer) bailout when all else fails' (Alexander, 2009, p. 91). Once established and understood generally to be resilient, that outcome would have obvious appeal. As is often the case, the journey is likely to be troublesome.

9.4 Monetary policy activism: interest rates

When a commercial bank needs liquidity, it turns to its central bank for refinancing. The refinancing rate is a key instrument of monetary policy. In recent decades, adjustments to the short-term refinancing rate have been central to attempts to manage aggregate demand.

With the crisis of 2008, central banks reduced short-term lending rates to the zero lower bound. Among further options subsequently tried, one is a commitment (forward guidance) to keep short-term rates low until a given macroeconomic benchmark is met.[14] Another is for a central bank to engage in an asset purchase programme, whereby government bonds (quantitative easing) and corporate bonds (qualitative easing) are bought from existing bondholders. To finance those acquisitions, a central bank issues base money. As bonds are purchased, bond prices are raised, long-term yields are lowered and former bondholders are left holding ever-larger volumes of deposits in their commercial bank accounts. By that monetary action, it was hoped that the former bondholders would raise their expenditure and that corporate bodies would increase their investments. In retrospect, the greater impact has been in raising property prices and equity values.

Even as world markets were showing faint signs of recovery into 2015, academic and practicing economists were evincing little confidence in the initiatives that had been taken. Note, for example, the review announced by a deputy governor of the Bank of England (2015): the launch by the Bank of new research agenda to encompass objectives other than price stability with policy instruments beyond that of interest rate variations. Perhaps more in hope than in expectation, new areas of research would relate to links between managing monetary policy, the regulation of banks and the stability of the financial system. As testimony to the impression that central bankers were bereft of ideas, one suggestion from the IMF belatedly caught some attention. This was a proposal to raise the inflation target above the conventional level of two percent (see as follows).

The manipulation of interest rates to steer aggregate demand raises issues relating to microeconomic adjustments. Interest rates are integral to a price mechanism that is vital in providing guidance to entrepreneurs. If it were possible to allow interest rates to find their natural levels across diverse markets, business entrepreneurs would face incentives and constraints that derive from spontaneous interchanges between suppliers and consumers. Within a liberal democracy, central price fixing is an anathema; but inter-temporal price fixing is inherent in every interest rate that is set.

In order to better anticipate consumers' requirements, entrepreneurs seek information as best they can. For example, where a commodity shows a forward price premium, the market is signaling that the commodity is likely to become in relatively short supply. Entrepreneurs then have an incentive to switch resources to the production of that commodity, the effect of which is to reduce the forward premium. This is the inter-temporal dimension to John Stuart Mill's 'law of one price'. If it were possible to achieve such spontaneous market outcomes (of real rates), it is unlikely that they would match those set by central bankers in deciding official lending rates.

The benchmark interest rate for markets in full equilibrium is a theoretical concept – *i.e.*, the natural rate of interest. At that rate, the cost of borrowing is equal to the marginal yield on capital. Where the borrowing rate is below the natural rate, there is profit to be earned by obtaining credit to finance the production of capital goods. As a theoretical concept, the natural rate is unobservable; but, in principle, it would vary with the capacity and the ease of production and the underlying willingness of income earners to save. In a money economy, where borrowing rates *are* observable, a key interest rate is the bank lending rate; i.e., in refinancing commercial banks, a central bank *must* set a nominal interest rate. So, how is that intervention to be judged?

In setting nominal interest rates, if the exercise of discretion by central bankers is motivated by macroeconomic concerns, it is more likely to distort the inter-temporal price mechanism and, thereby, to undermine sound husbandry and economic welfare. In the deepest recession, market mechanisms remain relevant because resources have value, even though they may not be in current use. By their decisions in manipulating the price of credit, central bankers face problems akin to those faced by central planners generally: where market signals are absent, coordination failures are more likely.

Where fiscal and monetary interventions may appear to lift an economy out of recession, those macroeconomic policy initiatives are not without unintended consequences and costs. Microeconomic price adjustments reflect the expenditure patterns that are encouraged by policy interventions.

As instigated by macroeconomic objectives, microeconomic adjustments are unlikely to prove sustainable. Even as a loosening of monetary policy ameliorates an economic recession, a chain of adjustments continues that adds to the legacy of inter-temporal price distortions.[15] In short, low interest rates and deficit spending to boost economic activity might perversely extend the duration of a recession. Added to which is the eventual requirement to repay the debts that are incurred by attempts to stimulate economic growth.

With short-term interest rates having long been held at the zero lower bound and after quantitative easing had borne down upon longer-term rates, a new proposition surfaced: that the policy target of two-percent inflation (as applied by central bankers in the US, Canada, Japan, the Eurozone and the UK) might be raised. First mooted in 2010 from within the IMF, a deputy governor of the Bank of England articulated its logic (see Broadbent, 2015). The rationale is as follows. When the metrics of the economy are good but the associated equilibrium levels of interest rates are low, there is little scope to cut rates if an economic downturn strikes. The conclusion drawn – that it would be better to set a higher target rate for inflation – has gathered steam. In noting that assessments of the 'neutral federal funds rate' were much lower than in earlier years, the Chair of the US Fed has acknowledged the potential for policy to

> be constrained by the zero lower bound more frequently than at the time that we adopted our 2 percent objective. So, it's that recognition that causes people to think we might be better off with a higher inflation objective, and that's an important set. This is one of our most critical decisions and one we are attentive to evidence and outside thinking.
>
> (Yellen, 2017)

This 'thinking' turns on the relevance and operational significance of the zero lower bound. Certainly, the negative money rate of interest that might accrue to bank deposits is avoidable, but the inconvenience of holding banknotes instead or the potential to ration their availability are the most obvious impediments. Within a month of Yellen's remark, a more obviously prudent precept was forthcoming from an authoritative UK source:

> With recessions and financial crises almost inevitable over a 50-year horizon, governments need to recognise the very high probability that they will have to deal with their costs at some point in the future. … So the public finances need to be managed prudently during more favourable times to ensure that when these shocks do crystallise they do not put the public finances onto an unsustainable path. This is all the more important given the rise in the stock of debt in recent years, and the greater sensitivity of future debt interest costs to changes in interest rates and retail price inflation.
>
> (Office for Budget Responsibility, 2017, p. 4)

9.5 Austrian business cycle theory

The potential distortions to inter-temporal price adjustments that are the result of monetary policy and commercial banking activity are enduring core issues for monetary theorists. In wrestling contemporaneously with concerns that are close to those expressed by Simons, Friedrich Hayek added important technical detail to the Austrian business cycle theory,[16] as rooted in the work of Eugene Böhm-Bawerk and Ludwig von Mises. It is regrettable that the evolution and exposition of Hayek's analysis of 'business fluctuations' were so slow and confused that their implications were lost to a generation, whose interest was taken by Keynes's analysis. Even for the University of Chicago, Hayek's economics were too peripheral for their economists to countenance his presence; for which reason, Hayek became a professor in the interdisciplinary 'Committee on Social Thought' where he worked from 1950 to 1962.

Only as Keynesian full employment policies proved inherently inflationary in the late 1960s did attention begin to turn to Hayek's criticisms of Keynes's theory. That revival of academic interest in Austrian business cycle theory followed in the wake of the surging popularity of Milton Friedman's Monetarism in the 1970s.[17] It was then that the repeated experience of credit-led booms and busts sparked new interest. Yet, Hayek would complain that his policy advice was sought only when it was too late to have any relevance:

> For forty years I have preached that the time to prevent a depression is during the preceding boom; and that, once a depression has started, there is little one can do about it. My advice was completely disregarded as long as the boom lasted. Now suddenly, when my prediction has come true and we have reached the stage where... little can be done about the inevitable reaction which has set in, people suddenly turn to me and ask for my opinion.
>
> (Hayek, 1975, p. 8)

In the citation for the award of the Nobel Prize in 1974, Hayek is described as 'one of the few economists who gave warning of the possibility of a major economic crisis before the great crash came in the autumn of 1929' (Royal Swedish Academy of Sciences, 1974). Hayek's argument is that a mild US recession would have terminated in 1927 but for the intervention of the authorities who 'succeeded, by means of an easy-money policy ... in prolonging the boom for two years beyond what would otherwise have been its natural end' (Hayek, 1935, p. 162).

Austrian business cycle theory shows how a discretionary cut that sets the interest rate below the natural rate causes a mismatch between consumers' demands and investors' plans. From an initial position of equilibrium (i.e., equal profitability) across investment projects, long-term projects become relatively more profitable than short-term projects. If those newly profitable investments are not resourced by real saving (i.e., by the availability of tangible resources), this new 'structure of production' carries the seeds of its own demise.[18] The implication is that if unnaturally low interest rates are set to stimulate a macroeconomic recovery, this is likely to exacerbate both the severity and the duration of a recession. The road to an economic recovery begins not with the provision of cheap credit, but with the liquidation of investment projects that are no longer viable. Yet, Hayek points to subtle changes in the consequences of an excess provision of credit in the 1970s, as compared with the 1930s when

> [i]n the misdirection of labor and the distortion of the structure during the past business cycles, it was fairly easy to point to the excessive expansion because it was, on the whole, confined to capital-goods industries. The whole thing was due to an over expansion of credit for investment purposes, so you could point to the industries producing capital equipment as those which had been over expanded.
>
> In contrast, the present expansion of money... has gone into entirely different channels. The additional expenditure has been much more widely dispersed.
>
> (Hayek, 1975, p. 20)

By those changes, it follows that malinvestments were unlikely to be confined to capital-goods industries. *Prime facie*, the impact of the greater dispersion of 'cheap money' on the course of a business cycle is an empirical matter. So, it is plausible to hypothesise that the long period of the Great Moderation may have been driven by a wider spread of spending opportunities that were fostered by low interest rates. That possibility raises concern with the near universal acceptance of the discretionary control of monetary policy: '[t]he Great Depression in the United States ... is a testament to how much harm can be done by mistakes on the part of a few men when they yield vast power over the monetary system' (Friedman, 1962, p. 50).

The utopian libertarian principle applied to money is a simple one: that it should not disturb real economic activity. In the jargon of economics, the objective is for money to be neutral in the sense that hypothetical barter transactions are unaffected by the presence of money. Although the practical means by which that outcome might be approximated has occupied many minds, the balance between possibilities – '[m]oney enormously enlarges the hurtful power of uncertainty at the same time as it enormously facilitates the beneficent power of specialisation' (Shackle, 1967, p. 137) – merely adds to that problem. A combination of spontaneous forces, authoritative rules, discretionary interventions and regulatory constraints, all of which operate upon an inheritance of institutional structures, determine the economic impact of money.

9.6 Assets and investments

In a lecture room, the mainstream presentation of macroeconomic theory is structured upon exogenous central bank money. Relatively little attention is given to the relevance of commercial bank lending and 'the need to examine how borrowers are able to fulfil their commitments and the economic consequences of systemically induced failures to meet them' (Minsky, 1980, p. 506). The adjacent concerns with short-term financing, as expressed by Simons, rest upon twin fears: (i) that payment commitments might exceed receipts, so that liquidity support becomes necessary; and (ii) that refinancing markets might lack resilience. As Simons is tightly focused upon the problems that can arise from the use of 'near moneys', Keynes's *General Theory* is singularly neglectful of that component. Indeed, Keynes is responsible for presentations in which commercial banking receives minimum attention and where (with fixed prices) base money faces no exchange risk. Clearly, this ignores all the complications that follow when commercial banking leverages upon exogenous 'narrow' money to create endogenous bank-credit money. As the latter is introduced, so, too, is the potential for bank insolvencies to lead to an economy-wide monetary contraction, bankruptcies and severe business recession.

Simons, Hayek and Minsky all agree that fractional reserve banking has an inherent tendency to foster economic instability. In drawing from Schumpeter's endogenous credit/financing theory of money, Minsky points to the potential damaging long-term consequences of over-exuberate capitalism, and he looks to fiscal and monetary interventions to stabilise the economy. Thus, where Schumpeter sees the extension of commercial bank credit as unambiguously positive, for Minsky it is inherently destructive. Although Minsky and Hayek both recognise the relevance of finance to the instability of capital investments, where Hayek builds upon Austrian theory to unify both phases of the business cycle, Minsky's focus is only upon the downside, when an overextension of credit is eventually brought to a halt in a 'Minsky moment'.

Business finance is necessary to resource the production of both consumption goods and capital goods. It is here that Minsky points to a distinction: there is short-term finance for investment processes and long-term finance for capital assets. With the former, corporate liabilities are met by 'the flow of profits or by funds obtained by a refinancing arrangement' (Minsky, 1980, p. 506). The repetitive entering into and repayment of bank loans relies upon the continuous creation of profits – i.e., upon a sequence in which bank credit money is routinely created and then destroyed as new profits are earned.

Receipts from the sale of consumption goods are largely driven by the level of personal income, but with capital goods 'a continued funding of debt occurs … by the financing arrangements of the purchasers of investment goods as capital assets' (Minsky, 1980, p. 509). A net financial position is defined by the difference between contractual commitments and the income ('quasi-rents') expected from capital assets. When business is good, the expectation of cash flows is more secure and there is less need for bankers and businesses to hold liquidity; but, if there is fall in expected returns ('quasi-rests'), there is a problem:

> [a]n increase in liquidity preference, which typically occurs when quasi-rents fail to validate debt structures or financial markets fail to refinance positions, will force attempts to reduce near-term payment commitments relative to expected quasi-rents. This will lead to a fall in the money price of capital assets.
>
> (Minsky, 1980, p. 509)

With the onset of a widespread financial crisis, there is a broad consensus that a monetary authority must act swiftly, to maintain the payments systems and, thereafter, to avoid chronic deflation. Yet, there is an awkward question, which may be couched in the context of 2008: 'If low interest rates, excessive borrowing and consequential bubbles in housing and equity markets landed the economy in a mess, how can quantitative easing, low interest rates, more borrowing and potential bubbles elsewhere provide a solution?'

The Credit Crunch of 2008 was met by unconventional measures from central bankers that will long be discussed. Yet, quantitative easing merely applied the familiar tool of open-market operations, but further up the yield curve. New suspicions have fallen upon a 'shadow banking system',[19] whose rapid growth has been driven by an ability to operate free of regulatory controls. Although 'shadow' refers to credit intermediation occurring outside the banking sector, 'non-banks' are frequently integrated within large banking groups. In recent times, the greater regulatory attention that has been considered necessary saw the creation in 2009 of the Financial Stability Board,[20] whose focus is upon the association of non-banks with 'systematic risk' and 'regulatory arbitrage'.

9.7 Shadow banking

Although the term 'shadow banking' was coined only in 2007, Hayek is among those who drew attention to the credit that is provided by unregulated banking institutions:

> In particular, it is necessary to take account of certain forms of credit not connected with banks which help, as is commonly said, to economise money, or to do the work for which, if they did not exist, money in the narrower sense of the word would be required. … The characteristic peculiarity of these forms of credit is that they spring up without being subject to any central control, but once they have come into existence their convertibility into other forms of money must be possible if a collapse of credit is to be avoided.
>
> (Hayek, 1935, p. 114)

Both with its timing and its content, Hayek's musings match the alertness of Simons to concerns that arise with the 'the reappearance of prohibited practices in new and unprohibited forms' (Simons, 1936, p. 17; 1948, p. 172). That those problems remain unresolved implies that the continuous evolution of the forms and practices of shadow banks is likely to continue to defeat regulation.

As is true for most bank lending, non-bank lending is secured by collateral. Shadow banking incorporates the activities both of the humblest pawnbroker who lends against the security of (say) a gold watch, and a building society that lends against the security of a house. If the borrower defaults, the collateral can be sold; and if 're-hypothecation' were possible, it would allow a gold watch to be repawned, so allowing pawnbrokers to obtain new funds to extend their core business. Of course, the constraint upon pawnbrokers is that their client expects to have the original watch returned.

With no access to central bank reserves, non-banks must look for alternative secure liquid assets as collateral. As commercial bank loans are a multiple of reserves, so non-bank loans are a multiple of collateral. At each round of commercial bank lending, the ratio of broad money to reserves increases. With each round of shadow bank lending, the ratio of loans to collateral increases. In both cases, that increase is at a diminishing rate. Therefore, a parallel exists between the money multiplier of economic textbooks (which is the ratio of broad money to base money) and the 'collateral velocity' that is associated with shadow banking (which is the ratio of loans to hypothecated collateral). When, for whatever motive, the supply of credit is curtailed, deleveraging is common to both.

Shadow banking is composed of diverse financial intermediaries whose existence may often be traced to state regulation. For example, US money market funds were a means to avoid Regulation Q – i.e., the prohibition of interest on bank demand deposits (1933–2011). Minsky cites money market funds as prominent in the emergence of a two-tier monetary system, the first part of which 'has the protection of bank equity, established channels for refinancing through the central bank, and deposit insurance' (Minsky, 1980, p. 510) and the second part of which lacks any safety margins.

Although Minsky had opposed the financial market deregulation of the 1980s, it is generic to all regulation (as to central planning generally) that, as it removes the market's way of moderating risk, regulation undermines the expectation that traders should take responsibility for the consequences of their decisions. Clearly, there are senior bankers who are alert to an essential truth – that 'Integrity can't be bought and it can't be regulated' (Carney, 2013, p. 13 fn. 9); in other guises, they tend to fall back upon the belief that regulators possess the know-how and capability to offset the systematic risk of financial intermediation. Even where they are able to achieve some moderation of *existing* practices, it is necessary for regulators to counteract the reactions and error-learning adjustments that inevitably follow.

For the UK, the Financial Services Authority (FSA) was responsible for financial regulation from 2001 to 2013, at which date its responsibilities were reassigned to two new agencies of the Bank of England: the Financial Conduct Authority (FCA) and the Prudential Regulation Authority (PRA). Where the FCA is charged to ensure 'fair, efficient and honest' dealing, the PRA is empowered to regulate UK banks, building societies, credit unions and investment firms. The task set for the PRA – to oversee accountability, solvency, capital requirements and structural reforms – is more obviously political: it can limit mortgage lending; it can demand affordability checks; and, by adjusting sectoral capital requirements, it can differentially affect lending on homes, credit cards and to businesses. By way of a general comment, financial stability appears so arbitrary, the tools so wide-ranging and the measures of stress so broad that it lacks a coherent framework.

A problem of modern complex capitalism is that rapid change and an overabundance of information makes it difficult to learn from the past. A comment by US Secretary of Defense Donald Rumsfeld will long be cited:

> Reports that say something hasn't happened are always interesting to me because as we know, there are known knowns: there are things we know we know. We also know there are known unknowns: that is to say we know there are some things [we know] we do not know. But there are also unknown unknowns - the ones we don't know we don't know. And if one looks throughout the history of our country and other free countries, it is the latter category that tends to be the difficult one.
>
> (Rumsfeld, 2012, xv)

Building upon an optimistic viewpoint, the Great Recession that followed in the wake of the Credit Crunch might be viewed as a perfect storm of unanticipated regulatory interactions; and these are unlikely to be repeated. A less sanguine view would be to treat that recent crisis and the response to it as warning signs that, at some stage, there may be worse to come.

Notes

1 Keynes's presentation of commercial banks as intermediaries channeling saving to investors is such that – 'except in conditions of full employment' – there is an increase in real income/output via the income multiplier (see Keynes, 1936, pp. 81–85). Bank credit money and the problem of 'near moneys' are not discussed.

2 Strictly, the nominal wage must rise more slowly than prices.

3 The original presentation of the neoclassical synthesis is that of comparative static analysis; i.e., there is no discussion of the 'traverse' between two points of equilibrium. With the introduction of representative agents, each of whom has rational foresight and an understanding of optimality, DSGE models redress that lacuna. Blessed with those prescient endowments, there is 'no reason for them to trade with each other, no reason why their decisions should be coordinated, and therefore no role for markets' (King, 2012, p. 2). As DSGE models address those defects, there emerges the virtual reality of a 'play-station' economy.

4 See Chapter 4, footnote 7.
5 With the classical quantity theory of money, the corollary of an excess supply of money is an excess demand for goods and services and demand-pull inflation.
6 From a Keynesian perspective, stagflation is associated with the 'cost-push' of a quadrupling of the oil price in 1973. Those taking a classical perspective point to the abandonment of gold convertibility of the US dollar in 1971 and to the monetary excesses of the UK 'dash for growth', 1972–1974.
7 Introduced in April 1980, the Medium-Term Financial Strategy set forward targets for the growth of money aggregates. By a steady deceleration in the rate of monetary growth and a reduction in the size of fiscal deficits, its aim was to reduce inflation over an extended period. In 1987, it was replaced by the policy of 'shadowing' the Deutschmark.
8 See Chapter 12, the section, 'Regulation and trust'.
9 After university libraries had closed, Simons often signalled his student to join him at the bar of the 'tavern at the corner of University Avenue and 55th Street' (Minsky, 2009, p. 201).
10 See the section, 'Austrian business cycle theory'.
11 Debt deflation theory was developed by Irving Fisher in the 1930s. Where low confidence is conjoined with a state of general over-indebtedness, then liquidations, distress selling and the repayment of bank loans tend to follow. This leads to a contraction of bank money, falling prices, profits, output and employment. As nominal interest rates fall, real rates rise, so causing further pessimism and financial retrenchment.
12 The interdependence of monetary and fiscal action is indicated by a tautological structure (see Chapter 8, the section, 'Broad money and its credit counterparts').
13 The previous month, the Bank of England had similarly concluded that 'The UK financial system remains highly resilient, with banks well capitalised and highly profitable' (Bank of England, 2007, p. 38).
14 In August 2013, for example, the Bank of England announced that it intended to hold the short-term rate at its historically low 0.5 percent, at least until the unemployment rate fell to 7 percent or below.
15 Even with output at below the full employment level, there is no Keynesian 'parallel universe' in which '[y]ou can have more of A without sacrificing B' (Brittan, 2009). Instead, there is a unique continuum of historical time, where future events are driven by everything that precedes them. Economists must never forget their concern for scarcity and value:

> [a]n analysis on the assumption of full employment, even if the assumption is only partially valid, at least helps us to understand the functioning of the price mechanism, the significance of the relations between different prices and of the factors which lead to changes in these relations. But the assumption that all goods and factors are available in excess makes the whole price system redundant, undermined and unintelligible.
>
> (Hayek, 1975, p. 103)

16 In the evolution of Hayek's exposition of Austrian business cycle theory, Monetary Theory and the Trade Cycle (1933) emphasises 'monetary causes which can start the cyclical fluctuations' (Hayek, 1933, p. 17); and Prices and Production (Hayek, 1935) focuses more closely upon 'successive changes in the real structure of production' that are the real phenomena of the trade cycle. These two publications together elucidate the impact of interest rate changes upon investment incentives (the 'interest rate effect'). Two subsequent publications, 'Profits, Interest and Investment' (Hayek, 1939a) and The Pure Theory of Capital (Hayek, 1941) give attention to the impact of prices upon investment incentives (the 'relative

prices effect' –i.e., final goods' prices in relation to capital goods' prices). That the theory was delivered piecemeal created considerable confusion.

17 Not to invite confusion, Friedman is not enamoured by Austrian analysis; see Garrison (1996).

18 Although the inter-temporal provision of capital is a central feature of market coordination, capital theory held little interest for those working within the mainstream: 'In the Cambridge tradition that governed Keynes's brief study of economics, the Mill-Jevons theory of capital, later developed by Böhm-Bawerk and Wicksell was not seriously considered. By about 1930, these ideas had been largely forgotten in the English-speaking world' (Hayek, 1983, p. 48).

19 In referring to the development of US money market funds in the 1970s, 'shadow bank' newly entered the lexicon, also coined by Paul McCulley (2007).

20 The FSB is the successor to the Financial Stability Forum, as established in 1999 by G7 finance ministers and central bank governors. The FSB has a key role in promoting international standards.

Bibliography

Alexander, J. (2009) 'Regulatory Arbitrage and Overregulation' in Booth, P. (ed.) *Verdict on the Crash: Causes and Policy Implications* (London: The Institute of Economic Affairs, in association with Profile Books Ltd), pp. 81–94.

Bank of England (2007) *Financial Stability Report*, Issue no. 21 April; http://www.bankofengland.co.uk/publications/Documents/fsr/2007/fsrfull0704.pdf (accessed 19 September, 2016).

Bank of England (2015) 'One Bank Research Agenda', February; www.bankofengland.co.uk/research/Documents/onebank/discussion.pdf (accessed 1 April 2015).

Basil Committee on Banking Supervision (2013) *Basel III: The Liquidity Coverage Ratio and Liquidity Risk Monitoring Tools*, January; www.bis.org/publ/bcbs238.pdf (accessed 15 July 2015).

Bernanke, B. (2007) 'The Subprime Mortgage Market', Speech at the Federal Reserve Bank of Chicago's 43rd Annual Conference on Bank Structure and Competition, Chicago, Illinois, May 17; www.federalreserve.gov/newsevents/speech/bernanke20070517a.htm (accessed 15 March 2017).

Booth, P. (2009) (ed.) *Verdict on the Crash: Causes and Policy Implications* (London: The Institute of Economic Affairs, in association with Profile Books Ltd).

Brittan, S. (2009) 'The Problem with All This Economic Doom and Gloom', *Financial Times*, 1 January.

Broadbent, B. (2015) 'The Economics of Deflation',Page Content *Bank of England Speech*, given at Imperial College Business School, London, 27 March; http://www.bankofengland.co.uk/publications/Pages/speeches/2015/813.aspx (accessed 8 August 2015).

Callaghan, J. (1976) 'Leader's speech, Blackpool 1976', *British Political Speech*; www.britishpoliticalspeech.org/speech-archive.htm?speech=174 (accessed 29 May 2015).

Carney, M. (2014) 'Inclusive Capitalism: Creating a Sense of the Systemic', *Bank of England Speech*, 27 May; www.bankofengland.co.uk/publications/Documents/speeches/2014/speech731.pdf (accessed 9 September, 2016).

Friedman, M. (1956) 'The Quantity Theory of Money - A Restatement', in Friedman, *et al.* (eds), 1956, pp. 3–21.

Friedman, M. (1962) *Capitalism and Freedom* (Chicago: Chicago University Press).

Friedman, M. (1968) 'The Role of Monetary Policy', *The American Economic Review*, vol. 57, no. 1, March, 1–17.

Friedman, M., P. Cagan, J. J. Klein, E. M. Lerner and R. T. Selden (1956), *Studies in the Quantity Theory of Money* (Chicago: University of Chicago Press).

Garrison, R. W. (1996) 'Friedman's Plucking Model: Comment', *Economic Inquiry*, vol. 24, no. 4, October, 799–802.

Greenspan, A (2002) 'World Finance and Risk Management', Speech at Lancaster House, London September 25; www.federalreserve.gov/BoardDocs/Speeches/2002/200209253/default.htm (accessed 28 July 2015).

Hayek, F. A. (1933) *Monetary Theory and the Trade Cycle* (London: Jonathan Cape); originally published in German in 1929 as *Geldtheorie und Konjunkturtheorie* (Wien: Verlag von Julius Springer).

Hayek, F. A. (1935) *Prices and Production*, 2nd ed., revised and enlarged (London: Routledge and Kegan Paul); 1st ed., 1931 (London: George Routledge and Sons); originally published in German as *Preise und Produktion* (Wien-Leipzig: Hölder-Pichler-Tempsky A.G.).

Hayek, F. A. (1939a) 'Profits, Interest and Investment', in Hayek, F. A. (eds) *Profits, Interest and Investment and other Essays on the Theory of Industrial Fluctuations* (London: Routledge), pp. 3–72.

Hayek, F. A. (1939b) *Profits, Interest and Investment and other Essays on the Theory of Industrial Fluctuations* (London: Routledge).

Hayek, F. A. (1941) *The Pure Theory of Capital* (London and Henley: Routledge and Kegan Paul).

Hayek, F. A. (1975) *A Discussion with Friedrich von Hayek* (Washington, DC: American Enterprise Institute for Public Policy Research).

Hayek, F. A. (1983) 'The Austrian critique', The *Economist*, 11 June, 45–48; reprinted in Hayek, 1995, pp. 247–54.

Hayek, F. A. (1995) *Contra Keynes and Cambridge: Essays, Correspondence*, vol. 9, edited by B. J. Caldwell (London: Routledge).

House of Commons Committee on H.M. Treasury (2012) *Accountability of the Bank of England*. 'Appendix: Response from the Court of the Bank of England'; www.publications.parliament.uk/pa/cm201012/cmselect/cmtreasy/1769/176905.htm (accessed 19 June 2017).

Keynes, J. M. (1936) *The General Theory of Employment Interest and Money* (London: Macmillan).

King, J. E. (2012) *The Microfoundations Delusion. Metaphor and Dogma in the History of Macroeconomics* (Cheltenham: Edgar Allen Publishing, Ltd.).

Lagarde, C. (2014) 'Economic Inclusion and Financial Integrity', an Address to the Conference on Inclusive Capitalism, London, May 27; www.imf.org/external/np/speeches/2014/052714.htm (accessed 27 July 2015).

Lahart, J. (2007) 'In Time of Tumult, Obscure Economist Gains Currency', *The Wall Street Journal*, August 18, 1.

Magnus, G. (2007) 'The Credit Cycle and Liquidity: Have We Arrived at a Minsky Moment?' *Economic Insights - By George*. UBS Investment Research, London.

McCulley, P. A. (2007) 'Teton Reflections', Global Central Bank Focus, September; www.pimco.com/en/insights/pages/gcbf%20august-%20september%202007.aspx (accessed 31 March 2015).

Minsky, H. P. (1980) 'Capitalist Financial Processes and the Instability of Capitalism', *Journal of Economic Issues*, vol. 14, no. 2, June, 505–23.

Minsky, H. P. (1982) Can "It" Happen Again? Essays on Instability and Finance (Armonk NY: Sharpe).

Minsky, H. P. (2009) 'Beginnings', *BNL Quarterly Review*, vol. 38, no. 154, September, pp. 211–22; cited from https://ssrn.com/abstract=2057575 (accessed 14 June 2013).

Office for Budget Responsibility (2017) *Fiscal Risks Report*, July, Cm 9459.

Phelps, E. S. (1967) 'Phillips Curves, Expectations of Inflation and Optimal Employment over Time', *Economica*, New Series, vol. 34, no. 3, August, 254–81.

Phillips, A. W. (1958) 'The Relationship between Unemployment and the Rate of Change of Money Wages in the United Kingdom 1861–1957', *Economica*, vol. 25, no. 100, 283–99.

Rawnsley, A. (2010) *The End of the Party: The Rise and Fall of New Labour* (Basingstoke: Viking).

Report on Economic and Monetary Union in the European Community (1989) http://ec.europa.eu/economy_finance/publications/publication6161_en.pdf (accessed 10 July 2015).

Royal Swedish Academy of Sciences (1974) 'The Sveriges Riksbank Prize in Economic Sciences in Memory of Alfred Nobel 1974, Gunnar Myrdal, Friedrich August von Hayek', Press Release 9th October; www.nobelprize.org/nobel_prizes/economic-sciences/laureates/1974/press.html (accessed 1 June 2015).

Rumsfeld, D. H. (2012) *Known and Unknown: A Memoir* (London: Penguin Books).

Samuelson, P. A. (1955) *Economics*, 3rd ed. (New York: McGraw-Hill).

Schumpeter, J. A. (1939) *Business Cycles: A Theoretical, Historical, and Statistical Analysis of the Capitalist Process* (London: McGraw-Hill).

Shackle G.L.S. (1967) *The Years of High Theory: Invention and Tradition in Economic Thought*, 1926–1939 (Cambridge: Cambridge University Press).

Simons, H. C. (1936) 'Rules versus Authorities in Monetary Policy', *Journal of Political Economy*, vol. 44, no.1, February, 1–30; reprinted in Simons, 1948, pp. 160–83.

Simons, H. C. (1948) *Economic Policy for a Free Society* (Chicago: University of Chicago Press).

Taylor, J. B. (1993) 'Discretion versus Policy Rules in Practice', *Carnegie-Rochester Conference Series on Public Policy*, 39, 195–214.

Yellen, J. (2017) Transcript of Chair Yellen's Press Conference, June 14, www.federalreserve.gov/mediacenter/files/FOMCpresconf20170614.pdf (accessed 21 June 2017).

10 Taxation

10.1 Motivation

Economists who set out to dispel their ignorance of Simons's legacy are most likely to find, sooner rather than later, references to the 'Schanz-Haig-Simons' measure of income (see Haig, 1921; Simons, 1938; von Schanz, 1896). This may be disappointing. Economists generally are not enthused by the analysis of the expropriation of value from an individual into the control of a sovereign power – i.e., by the rules of taxation.

Though, for many, taxation may remain inherently dull, economic principles can be brought to bear upon the subject in respect of: (i) the manner and the proportion whereby tax is taken from an individual; (ii) the impact which that expropriation has upon the decisions of an individual; and (iii) how the net difference between benefits and costs is affected by the structure and administration of a tax system.

In pointing to deficiencies in the provision of services by the free enterprise system, the US Treasury argues that the state is more effective in providing a limited array of services. National defence and police protection are prime examples. Antitrust legislation, general hygiene, pollution control, road networks, water supply and education follow if the list is extended.

Simons first elaborated a programme for tax reform in the late 1920s, and that interest was maintained throughout his life, primarily for one reason. Where the overriding ethos is that of market efficiency, for Simons there remained 'the virtues of greater equality most in need of emphasis'. So, his tax programme is dominated by a central theme: 'the role of taxation as the major instrument for mitigating the inequalities which arise in a capitalist society' (Director, 1946, p. 15). Many find it incongruous for Henry Simons both to embrace libertarian principles and to argue for greater income equality. However, if income inequality is to be mitigated, Simons's libertarian principles show in one core feature: taxation is the most appropriate means. Greater equality ought not to be achieved by undermining the economic well-being that accrues from free markets and competitive pricing.

Published in 1938, Simons's tract on taxation was drawn largely from work undertaken a decade earlier. Even setting aside the passages in German (without translation), *Personal Income Taxation* does not enamour itself to readers. Indeed, it opens with an apology for its hybrid nature in combining an 'academic treatise' with a 'tract for the times', which means that many of the details relate to US tax structures of the past.

Out of the hardships of the Great Depression, a consensus was emerging whose associated developments greatly worried Simons. He found it regrettable that the Republicans had fallen back upon the expediency of 'protectionist-tariff duties' and that the Democrats had adopted 'endless restraints upon free trade', A compendium of market interventions – 'fair wages, fair prices, parity prices and other derivatives of medieval conception' - carried a potential to undermine the liberal ethos:

> We are deliberately displacing competition within economic groups, which is essentially peaceful, orderly, productive, and mutually advantageous, by organized economic and political action which is inherently exploitive, destructive, and violent.
>
> (Simons, 1938, vii)

10.2 Evolution, not revolution

The relevant yardsticks for taxation are equity and efficiency, to which must be added the ease of administration and enforcement. Is it better for taxation to be levied upon income or upon expenditure? Simons complains that little attention had been given to income as a concept. For the greatest precision, definitions must focus upon specific problems. Keywords are 'regularity', 'rights', 'accruals' and 'value', i.e., the entitlement to receive regular payments that have value. Simons cites one view that '[i]ncome is the money value of the new accretion of one's economic power between two points in time' (Haig, 1921, chap. i; cited by Simons, 1938, p. 61). However, where Robert Haig places heavy emphasis upon the 'realisation' of values, Simons senses a problem. Decisions taken in relation to realisation are likely to be determined by their implications for tax liability.[1]

With the exception of consumables, realisation implies the exchange of one asset for another. In that context, Simons suggests that scenarios may be envisaged where '[o]ne may gain without realizing and realize without gaining' (Simons, 1938, p. 84). Where legal evaluations tend to focus upon the realisation of gains, Simons cites a few of the many anomalies that are possible.

What is the likely outcome from the adoption of a specific measure? Which measures are likely to achieve a given outcome? Those two key questions should focus minds upon goals, but goals are rarely addressed in advance of measures being imposed and which may be to the detriment of market transactions. For that reason, Simons dismisses market interventions as a tool for the purpose of achieving greater income equality. Progressive taxation is the better option, with the necessary proviso that a general consensus must first be achieved.

Simons rejects the option of an entirely analytical approach to taxation on the grounds that it would be futile to apply 'rigorous objective analysis' to determine a set of precepts for sound fiscal practice. The latter is necessarily a derivative of economic policy in its entirety. Any thoughts of 'revolutionary upheavals' must be forgotten. Taxation is an evolving system that is best motivated by the overriding objectives of achieving greater efficiency and certainty. It follows that reformers must be constrained to a considerable degree by 'the unlovely features of the system as it stands' (*ibid.*, p. 2; fn. 1).

The details of Simons's position on taxation are to be understood within the context of their likely impact upon economic policy, where evolving reforms are guided by precepts set down by Simons in *A Positive Program for Laissez Faire,* 1934. Although there had been historical relevance in protesting against the injustice of the 'tax-exempt nobility and clergy', the modern notion of 'taxation according to benefits' delivers no rational basis for deciding the apportionment of taxation. In respect of general welfare (which primarily relates to expenditure on civil policing and national defence), the benefit principle takes us 'nowhere at all'; and where taxation delivers the finance for general education and for the 'economically unfit', the benefit principle poses 'sheer contradiction' (*ibid.*, p. 4).

10.3 Equal sacrifice?

Much confusion had been created by the quest for equal sacrifice, which John Stuart Mill had wrongly suggested would minimise sacrifice across the whole community. Contrary to Mill's conclusion, the neoclassical social optimum requires equal *marginal* sacrifice. This would require a calculation to find the derivative of an (allegedly) inverse functional relationship between marginal utility and income. With the assumption that the marginal utility of income falls as income rises, optimal tax rates would be identified by the point elasticities of a non-linear relationship. With no evidence to support the assumption that individuals are equally efficient as pleasure machines, Simons is scathing about the readiness of academic writers to derive 'practical implications from the criterion of equality, or proportionality, of sacrifice precisely in proportion to one's knowledge of something which no one has ever known' (*ibid.*, p. 7). The assumption that individuals are equally efficient in converting their income into pleasure and that hedonism is a sensible driver for analytical welfare economics is challenged: 'hedonism derives a blessing which is unearned and undeserved and, indeed, unfortunate for economics as a discipline' (*ibid.* p. 10). Simons also empathises with the argument that satisfaction rests, 'not only on the absolute amount of the income, but also on the relation subsisting between it and the incomes of other people' (Pigou, 1928, p. 111).

The assumptions that drive academic analysis – and that buttress 'the pseudo-scientific statement of the case against equality' (*ibid.*, p. 10) – are often judged by the conclusions that follow. Simons's disdain for the utilitarian principle is echoed by Joseph Schumpeter who, in the twin contexts of universal suffrage and laissez-faire, states that 'preference plays so large a part in arriving at conclusions as to practical policy that it bends almost any analytic structure to its dictate' (Schumpeter, 1954, p. 133, fn. 18). Where there is wide support for public expenditure on targeted social welfare payments as the means to remedy income disparities, taxation is readily dismissed as a route to that same end. In describing this as 'an amazing achievement of academic reflection', Simons conjures different scenarios with different degrees of appeal before concluding that 'as from a conjurer's hat, anything may be drawn at will' (Simons, 1938, pp. 16–17).

In suggesting that more progress might follow if discussion turned on the effects that might be viewed as ethically or aesthetically desirable, Simons states his own case for progression, which is that 'the prevailing distribution of wealth and income ... is distinctly evil or unlovely'. In recognising the practical implications of the work disincentive of high rates of taxation, the policy issue becomes that 'of weighing the one set of effects against the other'. Simons is nothing if not bold with the colours that he nails firmly to the mast: 'if reduction in the degree of inequality is a good, then the optimum degree of progression must involve a distinctly adverse effect upon the size of national income' (*ibid.*, p. 19).

Simons acknowledges the negative impact of higher tax progression on the supply of services, the use of resources, the efficiency of enterprise and the accumulation of capital. He suggests that all, except the last of these, would have a negligible magnitude 'under any degree of progression which is politically possible or administratively practical for the significant future' (*ibid.*, p. 21). While greater income inequality is likely to produce a higher rate of capital accumulation, he insists that it is legitimate to engage in the trade-off between greater equality and lower growth.

Given that a higher rate of progressive taxation implies that fewer resources are allocated to capital investment, obligations to future generations must be weighed against obligations to those who are alive today. Justice and progress are costly luxuries, and the level of capital accumulation that presently exists must have been achieved at the cost of 'centuries of terrible poverty for the masses'. By implication, if progressive taxation were to further inhibit accumulation, 'the cost of justice will be a slowing-up of our material advance' (*ibid.*, p. 22). With a lower rate of progression and a higher rate of capital accumulation, more rapid economic growth might benefit the masses but, in the context of an epoch in which Bolshevism, fascism and chronically high unemployment were prominent features, it became a plausible proposition that the Western politico-economic ethos would be fortified by the 'mitigation of the grosser inequalities in the distribution of income'. If the security of a liberal economic system were enhanced by the alleviation of poverty, made possible by progressive taxation, the latter might retrospectively be seen as having served 'to sustain and strengthen the incentive to accumulate' (*ibid.*, p. 22, fn. 13).

10.4 Tracts for the times

From personal acquaintance, George Stigler describes Simons as

> closely tuned to the time and place in which he lived: America in the Great Depression. It was a time for great fears and bold reforms … and Simons frequently invoked imminent and utter catastrophe as the justification for his proposals.
>
> (Stigler, 1974, p. 5)

Analogous fears undoubtedly motivated Keynes's defence of 'the enlargement of the functions of government … as the only practicable means of avoiding the destruction of existing economic forms in their entirety and as the condition of the successful functioning of individual initiative' (Keynes, 1936, p. 380).

In a deep recession, where the desire to save is associated with damaging levels of hoarding, the concern that steeply progressive taxation might inhibit investment had little, if any, relevance. Setting aside that consideration, Simons argues that the case for progression is not to be weighed for its relevance against a dubious set of macroeconomic reforms. He makes it clear that he offers no support for the contemporary academic novelties of aggregate demand management. The 'sophistries recently propagated by Mr Keynes in England' (Simons, 1938, p. 23, fn. 14) were emphatically repudiated: 'a somewhat comprehensive socialisation of investment' (Keynes, 1936, p. 378) is not on the agenda set by Simons. Democratic governments could be trusted to use taxation to change the distribution of income 'without undermining the foundation of their own existence' (Simons, 1938, p. 29). With a gradual process of fiscal change, each small step on the road to greater equality can be assessed for its impact. Taxation *per se* places no inhibitions upon freedoms: businesses may freely pursue profit, the prosperous may freely exercise power, and market competition may freely determine prices. Natural monopoly is the single circumstance where Simons looks to the state to administer control over industry.

Where there are activities that enhance the general welfare, it does not follow that those activities must be undertaken by governmental bodies. The uses and the burdens of government funding require detailed scrutiny. It might be appropriate for the state to 'perform services for particular groups in the community', if that is a better option than the provision of subsidies. Decisions about which expenditures are properly chargeable to the state turn primarily on the distributional impact of taxation and other levies. Where such activities inadvertently afford special advantages to particular groups, it might be equitable to extract compensation from those so advantaged.

The situation is one that evolves, so that current decisions are necessarily built upon those previously implemented. From that position, Simons sees an 'element of truth' in the adage that 'old taxes are good taxes' (*ibid.*, p. 32);

i.e., long-established *ad rem* levies (charges that are purposefully and fittingly targeted) may have acquired the status of rules that shape behavioural choices. Any subsequent changes give rise to windfall gains/losses. For example, levies upon real estate that have become factored into market transactions are analogous to 'obligations under a special kind of mortgage held by the state' (*ibid.,* p. 33, fn. 20). If those obligations were then to be removed, real estate values would increase. So, where they have been firmly established over long periods, a case might be made for retaining property taxes 'permanently at the established level' (*ibid.,* p. 34).

Simons gives analogous consideration to windfall gains resulting (for example) from a rise in property values when (say) a new road affords improved access. It would be iniquitous to approve such windfall gains. Purely economic considerations require those who benefit, either directly or indirectly, to be levied accordingly. One clear exception relates to the net benefit of road networks to vehicle users. Given that private benefits accrue in direct proportion to the use of fuel, a duty on fuel provides 'a rare instance in which a decisive argument can be made for a commodity tax' (*ibid.,* p. 38).

There is one category of charges where, regardless of time or circumstance, there is no justification. Tariffs and excise duties vary merely in their degree of badness by their respective distortions to resource allocations and their contribution to inequality.

10.5 The base and the rates

The primary relevance of taxation is as 'an instrument of economic control, [and as] a means of mitigating income inequality' (*ibid.,* p. 41), where it is desirable for the tax base to leave a minimum of inequities and ambiguities. With those features and ends in mind, Simons points to three definitions of income: (i) the market values of products and services as they are sold; (ii) the values obtained in undertaking arbitrage (reselling items at prices exceeding their purchase price); and (iii) the nebulous concept of a community's net economic activity – i.e., social income. Simons's view of the latter is that it is theoretically dubious and practically useless:

> While commonly employed as though it denoted something quantitative, social income cannot be defined to any advantage in strictly quantitative terms. Economics deals with economy; economy implies valuation; and valuation is peculiarly and essentially relative. The prices with which rigorous economics deals are pure relations; and relatives cannot be summated into meaningful totals.
>
> (*ibid.,* p. 45)[2]

A further complication in attempting to deal with the concept of social income is the potential to conflate resources that are allocated to productive activities with those that are used for 'predation and mere waste'. Simons cites resources allocated to create and then to protect monopoly surpluses; and, more contentiously, activity that is associated with advertising – i.e., the 'ludicrous selling devices' of product promotion. That emphatic condemnation of advertising gives rise to many concerns, not least among which is a need to inform the market. There is no perfect knowledge upon which the tenet of 'perfect competition' rests. Perhaps the most erroneous of popular aphorisms is that, in building a better mousetrap, the world will beat a path to your door (as attributed to Ralph Waldo Emerson).

In the most general terms, personal income may be defined as an individual's acquisition of rights that command prices. Those acquisitions would be measurable either as a change in the stock of an individual's rights to property when his/her consumption is zero or by the level of consumption that leaves a stock of property rights unchanged. For income to be measurable by one or the other of those alternatives, it would be necessary for assets and commodities to be categorised under a number of homogeneous headings and for their complete revaluation at definitive market prices to be possible at the end of every taxation period: '[t]he essential connotation of income [is the] gain to someone during a specified period and measured according to objective market standards' (*ibid.,* p. 51). An individual's income would then be obtained by adding his/her level of consumption to the difference between wealth possessed at the end, and at the start, of a given period. All gratuitous transfers would be included.

Psychic income would be excluded because of the insurmountable measurement difficulties; or, alternatively, its relevance might be dismissed on the grounds that 'psychic income may be presumed to vary in a somewhat continuous manner along the income scale' (*ibid.,* p. 53). Income in kind, consisting primarily of activities within the household (cooking, childminding and nursing), is similarly excluded as is the notion of leisure income, which might otherwise be measured by the imputation of foregone earnings. Other illustrations, of a variety of different circumstances in which resources might be assigned to an individual for the purpose of levying taxation, point to an inevitable arbitrariness in many of the categorisations (see Simons, 1938, pp. 51–55).

Among the more prominent of additional considerations are: (i) defining allowable expenses that are deductible from investment income before the tax base is calculated; (ii) accommodating variations in the value of the monetary *numéraire*; (iii) adjustments to valuations in the absence of perfect markets; and (iv) the accommodation of 'gifts, inheritances and bequests'. The general rule recommended by Simons is to avoid arbitrary distinctions and complications. Thus, for example, a gift would be treated as an item of consumption for the benefactor and an item of income for the recipient. Against the objection of double-counting, Simons points to the absence of commensurate definitions of income across many different contexts that necessarily inhibit any *logical* aggregation of personal incomes.

The essential feature of income is personal gain: the enhancement of an individual's economic power. Contrasting with that abstraction is the practical notion of a 'realised gain', as defined by conventional financial accounting procedures. These have 'a markedly conservative bias', and Simons argues that such rules of thumb are too easily elevated into logical necessities, so that a 'professional conspiracy against the truth' is an 'unmixed evil, in a world of corruptible accountants' (*ibid.*, p. 81). In the broadest sense, the realisation of income is achieved only as consumption occurs – i.e., where there is 'a destruction, a using up, an end' (*ibid.*, p. 89), which does not commend itself to supporters of the realisation criterion.

In referring to differences between himself and Irving Fisher, Simons mostly attributes these to terminology rather than to logic. Simons compliments Fisher for the clarity of an exposition that is firmly anchored to capital and interest. Fisher's preference is to refer to earnings rather than income, but he is chastised for a 'double usage of the income concept' that at times is couched in terms of 'values realized in consumption' and, at other times, 'as the yield, rent or productivity sense' (*ibid.*, p. 90). Simons is emphatic that the realisation criterion is unhelpful. Although the outcome of a business venture is finalised only upon its completion, it is a dubious step then to argue that annual personal income should be defined entirely by realised transactions: 'in a world where ventures often have neither beginning nor end within the lives of interested parties, it is hard to argue that one may grow richer indefinitely without increasing one's income' (*ibid.*, p. 82).[3]

In developing 'capital and interest' as the context for defining income, Simons perceptively insists that an interest rate is not a price *per se*, but that it represents an inter-temporal relationship between prices. Then, because interest generally arises from the possibility of using a resource to produce a resource (*pace*, Austrian capital theory), either of alternative presentations has equal validity. With the first, the interest rate is determined by time-preference – i.e., the rate at which future goods are discounted (yields). With the second, the interest rate is determined by the rate of saving, which 'is really a problem of demand, not of supply'. However, the demand that is implied by current saving is more complex than that which is implicit in the 'sadly inadequate … idea of saving as postponed consumption'. The alternative perspective upon saving is that it delivers 'increased power, greater freedom, security, prestige, and respectability' (*ibid.*, p. 91).

Simons attaches no significance to the concept of an equilibrium rate of saving (or rate of capital accumulation). Instead, the expectation within competitive markets is for resources to be directed by decisions that not only set the overall level of saving, but also directs saving in such proportions that anticipated yields are equalised. In the terminology of Austrian theory (see, for example, Garrison, 1989), the structure of capital/production tends to equilibrium. In following that train of thought and in recommending an alternative to treating interest as a costly input into the production of a 'capital instrument', Simons contributes to the contemporaneous formalisation of investment appraisal.[4]

With 'recourse to simple algebraic statement', Simons prefers to start 'from the technical beginnings, treating outlays during construction as negative receipts and determining the rate of interest at which the full series of negative and positive receipts would discount to zero' (Simons, 1938, p. 92, fn. 78). Thus, a capital investment project has a construction ('gestation') period, when factor input values (negative receipts) – augmented by applying interest at a compound rate – are taken forward to time *t*. In viewing that aggregation of input values at time *t* as the 'cost' of the project, the discounted aggregation of earnings (positive receipts) over the subsequent ('payback') period is then set against that cost to determine the profitability (or otherwise) of the capital project at time *t*. In modern terminology, the capitalised value of an investment is the 'net present value' of a temporal flow of earnings.

The conclusion that emerges in setting income within the context of capital and interest is that there is no logical impasse – i.e., 'no circularity in the position that value determines income' (*ibid.*, p. 94). Rather, the relationship between the yield from any given capital project and its value is a two-way affair. With the focus upon income as the tax base, semantic difficulties are then diminished if the expression 'discounting future incomes' is avoided – or else, if a distinction is drawn between 'income *from* things (including human labor) and income *to* persons' (*ibid.*, p. 95). It then becomes appropriate to assign rising capital values to persons, from which perspective they are immediately liable to taxation, even as those rising capital values are associated with yields that are anticipated to accrue only in future periods.

Simons seeks to remove the ambiguities that are associated with consumption (viewed as current demand based on realised income) and saving. His preferred perspective is that income implies achievements – i.e., the acquisition of claims upon market values, where the market sets no distinction between claims to current goods and claims to future goods. Better to regard income not as something accruing over time, but 'as a result imputed to particular periods' (*ibid.*, p. 100). A complete revaluation of all assets and obligations must then be made at the end of each period. Even so, calculations would 'represent at best only estimates of a very tentative sort' (*ibid.*, p. 103), and how they are obtained would rest largely upon administrative expediency. From the evidence of taxation laws across many nations, it is clear that rules merely define items for inclusion and deduction. Where possible, cross-checking draws upon market valuations and information provided by third parties and business records, but schemes that function successfully are reliant upon 'the cooperation of taxpayers' and 'the paucity of ingenious lies' (*ibid.*, p. 100). Simons's concern to find consensus is clearly in evidence.

A 'broad conception' is necessary as a basis for any coherent response to criticisms of practice and proposals for tax reform. These must be 'obvious considerations of justice' in conclusions that are either explicitly reached or else implicit in a definition of income, and 'taxes should bear similarly upon persons similarly situated'. Yet, elements of arbitrariness are inescapable: in the delineation of income in kind; in the distinction between consumption and business expenses; and in a host of other details that are 'the inevitable consequence of compromise between ideal and feasible methods' (*ibid.*, pp. 106–7). The relevant practical focus of policymakers must be to avoid such shortcomings that allow systematic tax evasion and to secure a general perception that tax levies are equitable. The 'avoidance of obvious and flagrant inequality is imperative if income taxes are to be cheaply and efficiently administered' (*ibid.*, p. 109).

Simons cites some of the many inequities that arise as opportunities for evasion present themselves. These may occur within and between income groups, by occupations, by consumption tastes, by investments and by property held. In respect of wealth held as property, Simons is persuaded that, if 'a rate representing a conservative interest return' were applied to the capital value of property, this would determine a value approximating to the net return from ownership; and, if administrative costs were found to be disproportionately high in relation to the revenue so raised, that situation might be defended 'for its effect upon the equitableness of the income tax as a whole' (*ibid.*, p. 118). Even so, while that arrangement might find general approval, it would leave open the question of where to stop. For example, what case might there be for the exemption of 'yachts, art collections, automobiles and other more durable articles'? (*ibid.*, p. 122) The decision rests implicitly upon consensus:

> [t]he conception of personal income as the algebraic sum of the individual's consumption and the change in the value of his property rights during a period is … less ambiguous, more definite, and more readily intelligible than any alternative conception which merits consideration as a basis for personal taxation.
>
> (*ibid.*, p. 125)

In adopting that perspective, there would be achieved 'the most nearly equitable taxation' that raises a minimum of difficulties in respect of legal interpretation, systematic avoidance and administrative ease. In giving weight to that conclusion, Simons repeats it thus: 'the definition of taxable income as the algebraic sum of consumption and accumulation affords the best available basis for personal taxation' (*ibid.*, p. 130).

10.6 Reform

Reform of income taxation must be judged on the basis of a net improvement to the system as a whole. The framework upon which Simons builds is simply stated: 'income tax is not a tax upon income but a tax upon persons according to their respective incomes' where the objective is 'fairness among persons, not fairness among kinds of receipts' (*ibid.*, p. 128). Whether or not lottery prizes, gifts, inheritances or bequests *per se* are tax exempt is irrelevant to a decision about whether or not to include those categories within the income tax base. No levy has any special priority. With no single criterion for judging the reasonableness of a particular tax or of the tax system as a whole, the pragmatic approach is to settle for a structure in which imperfections in one area are seen to be counterbalanced by imperfections elsewhere.

As mutually consistent propositions: (i) where the inequitable treatment of taxation is the direct cause of an inequality of income, that is a fault to be remedied; but (ii) an income inequality *per se* is not necessarily inequitable. From that basis, none would disagree with Simons, when he writes that '[p]ersonal income taxation should seek to minimise inequities among persons' or when he writes that '[t]he criterion of equity by itself, leads only to a vague and elusive ideal, not a sound and workable income tax'. Between those two phrases sits the statement that '[t]he best guide for policy is the principle that income taxes should diminish systematically an objectively measurable kind of inequality' (*ibid.,* pp. 138–9). Whatever the degree of care that is taken in attempting to find a workable tax base, there will always be much that remains a matter of expedience or moral inclination (where the latter are fed by the education and/or persuasion that contribute to a broad consensus).

Inheritance tax violates the most basic of relatively few guiding precepts in that it is a charge upon a *category* of income rather than upon a component of the aggregate income of an individual. Yet, Simons applauds that outcome, which he excuses on the grounds that it is 'a disposition among legislatures to face inequality as a real problem' (*ibid.,* p. 130). Even so, there are so many exemptions that these are 'only feeble gestures' towards the proper inclusion of inheritance income. For any given threshold, an individual receiving bequests, each of which lies below the inheritance tax threshold, pays nothing. If, instead, inheritance were included within a broad income tax base, there would be greater objectivity and a more coherent set of internal checks leaving fewer opportunities for evasion.

A similar set of considerations applies to gratuitous receipts from which many, if not most, employees take inherent pleasure. In alluding to those innate satisfactions (and to the utilitarian ideal of graduating tax rates *pro rata* the relative pleasure derived from work activity), Simons finds a clear rationale in taxing gratuities: '[i]f it is impractical to graduate taxes according to the pleasure return from one's earning activity, it is hard to defend exclusion of certain receipts merely because one has done nothing or given nothing in return' (*ibid.,* p. 135). In further support of that position, Simons argues that any attempt to distinguish gifts from compensation must invite the 'dressing-up' of the latter as gifts. While administrative practicalities require a line to be drawn to exclude minor items, as a minimum requirement Simons would include items of real estate, investment assets and large items of 'consumer capital, such as yachts, motorcars, and valuable art objects' (*ibid.,* p. 136).

In respect of dependent children and aged relatives, Simons suggests that it is 'reasonable enough' to allow tax credits for 'minor dependents' to 'vary directly with family income … [with] … minimum and maximum credits per child' (*ibid.,* p. 137). Adults within that same household might be taxed according to their consumption (less contributions), with the householder's tax liability being adjusted accordingly. Consistency would require similar deductions in respect of any support afforded to persons living outside the household. In regard to concessions made to give equitable treatment to those with similar earnings but different family obligations, the criterion (as always) is to minimise inequities subject to the requirement for simplicity and definiteness. If confronted by a simple rule that brings worrisome consequences, the wrong choice would be to risk descending 'to a world of dialectic populated only by doctrines of ability, faculty, sacrifice, minimum social advantage, and their kind' (*ibid.*, p. 139). In regard to aged relatives, where the obligation to provide financial support to dependants might appear to be little different to making payments to creditors, Simons spins the argument around: those with the means to provide that support are better placed than others who 'must endure the spectacle of their distress' (*ibid.*, p. 140).

Simons is sympathetic to inheritance tax exemptions for widows, widowers and other dependants, but he is concerned that opportunities for avoidance might loom large. He would wish to minimise the incentive to consult specialists in tax avoidance and to neutralise any biases that influence the management and disposal of assets. His overriding fear is one of compromising the requirement for simple workable rules, even to the point of arguing for scaling down concessions in line with the age discrepancy (between the deceased and the surviving spouse) or the duration of the marriage.

Clear elements of social engineering are present as Simons senses 'something wrong with a system which gives great power to a few people, no matter how they use that power'; and where 'capable people are maintained in useless activities by the generosity of prosperous relatives';[5] and where the 'training of a few children is made the objective of expenditures involving a disproportionate share of the community's resources'. While it would be naive to expect the elimination of all 'inheritances in the form of special training, education, and social position', Simons applauds arrangements that 'cannot wisely permit depreciation deductions with respect to investment in personal earning capacity' (*ibid.*, p. 141).

Although any transfer of funds from the estate of the deceased is a realisation of gains that, alternatively, might have been imputed and taxed across a number of years, it would be a matter of regret (to Simons) if the state were to be deprived of the larger tax take on the accumulative total of such accruals. Therefore, while he looks 'for drastic changes in existing death duties', Simons does not 'call for abandonment of the old forms of levy'. With income as the appropriate context wherein to tax 'gifts inheritances and bequests', there is a strong case for a supplementary levy, because this kind of accumulation 'can be taxed with least adverse effect upon the morale of an enterprise economy; and opinion generally supports especially heavy taxation of "income" in this form' (*ibid.*, p. 144). Simons gives no further explanation of the rationale, but it is implicit that he finds justification for a levy where a consensus is already firmly established.

10.7 Variable income

The particular concern to find a clear principle by which taxation can be levied upon capital gains is among many that arise where disproportionate tax burdens accrue to individuals whose incomes fluctuate widely. Where these are driven by the variable receipt of gifts, inheritances and bequests, the heavier levies that arise have popular approval so that concerns are muted. Where receipts have more the flavour of earnings, problems have a higher profile. Evasion is often relatively easy. Simons cites bonds issued with a low coupon value and at a great discount. These may be liquidated at any time to deliver opportunely timed capital gains. Corporate dividends might also be withheld to similar effect. These sit within that category of problems that occur when realisation is the criterion for a tax liability.

Though wary of adding complications and as only a pointer to possibilities, Simons gives an illustrative proposal for dealing with highly variable incomes. His proposal is for individuals to be taxed annually, with the liability calculated against average income (say, on a cycle of five years). A hypothetical annual tax payment across that period of five years would then be calculated. Where the total is less (say, by more than ten percent) than the aggregate payments actually assessed for those years, the individual might be eligible to receive a rebate for the excess.

The general desire to avoid compounding complications applies to changes in money values when measuring capital gains and losses. Simons shies away from that consideration: 'some things are well let alone'! Beyond problems associated with index numbers, other questions relate to the disposal of assets after their prices have risen. Other impracticalities exist during periods of falling prices, where depreciation allowances could foreseeably exceed the original cost. It would be better, Simons suggests, for interested parties 'to join in the crusade for stable monetary conditions and in prayer for some intelligence in the regulation of financial institutions'. Simons gives short shrift to the idea that, in choosing between adjustments to tax provisions, the objective is to maximise revenue from taxation. As always, the primary objective is 'to secure an equitable, progressive distribution of tax burdens among individuals', and that end is not secured by the maximisation principle, nor is it served by 'arbitrary distinctions and casuistic definition of the tax base' (*ibid.*, pp. 155–7).

In practical terms, the realisation of gains and losses may be central to feasible systems and this is unobjectionable if it results only in the postponement of assessment or the cancellation of earlier profits/losses against subsequent losses/profits. Although the opportunity to postpone tax payments permits the reinvestment of paper profits, those gains remain subject to tax that, in a progressive system, would then be payable at a higher rate. That such practice permits future losses to offset current gains has the merit of mitigating the impact of progressive rates upon individuals with widely fluctuating annual incomes.

More fundamental is the question of why those in receipt of gifts should be permitted any deductions at all. Tax avoidance is too readily facilitated where the ownership of assets changes by gift, inheritance or bequest, not least where tax is assessed against those who are ordinarily subject to lower rates. Whether it is received by gift or by probate, every transfer should be treated 'as a realisation, at fair market value as of the date of transfer, by the donor' (*ibid.*, p. 166). By that interpretation, the option is removed of inter-generational gifts that can be made in perpetuity without incurring any tax liability.

10.8 Final thoughts

There is no case for the exemption from taxation of any category of income. Of those categories that were privileged with tax-exemption status in the 1930s, the 'most flagrant and least pardonable' (*ibid.*, p. 170) were interest and salary payments made by government bodies.[6] On constitutional grounds, interest on debt issued by the constituent states of the Union and by federal corporations was exempt from federal income tax. Also exempt were payments for services rendered to the constituent states. The primary concern was with tax-exempt securities, because of the opportunities that they presented for tax avoidance on a large-scale and that were available only to 'idle, passive holders of highly conservative investments' (*ibid.*, p. 172).

Any conclusion that the net effect of exemptions upon federal revenue is negligible misses the general point of principle: that income tax is 'a means for reaching persons equitably and progressively'. The pernicious impact of tax-exempt securities is most obvious among upper income groups, in that it gives favour to 'coupon clippers and against those actively engaged in business enterprise' (*ibid.*, pp. 175–6). With progressive tax rates, the advantage to holding tax-exempt securities is greatest to those with the greatest wealth

Simons accepts that the realisation criterion would continue to be used, but only because 'no workable scheme can require that taxpayers reappraise and report all their assets annually'. *Ad rem* levies should be retained for real property taxes and for vehicle fuel duty, but the proper source of revenue is the application of a simple levy to income taxation at a progressive rate, with a minimum of opportunities for avoidance or evasion. Income is defined as the periodic aggregation of consumption and accumulation (appropriately discounted). Difficult practical questions arise, not least in respect of income in kind from the use of capital by its owners and with minor gifts, but those difficulties must be addressed on the basis of 'careful experiment and experience' (*ibid.*, pp. 207–8). Where assets appreciate in value, they should be taxable at full value at the time of sale or probate; but no deductions should be made for losses on property transferred by gift. All acquisitions and disposition should be declared in an unbroken chain of valuations.

Although the freedom and responsibility of state and local government 'are indispensable for the preservation of representative political institutions' (*ibid.*, p. 215), there are inevitable dilemmas. A desirable objective is to obtain the same relative distribution of revenues that would obtain if the same tax base, the same personal exemptions and the same scale of rates were imposed upon every state. Arrangements might then be achieved that, 'besides enforcing a necessary uniformity among the states, would involve substantial centralisation and enforcement only in regards the technical administration and enforcement of the tax' (*ibid.*, p. 217).[7] In short, some degree of centralisation is not viewed as an ominous requirement, providing that state and local bodies retain control of their spending and receive most of their revenue from their own levies.

With an addendum to the final chapter of *Personal Income Taxation*, Simons pitches economic principles against the canons of a good tax system,[8] which are that it should be 'highly stable, regular, and reliable as to yield' (*ibid.*, p. 221). Simons is emphatic that those criteria are as meaningful as they are wrong, because countercyclical peaks and troughs in tax revenue serve the economic objective of smoothing money income. The means that are appropriate for implementing such rules lie in the power of government 'through exercise of its spending, taxing, and borrowing prerogatives' (*ibid.*, p. 222). This reopens the issues of monetary policy and reform, where Simons points his readers to his seminal paper of 1936: 'Rules versus Authorities in Monetary Policy'.

Notes

1 For Haig, accretion is 'a second best measure of true income'; the 'better measure' is consumption expenditure (see Wildasin, 1990, p. 649). Although Haig views true income as the flow of 'satisfactions expressed in terms of money' (Haig, 1921, p. 7), he concedes that it is an unrealistic goal to tax an ability to draw satisfaction from a variety of consumption items.

2 Here is evidence of distinct Austrian School undertones. Carl Menger (*Grundsätze*, 1871) emphasises that every choice is a costly experiment in which subjective values are established only at the moment of choice and that the combination of individuals' choices produces highly complex structures, knowledge of which is never complete or certain. More prosaically: 'there is no more sense in speaking of an economic system's total or aggregate demand and supply and, incidentally, of overproduction than there is in speaking of the exchange value of all vendible things taken together or of the weight of the solar system taken as a whole' (Schumpeter, 1954, p. 617).

3 Frank Knight's criticism of the period of production in the context of Austrian capital theory may have influenced this assessment by Simons: 'the production period has no beginning and no end, unless … the date of the end of the world is known from the beginning, and the entire social economy prepares from the beginning for the liquidation' (Knight, 1933, p. 222).

4 There are unambiguous relationships between the net income that is necessary to meet debt obligations and the market value of the debt instrument. Although the calculations that support valuations across periods of time date back to ancient times, the details by which flows of receipts are capitalised (most obviously to estimate stock values) received greater attention after 1929. Noteworthy publications are Irving Fisher's *The Theory of Interest*, 1930, and *The Theory of Investment Value*, published by John Burr Williams in 1938. The latter challenges the view

that asset markets are dominated by volatile speculations. Rather, the price of an instrument tends to reflect anticipated corporate earnings and dividends. *Note bene*: Simons *Personal Income Taxation* was published in 1938.

5 Against Simons, Hayek argues that unique advantages can flow from those with resources from family inheritance. With 'no material worries', they can develop a keener interest in 'the development of the art of living and of the non-materialistic values'. The alternative is action 'by collective agreement which must be limited to instances where previous efforts have already created a common view'. Hayek regrets the demise of that 'cultural elite within the propertied class' by which, 'wealthy men of affairs were able to take part in the movement of ideas' (see Hayek, 1960, pp. 126–30).

6 Three other categories of tax exemption were: receipts of real property used for own consumption; capital gains and losses; and gratuities.

7 This has close affinity with the conclusion of a lecture given by Hayek in 1976: 'Once it is generally recognised that government under the law and unlimited powers of the representatives of the majority are irreconcilable, and all government is equally placed under the law ... regional and local governments, limited by the same uniform laws with regard to the manner in which they could make their individual inhabitants contribute to their revenue, would develop into business-like corporations competing with each other for citizens who could vote with their feet for that corporation which offered them the highest benefits compared with the price change' (Hayek, 1978, p. 162).

8 Those canons have become extended since first elucidated by Adam Smith: 'The subjects of every state ought to contribute towards the support of the government, as nearly as possible, in proportion to their respective abilities; that is, in proportion to the revenue which they respectively enjoy under the protection of the state. ... The tax which each individual is bound to pay ought to be certain, and not arbitrary. The time of payment, the manner of payment, the quantity to be paid, ought all to be clear and plain to the contributor, and to every other person' (Smith, 1776, Book V, chap. 4, paras. 25–26).

Bibliography

Director, A. (1946) 'Simons on Taxation', *University of Chicago Law Review*, vol. 14, issue 1, article 4, December, 15–19.

Emmett, R. B. (1999) *Selected Essays of Frank H. Knight, "What is Truth" in Economics?*, vol. 2 (Chicago and London: Chicago University Press).

Fisher, I. (1930) *The Theory of Interest as Determined by Impatience to Spend Income and Opportunity to Invest It* (New York: Macmillan).

Garrison, R. W. (1989) 'The Austrian Theory of the Business Cycle in the Light of Modern Macroeconomics', *Review of Austrian Economics*, vol. 3, 3–29.

Haig, R. M. (ed.) (1921) *The Federal Income Tax* (New York: Columbia University Press).

Hayek, F. A. (1960) *The Constitution of Liberty* (London and Henley, UK: Routledge and Kegan Paul).

Hayek, F. A. (1978) *New Studies in Philosophy, Politics, Economics and the History of Ideas* (London and Henley, UK: Routledge and Keagan Paul).

Keynes, J. M. (1936) *The General Theory of Employment Interest and Money* (London: Macmillan).

Knight, F. H. (1933) 'Capitalist Production, Time and the Rate of Return', cited from Emmett, 1999, pp. 211–26.

Menger, C. (1871) *Grundsätze der Volkswirtschaftslehre* (Wein: Wilhelm Braumüller); https://archive.org/details/MengerCarlGrundsaetzeDerVolkswirtschaftslehre 1871299S (accessed 12 June 2014).

Pigou, A. C. (1928) *A Study in Public Finance* (London: MacMillan).

Schanz, G. von (1896) 'Der Einkommensbegriff und die Einkommensteuergesetze', *Finanzarchiv*, vol. 13, 1–87.

Schumpeter, J. A. (1954) *History of Economic Analysis* (Oxford: Oxford University Press).

Simons, H. C. (1934) 'A Positive Program for Laissez Faire: Some Proposals for a Liberal Society', published as *Public Policy Pamphlet no. 15*, (ed.) H. D. Gideonse (Chicago, IL: University of Chicago Press); reprinted and cited from Simons, 1948, pp. 40–77.

Simons, H. C. (1936) 'Rules versus Authorities in Monetary Policy', *Journal of Political Economy*, vol. 44, no.1, February, 1–30; reprinted in Simons, 1948, pp. 160–83.

Simons, H. C. (1938) *Personal Income Taxation: The Definition of Income as a Problem of Fiscal Policy* (Chicago, IL: University of Chicago Press).

Simons, H. C. (1948) *Economic Policy for a Free Society* (Chicago, IL: University of Chicago Press).

Smith, A. (1776) *An Inquiry into the Nature and Causes of the Wealth of Nations*; cited from a compilation by Edwin Cannan, 1904 (London: Methuen and Co. Ltd); www.econlib.org/cgi-bin/searchbooks.pl?searchtype=BookSearchPara&id=smWN&query=taxation (accessed 7 December 2016).

Stigler, G. J. (1974) 'Henry Calvert Simons', *Journal of Law and Economics*, vol. 17, no. 1, April, 1–5.

Wildasin, D. (1990) 'R. M. Haig: Pioneer Advocate of Expenditure Taxation?', *Journal of Economic Literature*, vol. 28, June, 649–60.

Williams, J. B. (1938) *The Theory of Investment Value* (Cambridge: Harvard University Press).

11 Islamic banking and finance

11.1 Central bank independence

The Great Moderation refers to a period (from the mid-1980s until 2008) when many thought that the diminished volatility of business cycles was permanent and that this could be attributed to the independence that had been afforded to central banks in setting monetary policy. When the Maastricht Treaty was signed in February 1992, its immediate purpose was to achieve economic convergence between those European Union states that aspired to adopt the euro as a single currency. 'Convergence' was defined in terms of key variables, most notably those relating to fiscal borrowing, sovereign debt, currency exchange rates and price inflation. It was also considered essential for national central banks to be free from political influence in setting the parameters of monetary policy. Primarily for that reason, the Maastricht Treaty enshrined the status of the ECB and the national central banks of the Eurozone as independent bodies.[1]

There are three features whereby greater economic stability has been viewed as 'deliverable' by an independent central bank: (i) the empirical evidence of a negative association between the independence of central banks and price inflation; (ii) the explanation that independence insulates monetary policy from political influence; (iii) the concept of time inconsistency, which implies an inflationary bias if a central bank is not independent.

Time inconsistency refers to the temptation to cheat after a pre-commitment to an inflation target has been announced. As rational economic agents adjust their expectations towards an announced inflation target, a political authority faces the temptation to deliver a short-term boost to employment by allowing inflation to rise unexpectedly above the target level. Yet, this must undermine the credibility of pre-announced targets. In order to strengthen that credibility, legislation is enacted such that the determination of monetary action is independent of political influence. The objective is to remove the (time inconsistent) temptation to 'cheat'.

11.2 Banking structures

Together with policy pre-commitments, banking structures are also relevant to banking and financial stability. The economic narratives that explain how the downturn of a business cycle might be triggered are of two kinds; i.e., 'normal' activity may be impaired either by an exogenous real shock or by some endogenous monetary or financial perturbation. As particular institutional structures are relevant to the latter, comparisons have been drawn between the structures of Western and Islamic banking. With the rapid growth of Islamic banking that has occurred over recent years and which is expected to continue, competition with Western banks is likely to grow. Although both bank types may face similar risks, the manner in which those risks are countered will vary, not least by the interpretations of Islamic precepts by regulatory Shariah Boards.

As the Great Recession entered its tenth year, with doubts about enduring recovery and excessive private and public debt remaining to be addressed, many decades had passed since Henry Simons implicitly endorsed advantages that many now find in Islamic banking and finance; i.e., that if 'there were no fixed money contracts at all – if all property were held in a residual-equity or common stock form', then 'no one would be in a position either to create effective money-substitutes … or to force enterprises into wholesale efforts at liquidation' (Simons, 1933b, cited from Friedman, 1967, p. 6). That these are redolent of Islamic precepts as applied to banking and finance provides the rationale for the present chapter.

The relative stability and/or riskiness of Western and Islamic banking are matters for empirical inquiry, where comparative studies of the performance of Islamic and Western banking systems tend to be heavily statistical in their approach. By implication, qualitative differences are less intensively investigated. Given the requirement to accommodate a large number of non-stationary qualitative factors, including 'a sound legal framework, a well-designed governance structure, and robust accountancy practices' (Mejía et al., 2014, p. 2), cross-country differences in the rulings of Shariah Boards warrant closer attention.

Perhaps the most pertinent question relates to whether the structures of Islamic banking (not least, the prohibition of *riba*) match any of the details of the Chicago Plan, where the payment of interest on deposit accounts would be displaced by a payment for warehousing clients' liquid assets. With the protection afforded by 100 percent reserve banking to a panic withdrawal of deposits, similar characteristics within Islamic banking may deliver a similar degree of stability. Yet, where financial probity may give protection to gains that have been won, those same characteristics may inhibit the potential to achieve the most advantageous of entrepreneurial gains.

The core Islamic principle is that of sharing profit and loss, where a number of equity-like financial arrangements exist. Although there is no agreement on the exact meaning of *riba* (i.e., usury, meaning an 'excess'), most Islamic jurists describe two kinds: interest charged (as money or in kind) for a loan; and the exchange of unequal quantities or qualities. A formal definition of 'interest' now serves as a prelude to a better understanding of Islamic prohibitions and their possible relevance to the relationship between financial stability and economic prosperity.

11.3 Yields: a Keynesian perspective

A concise formulation of 'the essential properties of interest and money' may be found in Keynes's *General Theory*. For all transactions that are processed over a period of time, an inter-temporal price ratio is obtained as the value placed upon a commodity unit at the date of future sale divided by its current valuation. It is that calculation – which signals the anticipated profitability of business activity – that is close to the Islamic principle of *murabaha*, as described in the next section. For every inter-temporal gain or loss from undertaking such a transaction, Keynes shows how a positive or negative yield is implicit in the outcome. If they so choose, traders may hedge their anticipated yield by dealing in competitive spot and forward markets. Across a full range of investments, competitive trading would be expected to drive a tendency for the equalisation of net returns; i.e., John Stuart Mill's law of one price as applied to yields.

As an illustrative example, Keynes cites investments in wheat (which has a positive 'carrying cost in terms of itself': i.e., any spoilage that devalues the wheat) and housing (where the 'carrying cost and liquidity premium are negligible': *n.b.*, a liquidity premium is the price discount on a relatively short-dated security). In Keynes's presentation, an interest rate is calculated as the total return expected from the ownership of an asset over a period. This is equal to its yield (q) *minus* its carrying cost (c) *plus* its liquidity premium (l), so that $r = q - c + l$, where r is the own-rate of interest of any commodity and q, c and l are measured using the commodity itself as the standard.

Although any commodity might serve as a unit of account, Keynes takes money 'as our standard of measurement' (Keynes, 1936, p. 227). In equilibrium, the own-rate of interest (r_j) for any commodity (j) is related to the rate of interest on money (r_m) as

$$r_j = r_m + a_j \quad \textit{for all } j$$

where a_j is the rate of appreciation of the money price of commodity j. In a competitive economy, any deviations from this equality are corrected by the reallocation of resources to produce commodities with higher total returns. Then, as the production of commodities rises generally so, by their greater abundance, returns tend to fall 'to levels at which one asset after another falls below the standard of profitable production; – until, finally, one or more own-rates of interest remain at a level which is above that of the marginal efficiency [yield] of any asset whatever' (*ibid.*, p. 229).

As argued by Keynes, the benchmark asset is money or, more strictly, 'any asset of which the own-rate of interest is reluctant to decline as output increases' (*ibid.*). The 'peculiar significance' stressed by Keynes is that

> [t]he money-rate of interest, by setting the pace for all the other commodity rates of interest, holds back investments in the production of these

> other commodities, without being capable of stimulating investment in the production of money, which by hypothesis cannot be produced. … [and] … men cannot be employed when the object of their desire (*i.e.*, money) is something which cannot be produced and the demand for which cannot readily be choked off.
>
> (*ibid.*, p. 235)

The perversity that Keynes attributes to the 'money-rate of interest' is that, during periodic business recessions, that money-rate tends to exceed the returns on other investments. In that situation, it is most profitable to hoard money. By that rationale, Keynes's liquidity preference theory of interest rate determination is at the core of *The General Theory*. Investors structure their asset portfolios according to their perceptions of the future valuations of its components. If asset prices are perceived to be more likely to fall than to rise, that anticipation of a capital loss causes a rise in the 'speculative' demand to hold money (i.e., a rise in liquidity preference implies a rise in money hoarding). It follows that any speculation of a general fall in asset prices acts as a deterrent to investment.

Keynes's desire to determine and then to implement policy that would gain and then sustain full employment was as much to avoid 'the destruction of existing economic forms' (Keynes, 1936, p. 380) as 'to mitigate economic distress' (*ibid.*, p. 382). An analogous mix of considerations may be relevant to Islamic precepts of virtue (*al-birr*) and justice (*al-qist*) for the community at large (*ummah*). In taking a narrow focus, Keynes's presentation of the speculative demand for money (which prevents yields falling sufficiently to encourage necessary investment expenditure) might be compared with the Islamic prohibition of *riba*. It is the liquidity premium of money (the money-rate of interest) that is the villain in each of those contexts.

11.4 Yields: an Islamic perspective

Within a general Islamic perspective, prohibited industries and activities include transactions based on interest, speculation, gambling, alcohol, illegal drugs, tobacco, pork products, non-halal meat, pornography, erotic art and certain music and cinema. In taking a more focused view, there are aspects of Simons's writing that resonate with that ethos. These include his aspiration for greater income equality and his concern over the moral hazard that exists in limiting the legal liability of business shareholders. Most notable, however, is the Islamic prohibition of *riba*, which precludes fractional reserve banking, at least as practiced in the West.

The prohibition of usury is general: interest cannot be paid on Islamic savings or current accounts, or charged on Islamic mortgages. This has prompted a number of options that allow *Sharia*-compliant accounts to be structured in diverse ways. For example, with (i) *ijara*, a trust is established as the owner of property, which is then leased to a customer who pays rent; and, although the customer may forego the option, there is an entitlement to buy the property; (ii) *murabaha*, a bank buys commodities for a customer who makes deferred payments at a higher price; (iii) *musharaka*, a bank and a customer jointly fund an investment or purchase, with an agreement to share the returns and risks in predetermined proportions; (iv) *wakala*, a bank acts as agent, receiving fees for managing the customer's *Sharia*-compliant trading activities.

The structures that have been approved for modern Islamic banking are founded upon the *Qur'an*, where scholarly interpretations can vary. General patterns that have emerged are those for which close parallels now exist between newly established Islamic practice and long-established Western practice. Many of these new formulations are not without their critics, who may dispute that Islamic principles are truly met by 'sham Shariah-compliant instruments that flooded the market in the decade before the crisis; these were window-dressing pseudo-Islamic financial instruments that were mathematically equivalent to conventional debt and mortgage contracts' (Buiter and Rahbari, 2015, p. 148).

Such pointed criticism might be more widely heard were it not for the opprobrium that can bear down upon those who would question the authority of Islamic scholars. Not least for the potential that exists for seeking greater clarity, the relatively few attempts made would suggest that religious commitment inhibits academic interest. The core requirement that a central bank supplies base money on demand (a provision for which it is compensated) surely creates a conundrum.

11.5 Islamic banking: base money

The instrument commonly used by Western commercial banks for obtaining liquidity from a central bank is the repurchase agreement (repo), whereby the bank sells a security to the central bank (in exchange for central bank reserves) with an agreement to repurchase that security at a later date. The difference between the repurchase price and the sale price is the interest charged by the central bank: the interest rate is the central bank's policy rate and it is the marginal cost of liquidity to the banks.[2] Competitive behaviour among the banks ensures that rates for inter-bank lending remain close to this official rate.[3]

Although the repo transaction is not *Sharia* compliant, a near-identical outcome is achieved within the Islamic inter-bank money market by a 'sell and buy back agreement'. This engagement follows the form as described previously, except that the same payment is made for the debt instrument in both directions, but with the central bank *charging a fee* for the transaction.

Among recent developments, in 2014 a group of Indonesian banks devised a standard master contract template, which requires sovereign Islamic bonds (*sukuk*) to serve as collateral for tenors of no more than one year. The critical *Sharia* element is the requirement for both parties to have 'some skin in the game', which is achieved by a provision whereby injured parties may claim compensation for losses arising from the non-fulfilment of a promise.

Another illustration is *provided by* the circumstances in which the UK became the first country outside the Islamic world to issue sovereign *sukuk*, in 2014. Orders totaling around £2.3 billion were received for £200 million *sukuk*, to mature in 2019. In following Islamic practice, a profit rate (of 2.036 percent) was set in line with yields prevailing on gilts of similar maturity; and the commonly used *sukuk al-ijara* structure was used.[4] Rental payments on three properties provide income for investors. Since it is always possible for unforeseen (or unforeseeable) events to cause variations in rental income, *Sharia*-compliance is met by the agreement that both parties to the transaction have a stake in that outcome.

General conclusions to be drawn from this are that: (i) the argument that *Sharia*-compliant financial arrangements do not permit *riba* is not the core issue; (ii) the focus upon interest *per se* is undermined by the truism that any inter-temporal price ratio defines an equivalent yield; (iii) the distinctive feature of *Sharia*-compliant finance is that an equity partnership should exist between a debtor and creditor.

11.6 The social perspective

The abhorrence of *riba* derives from the perspective that any society exists only by the acceptance of rules that govern behaviour. Yet, rules change. The moral certainties that bind small closed societies evolve over millennia. For example, the schism that gave the Islamic denominations of *Sunni* and *Shia* occurred almost 1,400 years ago, since when many events have directed the respective courses of their evolutionary paths. Even within those sects, each has four schools of jurisprudence whose broad similarities coexist alongside important differences. The outcome is that Islamic jurisprudence does not necessarily deliver definitive judgements.

Evolving societal practices promote the growth of human relationships beyond any intellectual vision or plan. Practices that are successful generally survive through imitative learning, when many may become enshrined as law, so that individuals, corporate bodies and governments understand how they must act under the same legal constraints. Within small groups, that cohesion is enhanced by tribal affiliation where morality is determined through a consensus on end goals. In that context, distributional justice is meaningful, because the consequences of any action may be generally anticipated. This is not the case within the extended order of a modern economy, where every action has diverse and unintended consequences that extend far beyond the comprehension of any aimed *directly* at definitive outcomes. Indeed, the pursuit of distributional justice across extended socio-economic relationships might then become both futile and damaging. Hence the aphorism: 'the road to hell is paved with good intentions'.[5]

Within Western market economies, entrepreneurship drives continuing adjustments between factor market prices and product market prices. Entrepreneurs acquire (what they believe to be) the least-cost services necessary to produce their prospective products. As entrepreneurs contract to buy inputs, their products and their prices exist only in the imagination. Factor inputs are purchased in anticipation of prevailing future prices. Entrepreneurship is necessarily speculative, which contrasts with Islamic aspirations whereby central bank officials purport to be able to provide definitive guidance on *Sharia*-compliant opportunities and yields.

More than two centuries have passed since feudal agriculture gave way to Western capitalism. However, there are many aspects where Islam remains set within the constraints of earlier stages of socio-economic development. Though the aspirations may be laudable – encompassing equitable shares, fair trading, the judicious use of wealth and community well-being – traditional Islamic practices raise concerns that invite re-examination.

The Islamic ethos stipulates that affluent families should not gain at the expense of those who are poor. Few in the West (and generally) would wish that to be otherwise. Nor are there likely to be many who would argue with the expectation that the wealthy should meet charitable obligations or that 'women and children must be evacuated first'. These are illustrations of decision-making that go beyond resource cost calculations, even within settings that are generally market-oriented. However, the ubiquitous relevance of market prices (and the yields that are implicit therein) is that exchange-values are essential to capital-using production. They are essential because '[t]he human mind cannot orientate itself properly among the bewildering mass of intermediate products and potentialities of production without such aid' (Mises, 1920, p. 103). If changing market prices have a role within Islamic culture, then the implications for the interpretations of *riba* remain to be readdressed in the context of that modern world view.

In a Western context, loan contracts are generally agreed in terms of a fixed money rate of interest. Setting aside debtor insolvency, a lender expects to receive that predetermined payment of interest, regardless of the success or otherwise that is achieved with the loan. Under Islam, that is viewed as giving too much advantage to the lender. The alternative is for the net proceeds of an investment to be shared equitably between, say, a bank (in providing finance) and an entrepreneur (in undertaking a business activity). Entrepreneurs are then expected to compete to become the 'agents' of those who possess financial capital, with the latter scrutinising the projects and their management teams. Within that decision-making process, the risk of asymmetric information is diminished by the sanctity of contractual obligations and the requirement for a full disclosure of information. Less persuasive to Western ears is that the selection from among investment opportunities is based upon hypothetical returns to different categories of investment, as predetermined by the authority that is vested in an Islamic central bank.

The general implication of that traditional structure is that an Islamic central bank oversees financial policy rather than monetary policy. Its key functions include: participation in the preparation of a national economic development plan; setting and informing individual banks of the priorities for investment projects; assessing project risks and determining the relative profit share of banks across different sectors and regions; and the inspection and supervision of investment projects. Islamic banks are also expected to act to reduce general unemployment; and a central bank gives priority to projects that are most closely compatible with the central economic plan. Once feasibility and profitability are decided, projects are eligible for finance. It not only follows that the monitoring costs of Islamic banking are (or have been) much higher than those associated with Western practices, but that centralised Islamic banking constraints are fewer and much lighter than the regulation imposed upon, or proposed for, Western banking.

11.7 Culture, entrepreneurship and economic advance

In the wake of the 2008 financial crisis, greater attention has been given to Islamic approaches to finance and investment. That crisis was preceded by a surge in property prices, as first triggered by events in the US. In 1977, the *Community Investment Act* had the effect of forcing US banks to make low interest and easy-term home loans. The objective was to give greater encouragement to home ownership among low-income households. By that coercion, it might be argued that central authorities brought US banking one step closer to Islamic practice; but it did not endure, and much detail has been written on how that drive for greater social equality became unsustainable. As a thumbnail sketch, investors were driven by the siren call of house prices that appeared to be inexorably following an upward trend. As that incentive was acted upon by an ever-growing number of households, the result was an unsustainable speculative game that stripped valuations of any meaningful relationship to 'the fundamentals'. Such non-sustainable investment surges have not been confined to property developments.

In general terms, 'bubble' relates to the inflated valuation of an asset. Cheap credit is often a prime suspect. That a speculative bubble will eventually burst is guaranteed when it has the characteristics of a Ponzi scheme. Otherwise, the bubble may simply deflate, though with varying degrees of rapidity. Although minor bubbles may gently inflate before gently falling away, the implosion of the sub-prime mortgage bubble triggered the worst financial collapse since the Great Depression.

Under Islam, speculation is denounced as a non-productive or wasteful activity. Yet, all rational action is directed to improving expected outcomes and, because uncertainty is all-pervasive, rational action necessarily drives decisions that are speculative. Gambling can be profitable, but it is perceived to provide no net additional wealth for the community. Any mutual gain from enjoying a day at the races must be discounted, but should the same categorical prohibition apply to aspects of trading in financial markets? Might not speculative trading in foreign exchange make it easier for end users to find counterparties in the market? Might purposeful competition not narrow the bid-offer spread, so reducing transaction costs?

11.8 A trade-off: innovation or stability?

The attempt to regulate the dynamics of rapidly evolving financial instrumentation presents no easy task. With the close monitoring of investment activities and the absence of credit leverage, Islamic banking can appear to be less exposed to periodic financial crises. Where commercial banking in the West is criticised for the moral hazard of being a cornerstone of the payments system, a number of additional problems arise under Islam. When the potential profitability of investments is determined by Islamic central bankers, it is inevitable that the *minutiae* of local circumstances are neglected. Differences in the acquisition of (and the response to) new information and in making adjustments to retain competitive advantage produce wide variations in profitability. Although, by comparison, Islamic practices may achieve more closely coordinated activities, less desirable consequences may follow. Inherent within conservative practices is a tendency to neglect the value that derives from dispersed local knowledge: '[t]he function of competition… is precisely to teach us who will serve us well' (Hayek, 1946: 1949, p. 97). The nub is that Islamic practices that follow traditional mores may enhance the coordination of activity at the cost of lowering the pace of innovation. That the reverse may hold for Western practices must be acknowledged.

Between the Western liberal ethos and the ethos of Islam, it becomes clear that the notion of entrepreneurship raises difficult issues. Entrepreneurial decisions have both an individual and a social context. Robinson Crusoe adduces entrepreneurial considerations when he weighs the pros and cons of an expedition to the far side of his island. As a lone individual, 'the entrepreneurial element consists in noticing the existence of opportunities despite the presence of discouraging uncertainties' but, if Crusoe has neighbours, the situation is changed 'by the configuration of the anticipated actions of others (and by the individual's own convictions concerning the ethical significance of the interplay between his own actions and those of others)' (Kirzner, 1992, p. 91). Whether Crusoe acts in isolation, or has neighbours who might react, entrepreneurial activity is necessarily speculative. Every response to an opportunity for purposeful action is an entrepreneurial act: the Misesian insight that 'in any real and living economy every actor is always an entrepreneur' is simply an implication of what it means to live in a world of radical uncertainty (*ibid.*, p. 102, fn. 6).

Notes

1 The literature on central bank independence might gain clarification if the tautological presentation of monetary and fiscal policy were explicitly acknowledged. See Chapter 8, the section, 'Broad money and its credit counterparts'.

2 As the result of quantitative easing, Western banks (with exceptions such as in Greece and Portugal) hold large amounts of excess reserves, which means that they borrow very little from their respective central banks. The opportunity cost of liquidity is therefore the operative official rate (Bank Rate in the UK), i.e., the rate paid on excess reserves.

3 When there is counterparty risk, as in 2008, inter-bank rates depart from official rates or may lead to the complete cessation of inter-bank lending beyond the very short term.
4 The term *ijara* applies to two situations. With the first, *ijara* means to transfer the usage (*usufruct*) of an asset or property in exchange for rent. This is analogous to 'leasing' between a lessor (*mujir*) and a lessee (*mustajir*) and a payment of rent (*ujrah*). With *ijara wa iqtina*, the lessee becomes the owner of the asset, by purchasing it from the lessor either during or at the end of lease period. With the second, *ijara* means a transaction involving a payment for hired services between an employer (*mustajir*) and an employee (*ajir*).
5 Although it is often credited to Samuel Johnson, the earliest attribution – as 'hell is full of good intentions' – is to Saint Bernard of Clairvaux (1091–1153).

Bibliography

Buiter, W. H. and E. Rahbari (2015) 'Why Economists (and Economies) Should Love Islamic Finance', *Journal of King Abdulaziz University: Islamic Econ.*, vol. 28, no. 1, 129–50.

Friedman, M. (1967) 'The Monetary Theory and Policy of Henry Simons', *The Journal of Law and Economics*, vol. X, 1–13; reprinted in Friedman, 1969, pp. 81–93.

Friedman, M. (1969) *The Optimum Quantity of Money and Other Essays* (Chicago, IL: Chicago, Aldine Publishing Co.).

Hayek, F. A. (1935) *Prices and Production*, 2nd ed., revised and enlarged (London: Routledge and Kegan Paul); 1st ed., 1931 (London: George Routledge and Sons); originally published in German as *Preise und Produktion* (Wien-Leipzig: Hölder-Pichler-Tempsky A.G.).

Hayek, F. A. (1946) 'The Meaning of Competition', Stafford Little Lecture, Princeton University, May; cited from Hayek, 1949, pp. 92–106.

Hayek, F. A. (1949) *Individualism and Economic Order* (London and Henley: Routledge).

Keynes, J. M. (1936) *The General Theory of Employment Interest and Money* (London: Macmillan).

Kirzner, I. M. (1992) *The Meaning of the Market Process: Essays in the Development of Modern Austrian Economics* (London and New York: Routledge).

Mejía, A. L., S. Aljabrin, R. Awad, M. Norat, and I. Song (2014) 'Regulation and Supervision of Islamic Banks', IMF Working Paper WP/14/219 December; www.imf.org/external/pubs/ft/wp/2014/wp14219.pdf (accessed 28 November 2016).

Mises, L. von (1920) 'Die Wirtschaftsrechnung im sozialistischen Gemeinwesen', *Archiv für Sozialwissenschaften*, vol. 47; cited from 'Economic Calculation in the Socialist Commonwealth', in Hayek, 1935, pp. 87–103.

Simons, H. C. (1933) Unpublished mimeographed memorandum, November; cited from Friedman, 1967.

12 Final comments

A set of concluding observations is delivered under nine headings. As economic crises (*Markets and mayhem*) invoke thoughts of a better way, *Keynesian options* and *Monetary reform* remain prominent among the agenda, today as in the 1930s. Even as markets have crashed, regulation undermines the force of trust (*Regulation and trust*), without which free societies cannot function. It is understandable that the lay public should ask why no one had anticipated the 2008 debacle. An associated question is *Does the discipline of economics progress?* Without doubt, Simons would have considered it to be 'progress', had he lived to see how *The epoch of aggregate demand management* lost ground to *Friedman's Chicago revival.* Nevertheless, there is great irony that Simons' general endorsement of policy rules in preference to discretionary action has such prominence in the concept and application of the Taylor rule. By the metrics of a benchmark inflation rate and a theoretical measure of an aggregate output gap, the Taylor rule is obviously a device intended for aggregate demand management. That it may continue to feature within academic journals than in the making of policy is for discussion elsewhere.

It is understandable that the relevance of earlier generations of economists to current issues should fade. Even where names are referenced, contributions tend to be misrepresented by practitioners who discount the time and effort to absorb the detail or the force of their work. Where this applies to the writing of, say, Maynard Keynes and Friedrich Hayek, that outcome is escaped by Henry Simons because his work is so highly marginalised. The opening paragraph of the preface to this book lists Simons's contributions. The intervening chapters attempt to examine and to explain some of the detail, where the objective is not only to incite or to broaden an appreciation of his writing, but also, as importantly, to draw others into the conversation. A summary of that detail is recounted under nine headings.

In *Markets and mayhem,* the ubiquity of business failure – as a necessary component to the progress that is possible within a liberal market order – is contrasted with infrequent major economic crises that invoke thoughts of a better way. Once markets have crashed, two features are common in the response to the mayhem that follows. After staring closely in their rear-view mirror, the authorities set regulatory constraints by which they hope that past malfunctions will be held firmly in check. Yet, there is a trade-off. The moral hazard that is associated with regulation undermines the force of trust, without which free societies cannot function. This is the motivation for the section that follows on *Regulation and trust.*

Another common response to major economic crises is to undertake a review of possible policy interventions. *Keynesian options* are typically most prominent among the agenda, where contentious issues relate to fiscal austerity and fiscal stimulus. Those scenarios are so well-rehearsed that they generally present nothing that is new. That is not the case with proposals for *Monetary reform*. By the pace and novelty of innovation in banking and finance, monetary reform is as prominent among the agenda for the 2020s (post Credit Crunch) as it was for the 1930s (post Wall Street crash).

In expressing general concerns with overall macroeconomic performance, the man in the street (and even H. M. the Queen) have good reason to ask why no one had anticipated the 2008 debacle. Less politely, the question they might put is, 'what is it that economists do?' The final four sections touch upon that inquiry and an associated question: *Does the discipline of economics progress?*

Unlike the physical sciences, progress within social science is aided by a capacity to understand human motivations through introspection (*verstehen*). Yet, though action is motivated by subjective evaluations, it can be categorised by type; and upon the basis of those categorisations, broad 'pattern predictions' may be modestly aimed to identify general tendencies. The guidance of 'pattern predictions' is far removed from that of the aggregate demand forecasting upon which Keynesian interventions are structured. Although, in principle, the pattern of growth and function of a complex system might be understood, without knowing the many specific details of particular circumstances, precise predictions are likely to fail.

A 'definitive blueprint' for achieving economic prosperity is an unlikely prospect. Given that situations are too fluid for optimisation principles to apply, David Laidler and Mervyn King have independently invoked the notion of 'coping strategies' to deal with diverse events as they unfold and interact. Although it is clearly desirable to find means to ameliorate the *Boom and bust* of the business cycle, the suspicion is strong that many academic economists have abandoned that quest. By the current fashion of the sophisticated tinkering with Keynesian DSGE and other mathematical models (*Economic policy; models and practice*), goals within academia are more obviously directed to enhancing an individual's career prospects.

12.1 Markets and mayhem

The association between individual freedom and economic prosperity is well-documented. The spontaneous screening of error-learning behaviour fosters positive developments, so that the criticism from those whose focus is upon the inevitable failures is poorly based. Free competition largely rewards those who find themselves in a position to satisfy new demands as they arise from changing circumstances:

> It does not matter through what process of reasoning or motivation such success was achieved. The fact of its accomplishment is sufficient. This is the criterion by which the economic system selects survivors: those who realize *positive profits* are the survivors; those who suffer losses disappear.
>
> (Alchian, 1950, p. 213)

As the majority of entrepreneurial ventures fail, economies advance through the competitive diminution of the profits that accrue from the relatively few successful innovations. Where societies are heavily conservative, established structures deliver greater certainties, but that stability is achieved by inhibitions that discourage risk-taking. The trade-off is obvious: 'by its very nature', conservatism 'cannot offer an alternative to the direction in which we are moving' (Hayek, 1960, p. 398). Setting to one side all the *minor* failures that are integral to market competition, *spectacular* failure is an infrequent, but recurring, experience.

On a visit to the London School of Economics in 2008, H. M. the Queen asked 'why had nobody noticed that the credit crunch was on its way?' (Besley and Hennessy, 2009). Some eight months later, a reply was forthcoming in a letter written on behalf of the participants in a forum convened by the British Academy. The summary response was that, in the period to 2007, low interest rates had caused indebtedness to soar. Yet, financial analysts believed that ways had been found to reduce the associated risks to manageable levels:

> Everyone seemed to be doing their job properly on its own merit. And according to standard measures of success, they were often doing it well. ... the failure to foresee the timing, extent and severity of the crisis and to head it off ... was principally a failure of the collective imagination of many bright people, both in this country and internationally, to understand the risks to the system as a whole.
>
> (*ibid.*)

The boom that had preceded the financial crash of 2008 largely centered upon property development. The salient details are that, as financial institutions extended cheap loans, new demands and rising property prices encouraged prospective purchasers to believe that these were opportunities not to be missed. As mortgage lenders structured new debts to create 'mortgage-backed securities', those who purchased those instruments believed their risks to have been astutely spread. The core problem is that of ignorance. With securitised assets, investors are ignorant of whose debts are incorporated within multiple tiers of assets and of how risks (and values) might be assessed. In lieu of that information, financial institutions rely upon seals of approval that are readily provided by credit-rating agencies.[1] Given the profitable opportunities in selling testaments of quality, the temptation for agencies to 'over-egg' credit ratings is obvious. *Quis custodiet ipsos custodes?*

Once the financial crash had occurred, a number of central banks became engaged in quantitative easing to counter the recession. After central bank action had taken short-term interest rates to their zero lower bound, that same action was applied to reduce long-term rates. The effectiveness of altering the ownership and term-structure of sovereign debt, by the substitution of base money for long-dated bonds, is an empirical issue. The recommendation from Simons to address the severe downturn that followed the 1929 Wall Street crash, was for direct fiscal measures to be implemented – i.e., cuts in taxation, not central bank open-market operations.

The distortions that quantitative easing imposes upon the price system are too rarely considered. Stock-market and house prices surged as former bondholders rebalanced their asset portfolios and as households were encouraged to enter into more debt. Pension funds and insurance companies saw the capitalised value of their liabilities raised in relation to the market value of their assets. As businesses diverted funds to support company pension schemes and as savers' incomes fell, other expenditures were curtailed.

By their training in microeconomic theory, economists are alert to the allocative implications of tampering with market prices. Yet, that judgement tends to be lost as their attention turns to macroeconomic issues. The core of Austrian business cycle theory is that inter-temporal price distortions are implicit when interest rates are lowered in order to stimulate economic recovery. In setting a bias that favours longer-term investments, such projects would be unlikely to prove sustainable.[2]

When interest rates are low and activity within the economy is below the full employment level, it has become a familiar *canard* that the government should borrow in order to spend its way to growth. While the lay public and its politicians might be excused for warming to that idea, others ought to know better. It is a matter for regret that so many economists continue to give professional support to Keynesian thinking.

A London School of Economics report argues that low interest rates give an opportunity for the state to undertake infrastructure investment (see Zenghelis, 2016). The claim is that this would boost growth, raise returns to private investors, strengthen the stability of public finances, reduce the risk of house-price 'bubbles' and have no impact upon inflation. Little wonder that, in the month following that report, the UK Shadow Chancellor should commit a future Labour government to establishing a national investment bank, with £100 billion borrowed 'at the cheapest rates in our history' (McDonnell, 2016). There are a number of reasons why such arguments are insubstantially based.

When corporations borrow, they expect to make a return from which to repay the debt. If governments are usually able to borrow more cheaply, it is because market participants understand that taxpayers underwrite the debt. If that privilege allows perceived societal needs (including infrastructure) to be met with no market return, the call to socialise investment projects must be tempered. Taken too far, credibility in the viability of such action can too easily dissipate even to the extent evidenced for Greece, Venezuela and Zimbabwe.

A second objection to borrowing at low rates is the track record of government projects. Cutting deals is no *forte* of civil servants or politicians. In 2011, the House of Commons Committee of Public Accounts complained that 'deals look better value for the private sector than for the taxpayer' (House of Commons, 2011). The Committee could only appeal to H. M. Treasury and other government departments to find ways to improve their business skills.

A third reason for doubting this modern widow's cruse is that, as state projects make use of scarce resources, the cost of those resources rises, so inhibiting private entrepreneurship. No matter how low the interest rate, investment projects should be weighed against competing alternatives. Prospects for an enduring return are more carefully calculated when entrepreneurs have their own 'skin in the action'. Yet, by the rapidity and willingness of the authorities to intervene in reacting to failure, the opposite tendency exists. As a response to the Great Recession, layers of new regulations have been, and continue to be, imposed upon banking practice, in the attempt to shield taxpayers from having to sustain the payments system in the event of new crises. Even as 'ring-fencing' purports to provide that protection by requiring retail banks and investment banks to operate as separate independent entities, inherent dangers remain when practitioners are absolved from responsibility merely by their adherence to regulatory checklists.

12.2 Regulation and trust

In respect of the development of money and banking into the early years of the twentieth century, an overcautious issue of base money had 'encouraged private agencies to provide what government itself blindly failed to provide' (Simons, 1942, p. 175). As the legacy of that rapid expansion and diversification of commercial banking, financial stability had become threatened by 'a mass of ersatz moneys', whose acceptance is built upon the illusion that they are 'really convertible into the real thing'. Base money *per se* is 'highly amenable to democratic legislative control', but base money

> is not easily manageable alongside a mass of private debt and private near-moneys whose aberrations fiscal policy must work against, or alongside a mountain of debt, short-term and long, which rises prodigiously in emergencies and is not reducible at other times.
>
> (*ibid.*, p. 176)

As they periodically overextend their provision of credit, commercial banks turn to the central bank for support. Against that pattern, regulation presents itself as a solution. With property prices already falling, an unprecedented sharp oil price rise of November 1973 left a number of secondary banks facing insolvency. In attempting to draw from that experience, the Banking Act of 1979 gave the Bank of England statutory responsibility for the supervision of the UK financial sector. At which point, regulators took their cue.

In 1980, there was one regulator for roughly every 11,000 employed in the UK financial sector. By 2011, the ratio had fallen to one for every 300 employed. In 1988, the initial Basel I financial regulatory framework covered thirty pages. In 2004, Basel II covered 347 pages and, by 2012, Basel III had been extended to 616 pages (see Haldane and Madouros, 2012, pp. 6–9). Not only does regulation have a poor track record, it is very costly and it opens the possibility of regulatory capture.[3] More generally, '[b]y encouraging a culture in which compliance with detailed regulations is a defence against a charge of wrong-doing, bankers and regulators have colluded in a self-defeating spiral of conspiracy' (King, 2016, p. 260).

If there were no alternative to rigorous supervision with associated penalties being applied to meet every transgression, human activity would be prohibitively costly. The alternative ethos that might be expected to deliver a workable system at low cost is a set of moral values, good faith, trust and reputation:

> Ultimately, of course, social capital is not contractual; integrity can neither be bought nor regulated. Even with the best possible framework of codes, principles, compensation schemes and market discipline, financiers must constantly challenge themselves to the standards they uphold.
>
> (Carney, 2014, p. 9)

A well-founded societal order rests upon accepted standards of behaviour and the ostracism that is faced by miscreants. The best that might be said of the UK honours system is the possibility of recipients being stripped of their accolades. On the downside, any leniency in the face of mishap invites morale hazard. The low cost of administering simple rather than complex rules and the advantages to be drawn from consensual understandings are among the cornerstones of the *credo* that motivates Henry Simons. That the alternative ethos of more elaborate state control took hold was, for Simons, an abomination, as was his distaste for Keynesian fiscal interventions.

12.3 Keynesian options

In a thirty-six page review of Alvin Hansen's *Fiscal Policy and Business Cycles*, Simons reflects upon the fiscal requirements that would most likely deliver a stable currency. The key point is that, where sovereign expenditure is considered to be necessary, it ought to be financed by raising taxation, for the simple reason that there is no alternative to providing *real* resources. Since borrowing merely defers taxation, it is justified only as a temporary expedient (most notably in withdrawing purchasing power to check incipient inflation) pending the necessary adjustment of a permanent rise in taxation.

Simons further argues that deflation is more readily countered than inflation because of 'a persisting confidence that prosperity would sometime follow upon depression and that great bargains were to be had by those who took the long view'. However, there is 'no corresponding ceiling to inflation, once governments have squandered their borrowing powers and undermined the confidence of their creditors in the future of fiscal policy' (Simons, 1942, p. 177). Sovereign expenditure can become an indulgence that is all too easily facilitated by borrowing. Although it might be decades in coming, the addition to debt that 'we shall owe to ourselves' has the inevitable result of 'political instability and exposure to revolution' (*ibid.,* p. 174). Simons is concerned that the pursuit of Keynesian options invites 'a future of free spending..., of taxes near the limit of taxable capacity ... and of huge debt, growing at an uneven rate but always growing', which then 'facilitates a dangerous muddling of monetary questions and questions of socialization' (*ibid.*, pp. 177–78).

Given the combination of a 'promiscuous intrusion of governmental enterprise all over the place' and the ready notion that 'the rate of increase [of sovereign debt] should be adjusted to the degree of unemployment', private investors are then likely to find that higher yields can be obtained from sovereign bonds. It is a situation that bodes ill:

> Presumably the private economy is to struggle along as best it can, whatever happens to wage rates, the unemployed being absorbed continuously into public employment, i.e., into an expanding socialized sector which, supported out of taxing and borrowing, need not be seriously concerned about relations between wage rates and productivity.
>
> (*ibid.*, p. 178)

Even if some respite might be found in the greater flexibility that exists in delivering variations to taxation rather than variations to expenditure, the general resistance from pressure groups to expenditure cuts carries a likelihood of ever-expanding government activity in a vain attempt to achieve full employment. Chronic inflation is then inevitable. Given those consequences of Keynesian interventions, Simons saw a paramount need for monetary reform.

12.4 Monetary reform

The commitment of a central bank to provide reserves on demand delivers confidence in the payments system. It also creates moral hazard: buttressed by the expectation that liquidity needs will be met, it is rational for bankers to take greater risks, so making monetary instability more likely. Simons considers the abolition of short-term borrowing to be the ideal reform, from which derives 100 percent reserve banking as the core feature of the Chicago Plan. Simons shows prescience with his awareness that banking innovations of the kind now termed 'shadow banking' are likely to undermine that new discipline.

With bank capital containing a low ratio of equity to unsecured debt as another potential source of instability, Simons argues that bank capital should be held only as common stock (i.e., equity shares). He also views the many different maturities of sovereign debt as serving no useful purpose. In arguing that they merely incite confusion, Simons suggests that sovereign borrowing should take the single form of 'contracts in perpetuity'. Unlike shorter-term sovereign debt, those 'consols' have little direct appeal as money substitutes. In contradiction of Simons, however, their use as shadow bank collateral offers an obvious loophole.

Independently of Simons, Hayek also recognises the potential for bank credit to foster monetary instability and business fluctuations, but he draws no policy guidelines. Hayek's greater concern is that '[t]he stability of the economic system would be obtained at the price of curbing economic progress' (Hayek, 1933, p. 191). In returning repeatedly (Hayek, 1960, 1976, 1978, 1986) to the issue of the most benign form for a monetary system, Hayek's final position is that governments should surrender their monopoly of the note issue (see Hayek, 1978, p. 27, fn. 1). Alternative private moneys would be distinct and each competitor would attempt to regulate the supply of its own particular brand of money, in order to make theirs the most acceptable of those in circulation. With each competitor exercising control over the unique characteristics of its own money, individual choice, free competition and flexible rates of exchange would provide a natural check to the falling purchasing power of individual currencies.

In their respective recommendations, it is clear that Simons and Hayek are poles apart. For Simons, money would ideally consist only of sovereign currency; for Hayek, it would be better for diverse moneys to be supplied by competing entrepreneurs. Where Simons is fearful of entrepreneurial innovations that would undermine 100 percent reserve banking and the sovereign monopoly of money, Hayek would give full rein to the forces of competition.

It is important to understand that the respective contexts in which such radically different views were formed were also radically different. Institutional structures underpinning money, banking and international transactions in the 1940s and in the 1980s bear little comparison (*note bene*: Simons died in 1946 and Hayek in 1992). The epoch in which Simons had formulated his ideas was one of deference, a tightly ordered social *milieu* and limited access to banking services other than by those within the upper echelons of society. In sharp contrast, the new pace of developing technologies and innovations rapidly overtakes yesterday's practice. In the two citations that follow, prospects outlined for the future are in close alignment:

> It is reasonable to expect that innovations in electronic communications and exchange will continue to shape the provision of financial services. … future developments might enable registers of individuals' asset portfolios (comprising not only financial assets of every kind, but also real assets) with opportunities to make virtually instantaneous withdrawals and deposits. … It is likely that advances in communication, information technology and financial services will raise the advantages and reduce the hazards of a money economy to the point where - in effect - arrangements would exist to allow the *barter* of assets and commodities alike;
>
> (Steele, 2001, p. 204)

> With high-speed electronic transfers it is becoming feasible to transfer stocks and shares and other forms of marketable wealth from the buyer to the seller instead of money, so enabling buyers and sellers to avoid handing some of their wealth in the form that earns little or no interest. Pre-agreed instructions embedded in computer algorithms would determine the sequence in which financial assets belonging to the purchaser were sold and used to augment the financial assets of the vendor, also in a pre-agreed sequence. Assets used in this way could be any for which there were market-clearing prices in 'real time'. Someone buying a meal in a restaurant might use a card, as now, but the result … would be a sale of shares from the diner's portfolio and the acquisition of different shares or other assets, to the same value by the restaurant. There would be no unique role for something called money in order to buy 'stuff.'
>
> (King, 2016, pp. 283–84)

The notion of some utopian monetary design is an unlikely prospect. Rather, the evolution of processes for payments and debt provision would suggest that enduring policy rules are unlikely to emerge:

> It seems instead that the problems of creating and maintaining a coherent monetary order, and hence of providing the monetary foundations for economic prosperity and political freedom, are not to be solved once and for all by developing and then following a definitive blueprint embodied in a set of policy rules based on today's ideas. Rather, it implies that they are problems constantly to be coped with over time as events and ideas unfold and interact.
>
> (Laidler, 2016, p. 21)

12.5 Economics moves on

Given the current ethos within academia – that of achieving peer-reviewed publications in 'top-rated' journals – scholarly inquiry is unlikely to contribute much towards the elucidation of coping principles. The blinkered reliance upon quantification shows in ever-higher layers of mathematical sophistication of a kind that were deprecated by notable scholars of earlier times:

> Too large a proportion of recent "mathematical" economics are mere concoctions, as imprecise as the initial assumptions they rest on, which allow the author to lose sight of the complexities and interdependencies of the real world in a maze of pretentious and unhelpful symbols;
>
> (Keynes, 1936, p. 298)

> Unfortunately, any one capable of learning elementary, or preferably advanced calculus and algebra, and acquiring acquaintance with the specialized terminology of economics can set himself up as a theorist. Uncritical enthusiasm for mathematical formulation tends often to conceal the ephemeral substantive content of the argument behind the formidable front of algebraic signs;
>
> (Leontief, 1970, p. 2)

> Ceteris paribus, one cannot prefer less to more rigor, lesser to greater generality, or complexity to simplicity; but other things are not equal, and in the estimate of many members of our Association the cost of that mathematization sometimes outweighs its benefit.
>
> (Debreu, 1991, p. 6)

It would be an understatement to say that those warnings have fallen upon deaf ears. On the contrary, obtuse modelling increasingly dominates the most prominent economic journals. A pause along the track to the current mainstream might have been achieved by the Lucas critique of the policy-oriented econometrics of the macroeconomy:

> Given that the structure of an econometric model consists of optimal decision rules of economic agents, and that optimal decision rules vary systematically with changes in the structure of series relevant to the decision maker, it follows that any change in policy will systematically alter the structure of econometric models.
>
> (Lucas, 1976, p. 41)

Yet, all was not lost. Economic modellers are nothing if not resourceful, and they address the Lucas critique by modelling a set of *microeconomic* behavioural patterns for a set of representative agents. 'Calibration' sets the parameters of a model so that it accords with prior evidence; i.e., details are chosen that best serve as 'microeconomic foundations'. If, in so doing, the Lucas critique is deemed to be addressed, confidence in the potential for any meaningful direction of policy is small. In purporting to grow as a social science, economics has blinded itself to the inherent limitations of this approach.

There is a different way: the unassuming purpose of a theoretical structure is to represent an existing state of affairs, which might then form a basis from which to reach 'a prognosis of what is likely to happen in the future' (Hayek, 1941, p. 22). In the same vein as Lucas, Keynes argues that:

> [i]t is a great fault of symbolic pseudo-mathematical methods of formalising a system of economic analysis, … that they expressly assume strict independence between the factors involved and lose all their cogency and authority if this hypothesis is disallowed; whereas, in ordinary discourse, where we are not blindly manipulating but know all the time what we are doing and what the words mean, we can keep "at the back of our heads" the necessary reserves and qualifications and the adjustments which we shall have to make later on.
>
> (Keynes, 1936, p. 297)

The complexity of change and the commensurate need for institutional structures and policy also to change are ever-present. Unfortunately, economic analysis is now infiltrated by mathematical virtuosos and 'a growing mesmerization with technique for its own sake' (Lipsey, 2001, p. 171). This formalisation of interacting behavioural traits and policy rules has pushed 'more descriptive and factual material out of the curriculum', with the result that there is 'a declining level of empirical knowledge from generation to generation' (*ibid.*, p. 184).

As a consequence of those developments, the relevance of philosophy, political science, psychology and institutional structures are more heavily discounted by academic economists than ever before. And the mainstreams of modelling and estimation are strengthened by networking, peer assessment, box ticking and the journals that feed the rankings of the institutions within which economists build their careers.

Yet, serendipity still raises its head. Though it may require great resolution to detach oneself from fashion, interests driven by curiosity carry the reward of discovery. Among many aphorisms attributed to Albert Einstein is one where he sets imagination above knowledge, because imagination opens possibilities for new paths to be tried. The Popper question should be to the front of every researcher's mind. In commenting upon an endeavour to measure the length, breadth, thickness and weight of books in the British museum, Karl Pooper asks, 'Why is this problem absurd?' His own reply is that the problem has no interest 'because there is no reason to think it will throw light on the more pressing scientific problems of the day' (Popper, 1994a, p. 155). That rebuke runs close to the complaint from Harry S. Truman who, tired of platitudes and fatuous advice on the economy ('on the one had this, but on the other had that'), famously called for a one-armed economist.[4]

The desire of politicians for relevant insights into 'the economy' is caught by Truman's frustration, and the evident lack of practical relevance of formal models raises the most fundamental questions. Friedrich Hayek (for one) suggests that complex systems are not susceptible to the precise determination of socio-economic interrelationships, and he argues that the distinction between 'the relatively simple phenomena with which the natural sciences deal ... [and] ... the more complex phenomena of life, of mind, and of society' is defined by 'the minimum number of distinct variables a formula or model must possess in order to reproduce the characteristic patterns of structures of different fields' (Hayek, 1967, p. 26).[5]

Hayek cites evolution as 'the best illustration of a theory of complex phenomena which is of great value, although it merely describes a general pattern whose detail we can never fill in' (*ibid*., p. 31). Hence the view that the primary achievement of theories of social structures is to have shown that events that both guide and reflect human behaviour depend upon so many interdependent relationships that it is impossible to ascertain them all. Hayek warned against basing predictions upon 'pseudo-entities'. Precise prediction and control are generally beyond the reach of social science and, by implication, macroeconomic policy management.

12.6 The epoch of aggregate demand management

The Chicago School of the 1930s is identified as having held to the ethos of liberal market economics against the notion of macroeconomic management as presented in *The General Theory*. With an economy stagnating at below full employment, Keynes invokes the existence of a liquidity trap, where long-term yields are too low for capital investment to match the thriftiness of savers: 'there has been a chronic tendency throughout human history for the propensity to save to be stronger that the inducement to invest' (Keynes, 1936, p. 347). For that chronic scenario, Keynes argued that government spending is needed to lift output to the full employment level. Although such commitment might be limited by 'the particular conditions of the time' (Keynes, 1973, p. 122), as that spending is sustained the impact of ever-rising sovereign debt must be faced.

In the immediate post-war period, when the Bretton Woods regime of fixed exchange rates was implemented by Western democracies (albeit constrained by capital controls and permitting periodic revaluations), the core objective was to deliver sustained growth, thereby to moderate cyclical tendencies. For the UK, ever-rising levels of public investment needed to be reconciled with fluctuating levels of private spending, while periodic foreign exchange crises were met, not by currency depreciation, but by emergency cutbacks across the public sector. That feature of economic management was lampooned as a series of 'stop-go' repetitions, which by no stretch of the imagination could be viewed as a policy success.

The perceived necessity for a general reappraisal of banking and financial structures and of the rationale for monetary and fiscal policy had been evident in the 1930s with the presentation of the Chicago Plan. By the mid-1950s, similar perceptions had become rooted in the UK, such that a reconsideration of policy options became prominent among economic agenda. The deliberations of the Radcliffe Committee (upon an 'inquiry into the working of the monetary and credit system') did show some affinity with Henry Simons's 'fiscal focus' upon monetary action. One of the conclusions then reached for the UK economy was that '[i]t is not merely that monetary action and debt management interact so that they ought to be under one control: they are one and indivisible; debt management lies at the heart of monetary control' (Radcliffe, 1959, p. 224).

Although the relevance of commercial banking to economic activity, which is the core feature of the Radcliffe Report, also chimes with the perspective taken by Simons, the salient conclusion of the Report is aligned with Keynes's *General Theory*: monetary policy is unlikely to prove effective in lowering interest rates sufficiently to deliver sustainable full employment. That monetary policy did not matter became the ethos that shaped policy over the ensuing decade. So it was that

> [m]any economists on the Bank staff in the 1950s and 1960s learned economics during the period of "Neanderthal Keynesian" U.K. academic thought, with their views on monetary policy shaped further in that direction by the Radcliffe Report. Consequently, senior Bank economists during this period tended not to be monetary specialists. It is perhaps significant that when in 1968 the Bank hired an economist with a monetary economics background, the event was considered unusual enough to merit a news item in the London *Times*.
>
> (Batini and Nelson, 2005, p. 21)

That newsworthy appointment coincided with the breakdown of the Phillips curve – i.e., the negative association between inflation and unemployment that had been initially mapped for the UK economy (Phillips, 1958). The new experience of high inflation with high unemployment had been explicitly discounted by the assertions 'that an increase in the quantity of money will have no effect whatever on prices, so long as there is any unemployment, and that employment will increase in exact proportion to any increase in effective demand brought about by an increase in the quantity of money' (Keynes, 1936, p. 295). From the end of the 1960s, the empirical contradiction of those assertions brought: (i) a retrospective invocation of the Chicago School as an oral tradition that had remained committed to classical liberalism as others were taken by Keynesianism; and (ii) a rebranding of Friedman's quantity theory of money as the Monetarist[6] counter-revolution.

12.7 Friedman's Chicago revival

In popular presentations, this new epoch saw something of a gladiatorial positioning: Monetarists against Keynesians; demand-pull inflation against cost-push inflation; and market clearing against aggregate demand management.

By implication – and occasionally explicitly – Friedman's rekindling of classical monetary theory was simplistically presented as giving a different emphasis to macroeconomic demand management.

The key narrative for understanding the Monetarist rejection of Keynesian economics is Friedman's presidential address to the American Economic Association in December 1967 (Friedman, 1968). In that address, his focus is upon the objective of monetary policy and the criteria under which it should be applied. Friedman had previously argued that Keynes, Simons and 'most other economists of the time' had misread the role of money in the period 1929–1933. The crash on Wall Street had not been countered by 'aggressive expansionary policies by the monetary authorities'. On the contrary, the US money supply had been permitted to fall by one-third. Friedman's conclusion is that 'the Great Contraction is tragic testimony to the power of monetary policy – not, as Keynes and many of his contemporaries believed, evidence of its impotence' (Friedman, 1967, p. 3). In reviewing the evidence through to December 1930, Friedman absolves commercial banks from having presided over a contraction in 'near-moneys'. Rather, '[t]he monetary authorities not the private economy, were the major source of the deflationary pressure' (*ibid.*, p. 10).

Whatever the strength of Friedman's evidence, it must be clear that insolvency among commercial banks has a potential to undermine monetary stability. Whether in consequence of bank failure or central bank ineptitude, deflation was the economic challenge of the 1930s. From his consideration of alternative remedial measures, Keynes gives near-exclusive weight to the force of fiscal intervention, not simply to ward off deflation but for new government activity – boosted by the income multiplier process – to raise employment and output. The general ineffectiveness of monetary policy rests upon a liquidity trap that inhibits a fall in long-term interest rates.

For Simons, an economic downturn presents no case for setting aside the allocative mechanism of price adjustments across competitive markets. He therefore recommends cuts in taxation as the means to counter a general deflation. Friedman cites an unpublished memorandum written by Simons in 1933: 'at the present time, increase of expenditures or reductions in taxation would be far more immediately effective toward raising prices than conversion of the federal debt into the non-interest bearing form' (Simons, 1933; cited from Friedman, 1969, p. 8). Friedman argues that it is by 'such ideas as these… that the Chicago students were so much less susceptible to the Keynesian virus than their contemporaries' (Friedman, 1969, pp. 8–9).

Before publication of *The General Theory*, the broad concern of economists had been with price stability. After its publication, the primary focus became full employment. Friedman contrasts this with the emphasis of his own 'Monetarist' presentation, which is that monetary policy can peg interest rates and the rate of unemployment for a limited period only. If, in order to cut interest rates, a central bank buys bonds, then 'it also increases the quantity of reserves available to banks, hence the amount of bank credit, and, ultimately the total quantity of money' (Friedman, 1968, p. 6). As the growth of broad money then encourages spending, incomes and prices rise (albeit with different time lags) so that the initial impact – which is to lower both interest rates and unemployment – is eroded as the economy reverts to its initial settings. During the expansion phase, however, individuals will begin to anticipate rising prices so that, 'as Irving Fisher pointed out decades ago' (*ibid.*), if the real rate of interest is not to change, the nominal rate must rise. Hence, the empirical generality from Friedman's analysis is to expect excessive monetary growth to be associated with price inflation and rising nominal interest rates.

In extending the Monetarist narrative upon those lines, Friedman follows Simons in dismissing the Keynesian notion of aggregate demand management. Instead, the credible macroeconomic purpose is to protect the liberal order of a market economy by measures that work towards monetary stability. The crucial idea is to 'provide a monetary climate favourable to the effective operation of those basic forces of enterprise, ingenuity, invention, hard work, and thrift that are the true springs of economic growth' (Friedman, 1968, p. 17).

With like motivations, Simons had opposed Roosevelt's New Deal policies, arguing that government should set a framework for a free market economy and then withdraw. Don Patinkin describes the force with which Simons presented those policy recommendations:

> Market competition was to be assured by opposing with equal vigor all forms of monopoly, business as well as labor unions; a high degree of equality was to be achieved by a progressive income tax, applied to receipts of any kind - not only income, but capital gains inheritances, gifts as well; the instability of the banking system was to be solved by requiring 100 per cent reserves; and of course, mass unemployment - with the waste and sufferings that it represented - was to be prevented by a contra-cyclical policy of varying the quantity of money so as to stabilize the price level.
>
> (Patinkin, 1979, p. 214)

12.8 Boom and bust

After Keynesian interventions had incorporated the full paraphernalia of fiscal fine-tuning in the 1960s, the tightly regulated post-war model slowly gave way to that of global capitalism. Many attributed the reduced volatility of business cycles from the mid-1980s to institutional and structural changes. Among these was a lessening of political influence over monetary decisions, by the innovation of central bank independence. Alan Greenspan (Federal Reserve Chairman, 1987–2006) is closely associated with the epoch of 'Great Moderation'.[7] Greenspan's revealed predisposition is likened to having provided market traders with an exercise price, when a 'put option' allows a security to be sold at a given price. With the 'Greenspan put', the Fed Funds rate was systematically lowered whenever there was a sharp fall in equity prices: 'Key evidence in support of this view are the prompt actions taken by Mr. Greenspan to limit the crash of 1987 and the effects of the liquidity crunch of 1998, in both cases by cutting interest rates and pumping in liquidity' (Miller, Weller and Zhang, 2002, p. 171).

If the Greenspan put had led investors to feel protected against downside risk, the plausible consequence was that moral hazard became more firmly embedded. Thus, the Greenspan put may have been a contributory cause of the financial crisis of 2008, when '[a]fter the longest period of economic expansion in living memory, the crisis destroyed the credibility of economic policy and the reputation of the banking system of the advanced economies' (King, 2016, p. 368).

With similar events having been observed in earlier periods, it follows that that, if there is no one to order '*the punch bowl removed just when the party [is] really warming up*' (Martin, 1955, p. 12)[8], credit-led booms will proceed to the point where financial sectors threaten to implode under the weight of insolvencies. Whenever that event happens, and as partygoers look for palliatives as they nurse their sore heads, Austrian School economists might be forgiven if they draw some kudos in pointing to their business cycle theory. Without denying the legitimacy of that Austrian position, there is some mitigation: unique time-paths and their turning points are always uncertain.

12.9 Economic policy: models and practice

If there is any sense of a need for a radical rethink and a new direction, the performance of economic systems is more likely to deliver outcomes close to the goals of policy, when they build upon and re-enforce an evolving consensus. That, of course, is central to the broad thrust of Simons's ethos. Public announcements, forward guidance, established practice and tacit understandings are all relevant if policy is not to generate instability. Yet, where consensus is thin, regulatory impositions can only create resentments and reactions that are likely to raise the costs of administering policy.

When good order is perceived to derive from existing institutional structures, the potential to gain from radical reform is not pressing. Only in the face of new concerns or unwelcome major surprises (as with the crash of 1929 and the crunch of 2008) is debate likely to be roused over a perceived need for new regulatory devices. After listing the many reforms enacted post 2008, the warning follows that these can never be definitive: '[r]adical uncertainty means that the sentiment towards financial firms can change so quickly that regulations that appear too burdensome one moment seem too lenient the next' (King, 2016, p. 257). From that appraisal, monetary and financial systems need to be responsive to change, where successful adjustments are most likely to be discovered though an unending succession of trial and error.

If there is a *sine qua non* to achieving greater long-term economic stability, the following might prove salutary. It is that measures should be judged within the ethos of libertarianism. In particular, the elimination of moral hazard is a paramount objective that is best met by the perpetual re-enforcement of a consensus that individuals' losses should remain their private property.

Notes

1 Credit-rating agencies date from the early years of the twentieth century: the now-familiar AAA through D rating system was introduced by John Fitch in 1924.
2 See Chapter 9, the section, 'Austrian business cycle theory'.
3 The general conclusion from empirical studies is that there is a tendency for regulators to promote the interests of suppliers rather than consumers, i.e., of a regulator being captured by the regulated (see Stigler, 1971).
4 A similar sentiment is attributed to Margaret Thatcher: 'Standing in the middle of the road is very dangerous; you get knocked down by the traffic from both sides' (cited from Hurd, 2013).
5 When Sir Isaac Newton (as Master of the Royal Mint) set the silver price of gold too high, the gold standard was inadvertently brought into existence in 1717. George Stigler is reported as citing Newton's mistake 'as proof positive that economics really is more difficult than physics' (Laidler, 2016, p. 10).
6 Karl Brunner is responsible for this new branding of the quantity theory of money: '[t]he authors reject the Monetarist thesis that monetary impulses are a chief factor determining variations in economic activity' (Brunner, 1968, p. 9).
7 The Great Moderation saw a sharp decline in the variability of real output and inflation, in the US and many other major industrial countries (see Bernanke, 2004).
8 William McChesney Martin Jr. (1906–1998) was the ninth and longest-serving Chairman of the United States Federal Reserve Bank.

Bibliography

Alchian, A. A. (1950) 'Uncertainty, Evolution and Economic Theory', *Journal of Political Economy*, vol. 58, no. 3, 211–21.

Batini, N. and E. Nelson (2005) 'The U.K.'s rocky road to stability', Technical Report 2005-020A, Federal Reserve Bank of St. Louis; http://research.stlouisfed.org/wp/2005/2005-020.pdf (accessed 25 June 2015).

Bernanke, B. (2004) 'Remarks by Governor Ben S. Bernanke at the Meetings of the Eastern Economic Association, Washington, DC February 20'; www.federalreserve.gov/BOARDDOCS/SPEECHES/2004/20040220/default.htm (accessed 15 March 2017).

Besley, T. and P. Hennessy (2009) 'Letter to Her Majesty the Queen', 22 July; www.britac.ac.uk/news/newsrelease-economy.cfm (accessed 7 June 2016).

Brunner, K. (1968) 'The Role of Money and Monetary Policy', *Federal Reserve of St. Louis Review*, vol. 50, 9–25.

Brunner, K. and A. H. Meltzer (1976) (eds.) *The Phillips Curve and Labor Markets*, Carnegie-Rochester Conference Series on Public Policy, vol. 1 (New York: American Elsevier).

Carney, M. (2014) 'Inclusive Capitalism: Creating a Sense of the Systemic', *Bank of England Speech*, 27 May; www.bankofengland.co.uk/publications/Documents/speeches/2014/speech731.pdf (accessed 9 September 2016).

Debreu, G. (1991) 'The Mathematization of Economic Theory', *The American Economic Review*, vol. 81, no. 1, 1–7.

Friedman, M. (1967) 'The Monetary Theory and Policy of Henry Simons', *The Journal of Law and Economics*, vol. X, October, 1–13; reprinted in Friedman, 1969, pp. 81–93.

Friedman, M. (1968) 'The Role of Monetary Policy', *The American Economic Review*, vol. 57, no. 1, 1–17.

Friedman, M. (1969) *The Optimum Quantity of Money and Other Essays* (Chicago, IL: Chicago, Aldine Publishing Co.).

King, M. A. (2016) *The End of Alchemy: Banking, the Global Economy and the Future of Money* (London: Little, Brown Book Group).

Haldane, A. G. and V. Madouros (2012) 'The Dog and the Frisbee', Speech Given at the Federal Reserve Bank of Kansas City's 36th Economic Symposium, 'The Changing Policy Landscape', Jackson, Wyoming, 31 August; www.bis.org/review/r120905a.pdf?frames=0 (accessed 8 June 2016).

Hayek, F. A. (1933) *Monetary Theory and the Trade Cycle* (London: Jonathan Cape); originally published in German in 1929 as *Geldtheorie und Konjunkturtheorie* (Wien: Verlag von Julius Springer).

Hayek, F. A. (1941) *The Pure Theory of Capital* (London and Henley: Routledge and Kegan Paul).

Hayek, F. A. (1960) *The Constitution of Liberty* (London and Henley: Routledge and Kegan Paul).

Hayek, F. A. (1967) *Studies in Philosophy, Politics, Economics and the History of Ideas* (London and Henley: Routledge and Kegan Paul).

Hayek, F. A. (1976) *Choice in Currency*, Occasional Paper 48 (London: Institute of Economic Affairs).

Hayek, F. A. (1978) *Denationalisation of Money*, 2nd ed., Hobart Special paper 70 (London: Institute of Economic Affairs).

Hayek, F. A. (1986) 'Market Standards for Money', *Economic Affairs*, vol. 6, no. 4, 8–10.

House of Commons Committee of Public Accounts (2011) *Lessons from PFI and Other Projects*. Forty-fourth Report of Session 2010–12, HC 1201, September; www.publications.parliament.uk/pa/cm201012/cmselect/cmpubacc/1201/1201.pdf (accessed 14 February 2017).

Hurd, M. (2013) 'Margaret Thatcher: In Her Own Words', *Capitalism Magazine*, 10 April; http://capitalismmagazine.com/2013/04/thatcher-the-lady-who-was-not-for-turning/ (accessed October 2016).

Keynes, J. M. (1936) *The General Theory of Employment Interest and Money* (London: Macmillan).

Keynes, J. M. (1973) *The General Theory and After: Part II: Defence and Development*, vol. XIV, *The Collected Writings of John Maynard Keynes*, edited by D. E. Moggridge (London: Macmillan).

Laidler, D. (2016) 'Economic Ideas, the Monetary Order and the Uneasy Case for Policy Rules', Department of Economics Research Reports, 2016-4 (London, ON: Department of Economics, University of Western Ontario); http://economics.uwo.ca/research/department_working_papers_docs/wp2016/wp2016_4.pdf (accessed 16 January 2017).

Leontief, W. (1971) 'Theoretical Assumptions and Nonobserved Facts', *The American Economic Review*, March, vol. 61, no. 1, 1–7.

Lipsey, R. G. (2001) 'Successes and Failures in the Transformation of Economics', *Journal of Economic Methodology*, vol. 8, no. 2, 169–201.

Lucas Jr, R. E. (1976) 'Econometric Policy Evaluation: A Critique', in K. Brunner and A. H. Meltzer, (eds.), *The Phillips Curve and Labor Markets*, Carnegie-Rochester Conference Series on Public Policy, vol. 1 (New York: American Elsevier), pp. 19–46.

Martin, W. M. (1955) 'Address before the New York Group of the Investment Bankers Association of America', 19 October; https://fraser.stlouisfed.org/_scribd/?item_id=7800&filepath=/files/docs/historical/martin/martin55_1019.pdf (accessed 10 January 2017).

McDonnell, J. (2016) 'John McDonnell Unveils Plans to Borrow £100bn to Protect British Industry Post-Brexit', *The Independent*, 25 September; www.independent.co.uk/news/uk/politics/john-mcdonnell-labour-would-form-interventionist-government-and-abandon-belief-in-the-free-market-a7329646.html (accessed 3 May 2017).

Miller, M., P. Weller and L. Zhang (2002) 'Moral Hazard and the US Stock Market: Analysing the 'Greenspan Put', *The Economic Journal*, 112, c171–86.

Patinkin, D, (1979) 'Keynes and Chicago', *Journal of Law and Economics*, vol. 22, no. 2, 213–32.

Phillips, A. W. (1958) 'The Relationship between Unemployment and the Rate of Change of Money Wages in the United Kingdom 1861–1957', *Economica*, vol. 25, no. 100, 283–99.

Popper, K. (1994a) 'Models, Instruments and Truth', in Popper, 1994b, pp. 154–84.

Popper, K. (1994b) (ed.) *The Myth of the Framework: In Defence of Science and Rationality* (London: Routledge).

Radcliffe (1959) *Committee on the Working of the Monetary System, The Report*, Cmnd 827 H.M.S.O.

Simons, H. C. (1942) 'Hansen on Fiscal Policy', *Journal of Political Economy*, vol. 50, no. 2, 161–96.

Steele, G. R. (2001) *Keynes and Hayek. The Money Economy* (London: Routledge).

Stigler, G. (1971) 'The Theory of Economic Regulation', *The Bell Journal of Economics and Management Science*, vol. 2, Spring, 3–21.

Zenghelis, D. (2016) 'Building 21st Century Sustainable Infrastructure (Part 1): Time to Invest', The Centre for Climate Change Economics and Policy, Policy brief, August; www.lse.ac.uk/GranthamInstitute/wp-content/uploads/2016/08/Zenghelis-policy-brief-August-2016a.pdf (accessed 14 February 2017).

Index

For Product Safety Concerns and Information please contact our EU representative GPSR@taylorandfrancis.com Taylor & Francis Verlag GmbH, Kaufingerstraße 24, 80331 München, Germany